Business Plans Kit

for
dummies®
A Wiley Brand

5th Edition

by Steven D. Peterson, PhD, Peter Jaret,
and Barbara Findlay Schenck

for
dummies®
A Wiley Brand

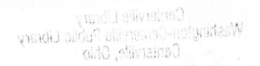

Business Plans Kit For Dummies®, 5th Edition

Published by: **John Wiley & Sons, Inc.,** 111 River Street, Hoboken, NJ 07030-5774, www.wiley.com

Copyright © 2016 by John Wiley & Sons, Inc., Hoboken, New Jersey

Published simultaneously in Canada

No part of this publication may be reproduced, stored in a retrieval system or transmitted in any form or by any means, electronic, mechanical, photocopying, recording, scanning or otherwise, except as permitted under Sections 107 or 108 of the 1976 United States Copyright Act, without the prior written permission of the Publisher. Requests to the Publisher for permission should be addressed to the Permissions Department, John Wiley & Sons, Inc., 111 River Street, Hoboken, NJ 07030, (201) 748-6011, fax (201) 748-6008, or online at http://www.wiley.com/go/permissions.

Trademarks: Wiley, For Dummies, the Dummies Man logo, Dummies.com, Making Everything Easier, and related trade dress are trademarks or registered trademarks of John Wiley & Sons, Inc., and may not be used without written permission. All other trademarks are the property of their respective owners. John Wiley & Sons, Inc., is not associated with any product or vendor mentioned in this book.

LIMIT OF LIABILITY/DISCLAIMER OF WARRANTY: WHILE THE PUBLISHER AND AUTHOR HAVE USED THEIR BEST EFFORTS IN PREPARING THIS BOOK, THEY MAKE NO REPRESENTATIONS OR WARRANTIES WITH RESPECT TO THE ACCURACY OR COMPLETENESS OF THE CONTENTS OF THIS BOOK AND SPECIFICALLY DISCLAIM ANY IMPLIED WARRANTIES OF MERCHANTABILITY OR FITNESS FOR A PARTICULAR PURPOSE. NO WARRANTY MAY BE CREATED OR EXTENDED BY SALES REPRESENTATIVES OR WRITTEN SALES MATERIALS. THE ADVISE AND STRATEGIES CONTAINED HEREIN MAY NOT BE SUITABLE FOR YOUR SITUATION. YOU SHOULD CONSULT WITH A PROFESSIONAL WHERE APPROPRIATE. NEITHER THE PUBLISHER NOR THE AUTHOR SHALL BE LIABLE FOR DAMAGES ARISING HEREFROM.

For general information on our other products and services, please contact our Customer Care Department within the U.S. at 877-762-2974, outside the U.S. at 317-572-3993, or fax 317-572-4002. For technical support, please visit www.wiley.com/techsupport.

Wiley publishes in a variety of print and electronic formats and by print-on-demand. Some material included with standard print versions of this book may not be included in e-books or in print-on-demand. If this book refers to media such as a CD or DVD that is not included in the version you purchased, you may download this material at http://booksupport.wiley.com. For more information about Wiley products, visit www.wiley.com.

Library of Congress Control Number: 2016938156

ISBN: 978-1-119-24549-0 (pbk); ISBN 978-1-119-24571-1 (ebk); ISBN 978-1-119-24569-8 (ebk)

Manufactured in the United States of America

10 9 8 7 6 5 4 3 2 1

Contents at a Glance

Table of Contents

Introduction

E veryone who wants to start a business — or grow one — usually starts with the same question. What's the key to success? Well, you need a good idea, of course. And you have to have a smart strategy to carry it out. But just as important, you need a solid business plan, one that lays out exactly what you hope to do and how you plan to do it. A good business plan sets your course and prepares you for the challenges that inevitably lie ahead in today's fiercely competitive world.

Today, companies large and small face the challenge of change like never before. New business models have transformed whole industries. Innovative technologies have completely altered the way business is done. Opportunities abound. But so do tough challenges. That's why the fifth edition of *Business Plans Kit For Dummies* is packed with fresh advice for navigating marketplace disruptions and finding a successful course through turbulent times. Along the way, you'll find practical advice on how to put a promising business idea to the test, how to recognize your own strengths and weaknesses, how to craft a successful competitive strategy, how to find funding, and much more.

This book doesn't *tell* you how to develop your business plan; it *shows* you how, walking you through the process with step-by-step action plans, examples, and do-it-yourself forms throughout the book, along with more than 100 additional forms online, which you can download at www.dummies.com/go/businessplanskit.

So whether you're planning to launch a brand-new business, kick-start an idling enterprise, run a successful nonprofit, or take a going concern to new heights, this book makes the planning process straightforward, easy, rewarding — and yes, even fun.

About This Book

Plenty of books out there offer business-planning theories and principles. This one is different. It cuts through the academics and steers clear of the jargon to provide an easy-to-grasp, step-by-step approach to putting a business plan together. It also offers dozens of forms to make the task easier and includes examples from all kinds of businesses — from freelancers and small retailers to online marketers and nonprofit organizations. It even provides a template to guide you as you assemble the right parts and pieces into a business plan that addresses your target audience, business goals, and one-of-a-kind situation.

We've updated every chapter of this new edition — and added two brand new chapters — to help steer you toward success in today's business environment, where start-ups abound and established businesses are transforming to adapt to the rapidly changing world around them.

We've added loads of tips on everything from structuring new businesses and business models to adopting the latest technology and social media resources to find, reach, interact with, and develop loyalty from customers. An all-new Chapter 8 helps you explore ways to find funding for your business. A brand new Chapter 12 zeroes in on planning and running a virtual organization. We've expanded our coverage of business models and the increasingly essential role of the Internet. On almost every page, you'll find fresh tips on pricing, promoting, and controlling costs and driving profits in today's business environment. With more people going out on their own or looking for opportunities to start small businesses, we've expanded advice on how to start a new business, raise cash, build brands, and overcome entry barriers. And with more and more nonprofit organizations doing good in the world, we've also updated Chapter 14 with advice on reaching potential donors and snaring grant money.

Foolish Assumptions

You've picked up this book, so we can safely assume that you're probably starting or growing a business. Chances are it's a small- to medium-size business because that's how most companies start. You may be a sole proprietor planning a one-person business, or you may be planning a company with a staff of dozens of people. Who knows, you may even be part of a very large company and writing a plan for your department or division. No matter what brings you to this book, we guarantee you will find a ton of helpful advice. Whether your company is big or small, whether you're just starting out or working for a long-established business, the basics of business planning are the same.

We also assume that you're probably approaching the planning process with more than a little anxiety, which is true of most of the people we work with in our day jobs as business consultants. But guess what: As soon as most business planners get going, they discover that planning isn't just challenging and interesting — it's even fun.

One last note: You don't need previous business experience to make your way through this book, although people with experience will also find plenty of good advice.

Icons Used in This Book

What would a *For Dummies* book be without the margin icons alerting you to all sorts of useful stuff? Here are the icons you find in this book:

TIP

Tried-and-true approaches to help save you time or trouble. This tip icon also points out forms and resources that we describe in this book. You can find them online at www.dummies.com/go/businessplanskit.

REMEMBER

This icon marks business-planning essentials you don't want to forget.

WARNING

Here are common problems or pitfalls to avoid.

EXAMPLE

These real-life examples provide useful lessons on business planning.

Beyond the Book

The book you hold in your hand is chock-full of all the information you need to develop and implement a killer business plan — one that will help turn your very good idea into a very successful business. But there's more. Online resources associated with this edition of *Business Plans Kit For Dummies* contain a wealth of forms that can help guide you, including a template that describes each of the sections your business plan should have, with pointers on where to find advice on developing them within the book.

To view this book's Cheat Sheet, simply go to www.dummies.com and search for "Business Plans Kit For Dummies Cheat Sheet" in the Search box. It offers additional bits of information to refer to as you put together your plan. You can access this material again and again as you need it.

Where to Go from Here

You don't have to begin with the first page and end on the last (although you're certainly welcome to read straight through the book). People turn to business planning for all kinds of reasons and with all kinds of goals in mind, so we organized this book to make it easy to roam around and find exactly what you need. Wherever you start, remember that you can use the handy index to jump quickly to the exact information you need at any time.

If you need some help locating exactly the information you need, flip to the table of contents or the index, find the topic that interests you, and turn to that chapter to start putting your business plan together.

1

Getting Started with Business Plans

IN THIS PART . . .

Recognize the all-important value of business planning, establish your business-planning starting point, and get an overview of the business-planning process that will lead to an effective plan.

Explore ways to hatch new business ideas, put them to the test, refine your choices, and find opportunities best suited to your personal traits, strengths and weaknesses, and marketplace realities.

Know where you want your business to go by giving your business its mission and vision, setting goals and objectives, putting principles into practice, and then designing a business model capable of turning your company into a profit powerhouse.

Lay the groundwork for developing a business plan that's grounded in the reality of market conditions and tailored to the wants, needs, tastes, and trends of your precisely targeted prospective customers. Whether you're launching a start-up, orchestrating a turnaround, or taking a business to new heights, this part helps you make sure you have the basics in place to begin creating a plan that keeps your business a step ahead of competitors and changing conditions.

Chapter 1

Powering Up for Business Success

The fact that you've opened this book means the idea of writing a business plan has made it onto your to-do list. That's a big step in the right direction. Now come the questions. What exactly is a business plan? What should it include? How should it be organized? And do you really need one?

This first chapter of *Business Plans Kit For Dummies,* 5th Edition, answers all those questions and more. It offers plenty of reasons why business planning is essential — when you start your business and at every growth stage along the way. It helps you think about the audience for your plan, what its key components should be, and how to go about putting it together. It also updates you on changes and challenges facing business planners in today's rapidly transforming business arena.

We won't pretend that writing a business plan is a breeze. It takes time and thought. But we wrote this book to make the process manageable and even fun. The fact that it's in its fifth edition, with hundreds of thousands of copies worldwide, suggests that a lot of readers have found it useful.

Now it's time to get going. This chapter gets you oriented and on the way to success.

Selling Yourself on the Importance of Business Planning

Nearly all business experts agree on one thing: the importance of drafting a business plan. Yet plenty of business leaders plunge into the competitive arena without a formal plan. Why? We've heard plenty of excuses posing as reasons. We've also heard from entrepreneurs so carried away by their enthusiasm that they figure their passion and optimism are enough to build a successful company. Others say they were just too busy to develop a formal business plan. But operating without a plan can prove even more time-consuming in the long run. These sections clarify in plain English the importance of having a business plan.

Tallying up the benefits of a business plan

Some of the benefits you can gain from business planning include

>> An opportunity to test your business idea to see if it holds real promise of success (refer to Chapter 2)

>> Clarity about your business mission, vision, and the values that can help you steer your business through times of growth or difficulty (check out Chapter 3)

>> A description of your *business model,* or how you plan to make money and stay in business, along with a road map and timetable for achieving your goals and objectives (see Chapter 3 for more information)

>> A portrait of your potential customers and their buying behaviors (flip to Chapter 4)

>> A rundown of your major competitors and your strategies for facing them (refer to Chapter 4)

>> A clear-eyed analysis of your industry, including opportunities and threats, along with an honest assessment of your company's strengths and weaknesses (head to Chapter 5)

>> Benchmarks you can use to track your performance and make midcourse corrections (turn to Chapters 5 and 17)

>> An explanation of your marketing strategies (flip to Chapter 7)

>> An analysis of your revenues, costs, and projected profits, along with cash flow projections that help you anticipate your funding needs until the time when revenues flow in to cover expenses (check out Chapter 8)

>> An assessment of risks and the forces of change that can threaten your success or present opportunities to capitalize upon (see Chapter 15)

>> A résumé you can use to introduce your business to employees, suppliers, vendors, lenders, and others (look in Chapter 17)

Knowing what can go wrong without a plan

The many benefits of having a business plan should be enough to convince you. But in case you're still wavering, consider what can go wrong if you don't take time to plan. You risk

>> Running out of cash because you haven't projected start-up or expansion costs and the amount of funding you'll need before sufficient revenue rolls in

>> Missing sales projections because you don't really know who your customers are, what they want, or how they shop and buy

>> Becoming overwhelmed or sidetracked by too many options because you never took the time to focus on a mission and vision for your company

>> Going bankrupt because you don't have a rational *business model* or a plan for how to make money

REMEMBER

Take our word for it: Time spent putting together a solid business plan is time well spent. Don't be overwhelmed by the task you're launching. The basic components of a business plan are fairly simple and the benefits are many.

Business planning as a test drive

Business planning sets the course that you intend to follow. But a good business plan also functions as a kind of test drive. It allows you to think about all the parts you need to have in place to turn an idea into a business success or to make a business run at peak performance.

Business planning is also your chance to anticipate bumps or sharp turns that may lie ahead, including economic uncertainties, competitors on the same racetrack, new technologies and innovations, and the way your particular strengths and weaknesses prepare you for the risks and opportunities ahead. Business planning forces you to detail the costs, resources, and timelines required to introduce a business, launch a new product or service, open a new market area, or implement a proposed strategy for growth or business turnaround. Many companies end up retooling their product, service, or strategy as a result of the business planning process.

The Anatomy of a Business Plan

Business plans are as varied as the companies that compile them. Some run dozens of pages. Others barely fill a few sheets. The next sections introduce the basic components that you can adapt to create a plan to meet your needs.

Business plan contents, beginning to end

Although business plans come in all sizes and formats, they typically share a similar framework. The following components, presented in the order they generally appear, are the elements you'll choose from as you build your plan:

>> **Table of contents:** This guide to key sections in your business plan is especially useful if your plan exceeds ten pages.

>> **Executive summary:** This summary of key points in your business plan is important if your plan runs more than ten pages, and you want to convey the major points up-front. You want to keep it clear, captivating, and brief — in fact, aim to keep it to no more than two pages.

>> **Business overview:** This section describes your company and the nature of your business. It may include your company's mission and vision statements as well as descriptions of your values, your products or services, ways your company is unique, and what business opportunities you plan to seize. (Turn to Chapter 3 for help defining your business purpose and developing your overview.)

>> **Business environment:** This section includes an analysis of your industry and the forces at work in your market; a description of your direct and potential competitors; and a close look at your customers, including who they are, what they want, and how they buy products or services. It describes forces beyond your control that affect your business success. (Count on Chapter 4 to help you zoom in on your environment and develop your analysis.)

>> **Business description:** In this section, include information about your management team, organizational structure, new or proprietary technology, products and services, business operations, and marketing potential. (Check out Chapter 6 for help with writing your description.)

>> **Business strategy:** This section is your road map to success. It brings together information about your business environment, business model, goals and objectives, and resources, and then lays out your strategy for start-up, growth, or turnaround. (As you prepare this section, Chapter 5 is an indispensable resource.)

- » **Marketing plan:** This section is where you describe your brand, value proposition, and how you plan to reach prospects, make sales, and develop a loyal clientele. (Chapter 7 helps you develop your marketing plan.)

- » **Financial review:** This section includes a detailed review of the state of your current finances and what you expect your financial picture to look like in the future. It typically contains financial statements, including an income statement, your balance sheet, and a cash-flow statement. (If any of these terms seem foreign to you, or if you want step-by-step financial planning advice, see Chapter 9 for all the details.)

- » **Action plan:** Here you detail the steps involved in implementing your business plan, including the sequence of actions and how they align with your goals and objectives. (Flip to Chapter 3 for advice on establishing goals and objectives, and then turn to Chapter 16 for information on how action plans ensure that you'll put your business plan to work.)

- » **Appendices:** This section includes detailed information that supports your business plan. It may include analyses, reports, surveys, legal documents, product specifications, and spreadsheets that deliver information that supports your business plan but which is of interest to only a small number of your readers.

TIP

For a business plan checklist, go to www.dummies.com/go/businessplanskit to download Form 1-1. It features the preceding lineup of business plan components. As you write your plan, use the list to tick off major components as you complete them.

Keep in mind: There is no single format for a written business plan. For that reason, we don't provide any rigid business-plan models in this book. Instead, in the following chapters you can find information on how to develop each of the major components, advice for how business plans tend to work for different kinds of businesses, and plenty of real-world examples to follow, including model mission statements, goals and objectives, financial statements, and business models. Then, in Chapter 16, we introduce a customizable business plan template that helps you bring together all the planning information referenced throughout this book. The result: a self-tailored business plan for your unique business-planning situation.

Business plan FAQs

If you're like most people who are launching the business-planning process, the following questions are on your mind:

- » **Do you really need to include all these sections?** Nope. Your business plan should include only what's important to you and your company. If your plan is short — or written mostly for your own purposes — you can skip the executive summary and table of contents, for example. Or if it's a one-person business, you may not need to describe its organization (unless you need a little help in getting organized!).

TIP

For most businesses, however, all the other sections are important. By putting your mission, vision, values, product offering, goals, and competitive advantages into words, you clarify and strengthen ideas about what you really plan to do with your business. That exercise can be extremely valuable for any company, no matter how big or small.

>> **Do you really need to write it all down?** The one-word answer is yes. Creating a written plan forces you to think through issues that you may otherwise ignore. For example, when you write your business plan, you commit to how you're going to make money; you define your customers and your strategy for reaching them; you analyze your competition and how your offerings compare to theirs; you list opportunities to seize and threats to protect against; and you establish a set of goals and objectives — along with your action plan for achieving success. And when you're done, you have it all in writing for quick, easy, and frequent reference.

>> **How long should your plan be?** As long as it needs to be — and not a single word longer. A business plan as thick as a good novel doesn't impress anyone. In fact, a plan that size is likely to scare people off. What really impresses investors, clients, employees, and anyone else who may read your plan is clear, straightforward, and to-the-point thinking. Don't go overboard in the cutting room or leave anything important out of your plan purely for the sake of keeping it brief, but do condense every section down to its most important points. Even comprehensive plans usually fit on 20 to 30 pages, plus appendices. Most 100-page business plans are about 75 pages too long.

Establishing Your Planning Objectives

To get your business where you want it to go, you need a map to follow, which is what your business plan is all about.

TIP

Imagine that your company is a ship about to set sail on an ocean voyage. Your business plan defines your destination and the route that you'll follow. It details the supplies and crew you have on board as well as what you still need to acquire. It forecasts the voyage's cost. It describes the weather and sea conditions you're likely to encounter and anticipates the potential dangers that may lurk over the horizon. Finally, your business plan identifies other ships that may be attempting to beat you to your destination.

The same kind of planning is necessary back on dry land. To navigate a new course for your company, you need to start with an assessment of where your business is right now. You may be putting your business together for the first time. Or your business may be up and running but facing new challenges. Or perhaps your business is doing well and about to launch a new product or service. After you assess your current situation, you need to define where you want to arrive and what financial, operational, marketing, and organizational strategies you'll follow to achieve success. The next sections lead the way.

Defining your starting point

Every business planner begins with a different set of issues and goals. You're likely beginning the planning process at one of these starting points:

» A good idea you want to turn into a business

» A side gig you want to turn into a business

» A business that needs funding to get off the ground or to expand

» An established business that's struggling and needs to get back on track

» An established business in need of better talent, partners, or customers

» An established business with growth that seems out of control

» An established business with growth limited by lack of scalability

» An established business launching a new product or service

» A business preparing for management transition or sale to new owners

TIP

To define your current business situation, download Form 1-2 at www.dummies. com/go/businessplanskit. It lists many of the situations that companies face as they embark on the planning process. Check off the situations that apply to your circumstances. Your business plan essentially will map the route you'll follow from your starting point to the goals you want to reach.

Zeroing in on the changes you want to plan for

Setting out your priorities in the form of a business-planning wish list can help you focus your efforts.

WRITE A PLAN; MAKE MORE MONEY

For proof that a business plan is important, consider this example. When the Kauffman Center for Entrepreneurial Leadership surveyed the annual winners of its Entrepreneur of the Year Award, it found that companies with written business plans had 50 percent greater sales growth and 12 percent higher gross profit margins than companies without plans. How's that for incentive?

TIP

Check out Form 1-3 for a list of top priorities shared by many businesses embarking on the planning process. Place a check mark beside the items that are on your wish list or use the provided space to enter your own unique desired outcomes. After completing the form, assign a priority (low, medium, or high) to the items you've checked. Keeping this form handy as you go through the planning process can help you stay on track to meet your planning goals.

Setting out your planning objectives

With a thousand issues clamoring for the precious hours in your day, committing time to plan your company's future isn't easy. But operating without a plan is even harder — and even more time-consuming in the long run. Two steps can help you get started. The first is to define your planning objective, whether it's to start or grow a business, launch a product, pivot to new strategies, or orchestrate a turnaround to get your business from where it is to where you want it to be. The second is to realize the ways that a business plan can heighten the odds of success for businesses in all stages.

Planning for a new business

Every new business — whether a tech start-up or new business in a long-standing arena — begins with a new idea and high hopes. A business plan helps you evaluate your new idea, potential market, and competition, addressing these critical questions:

>> Does this new venture have a good chance of getting off the ground?

>> How much money will the business need to get up and running?

>> Who are your customers, and what's the best way to reach them?

>> Who are your competitors, and what's the best way to outrun them?

>> Why will people choose this product or service over other options?

Count on Chapter 11 as you develop the plan for launching and growing a small business.

Planning for a solo business

Millions of people work for themselves in businesses called *sole proprietorships.* They range from accountants and attorneys to app developers, artists, and musicians. Many never consider drafting a business plan, which is too bad. A business plan helps zero in on key questions:

>> Are you prepared for running a company of one?

>> How can you turn what you love doing into a profitable business?

>> What resources do you need to get your business off the ground?

>> What should you charge for your product or service?

>> What affiliations could you explore to strengthen the business?

Chapter 2 includes a section on turning a side gig into a business, and Chapter 10 provides valuable information for planning, building, and running a one-person business.

Planning to address changing conditions

No business today is immune to change. New technologies, disruptive innovations, and global, economic, and political turbulence prompt many established businesses to plan how to retool themselves. In fact, one of the main reasons we've updated the book is to include new strategies for anticipating and dealing with change. The critical questions a business plan must address are as follows:

>> What are the drivers of change that present your business with internal or external threats or opportunities?

>> How can you reshape your business, its technology, its products or services, and its customer interactions to better compete in its transformed environment?

>> What steps do you need to take to achieve your goals for change?

Every chapter of this book helps you plan around the changes facing your business. Plus, Chapter 15 focuses entirely on proactively planning for change as a fundamental step in business planning. It helps you identify the drivers of change in your business arena so you can anticipate the likely impact and devise strategies to avert trouble and gain competitive advantage.

Planning for growth

Successful companies can't rest on their laurels. To remain successful, they have to maintain their competitive edge. And to grow, they need to seize new opportunities, whether by introducing products, expanding into new locations or market segments, improving efficiencies and profitability, or embracing new innovations. For companies charting a strategy to grow, a business plan must address several key questions:

» How are you planning to deepen customer loyalty?

» Where do the best opportunities for growth lie?

» If you're aiming to reach new market areas or new consumer segments, who are your competitors in these new markets?

» Can you take advantage of technological innovations?

» How can you revise operations and processes to scale into a larger business or to improve profitability?

» How can you best compete to grab new market share?

Turn to Chapters 5, 6, and 13 for advice as you plan to strengthen business capabilities and chart strategies to achieve your business growth goals.

Identifying Your Business Plan Audiences and Key Messages

Your business plan is the blueprint for how you plan to reach your business goals. To help focus your efforts, consider which groups of people will have the greatest impact on your success. Those groups will be the primary audiences for your business plan. For example, if you need capital investment, investors will be your primary audience. If you need to build strategic alliances, you want your plan to address potential business partners. You and your team are another key audience for the plan, of course, because it will serve as your guide.

After you know *whom* you want to reach with your business plan, you can focus on what those readers need to know and what messages you want them to receive. These sections help you define your audience and your messages before you begin to assemble your plan.

Your audience

All the people who have an interest in or who can help you succeed in your business venture — from investors and lenders to employees, customers, and suppliers — represent *audiences* for your business plan. Depending on the situation you face and what you want your company to achieve through its plan, certain audiences will be more important than others:

>> If your company seeks investment capital, your all-important target audience is likely to be filled with potential investors.

>> If your plan includes the introduction of stock options (possibly in lieu of higher salaries), your current and prospective employees and stakeholders are a primary target audience.

>> If you're launching a business that needs clients to get up and running — the sooner the better — major customers may comprise one of your plan's primary audiences.

>> If you're self-employed in a one-person business, your plan may be to focus on you and you alone as you chart your course and anticipate problems before they arise.

TIP

Check out Form 1-4 for a checklist of the most common audiences for a business plan.

Your message

After you target the audiences for your plan, the next step is to focus on the key messages you want each group to receive. For example:

>> A person who owns shares in a company wants to know growth plans.

>> A banker considering a loan request wants to see proof of strong revenue and profit prospects.

>> Employee groups want to see how they'll benefit from the company's growth and profits.

>> Regulators focus on operational and financial issues.

TIP

Take time to clarify the primary messages you need to convey to your key audiences. Refer to Form 1-4 for samples of messages that various audiences are likely to consider important. Then, use Form 1-5 as a worksheet as you identify the three most important audiences you intend to address with your business plan and the key points you want to convey to each.

For more advice on targeting and talking to key audiences, including information on which parts of the business plan various audiences turn to first and how to address multiple audiences with a single plan, head to Chapter 16.

Establishing Your Plan's Time Frame

Your *time frame* represents how far into the future you want your business plan to reach. You want your business to grow successfully for years and years into the future, but each business plan covers a unique planning period. Some are designed to get a company to a defined sales level, a funding objective, or the achievement of some other business goal. All good plans should span a time frame that has a realistic start and finish, with a number of measurable checkpoints in between. The sections that follow help you determine how far into the future your plan should extend and the milestones that you can use to chart your progress.

Setting your schedule

How far out your planning horizon should span depends on the kind of business you're in and the pace at which your industry is moving. Some ventures have only six months to prove themselves. At the other end of the spectrum, organizations with substantial endowments, such as nonprofits, are in for the long haul with business plans that look at five- or ten-year horizons. Typical business plans, however, tend to use one-year, three-year, or five-year benchmarks.

REMEMBER

Business planning is an ongoing process. At least annually — and sometimes more often — most companies review, revise, and even completely overhaul their plans. As you establish your time frame, don't cast it in cement. Instead, think of your schedule as something you commit to follow unless and until circumstances change and you make a conscious decision to revise it.

Defining milestones

Establishing goals and establishing measurable objectives is a critical part of business planning. (Take a look at Chapter 3 to find out more about setting goals and objectives.) But knowing your goals and objectives isn't enough. You also need to establish and hold yourself accountable to a schedule that includes specific milestones to reach along the way to success.

EXAMPLE

Figure 1-1 shows how a retail store specializing in digital equipment answered five questions in order to establish a reasonable time frame for its expansion plans. Based on their answers, the owners determined that the business would need one year to open new stores and achieve profitability. Over that yearlong planning period, they defined a number of milestones:

>> **Month 1:** Complete business plan.

>> **Month 2:** Secure business loans.

>> **Month 3:** Lease and begin development of retail spaces.

>> **Month 5:** Begin hiring and training.

>> **Months 6-7:** Open shops; produce holiday ads.

>> **Month 8:** Holiday shopping season begins.

>> **Month 12:** New stores become profitable.

FIGURE 1-1:
These questions, included in the downloadable Form 1-6, help determine your business plan time frame and milestones.

Business Plan Time Frame Questionnaire

1. Identify three milestones that represent essential steps you need to take to get your business off the ground or to the next level of achievement. Estimate a time frame for each.

- **Milestone 1:**   Secure business loans.   (2 months)
- **Milestone 2:**   Lease and develop four locations.   (5 months)
- **Milestone 3:**   Get all shops up and running.   (8 months)

2. Is the success of your business tied to a major business trend? If so, what is the time frame?

The emerging market for digital devices — already underway, with new products scheduled for release every quarter.   (5 months)

3. Is your business seasonal in nature? When do you need to have your product or service available to take advantage of the peak season?

Holiday sales represent 50 percent of our revenue.   (8 months)

4. How soon do you need to make your product or service available to stay ahead of your competition?

Consumer electronics is extremely competitive.   (ASAP)

5. When do you absolutely need to start making a profit or meet your profit projection?

Moderate financial pressure on the company.   (Within 1 year)

Download and answer the planning questions in Form 1-6. Then use your responses to establish your business plan time frame, along with key milestones that take into account your business trends and cycles and the competitive and financial realities of your business.

Launching the Planning Process

You're about ready to dive into the business-planning process. By now you're pretty certain about the purpose and benefit of your plan, and you have a fairly clear idea of who you want to read your opus when it's ready, and what you want them to do as a result. You may even have a preliminary idea of your planning timeline. (If any of that sounds like Greek, look back at the preceding sections in this chapter.)

Before you turn to Chapter 2 and dive into the planning process, however, take a minute to become aware of some of the resources you can turn to for additional tips and tools.

Locating informative resources

You're certain to have plenty of questions as your business planning gets under-way. We attempt to answer most of them, but here's a list of other places you can check out:

>> **The Internet:** You can find tons of information on markets, customers, competition — you name it. Just make sure the material is current and from reliable sources. Reputable industry, government, or university reports are among the best resources for tracking market shifts and trends.

Also, spend time studying customer comments on review and rating sites. Look to see what customers like and don't like about products and services already on the market. Study your own customer reviews, if you have them, and also study what people say about competing offerings. Every complaint you see represents a potential business opportunity.

>> **The library:** The periodical section of most libraries has business journals and other useful publications, and the reference shelves contain books on demographics, industry trends, and other factual resources.

>> **Business schools:** Colleges, universities, and organizations (including the Small Business Association [SBA]) offer courses that can develop your planning, financial, and management skills. Also, many business school professors are willing to discuss specific planning issues.

- >> **Industry trade journals:** Yes, the subscriptions can be pricey, but they're often worth the investment and sometimes available at libraries.

- >> **Newspapers:** No matter your business, *The New York Times, The Wall Street Journal,* and local papers keep you on top of issues and trends.

- >> **Trade shows and industry symposiums:** These gatherings are usually great places to get news about products, services, customers, and competitors — all under one roof.

- >> **US Small Business Administration (SBA):** This rich resource is for just about everything you want to know about starting and running a small business. Look at www.sba.gov.

- >> **Search and research companies:** Using these resources comes with a price, but sometimes a LEXIS/NEXIS search or a market-research study is the only way to access must-have data.

- >> **Professional groups:** Almost every profession has a guild or group, from the American Medical Writers Association to the Society of Wetlands Scientists. Find the group that serves your business arena and check out the website and membership requirements.

- >> **Business networking groups:** These groups are comprised of members with experience, insights, and even business referrals to share.

- >> **Local business organizations:** Your local Chamber of Commerce and economic development organization are good vehicles for networking, staying abreast of local and state issues, and obtaining business and regional information.

Seeking expert advice

When you can't find answers to specific questions, ask for advice. For example, if you're thinking of starting a business, ask someone who runs a similar business to fill you in on what you need to know. If you want to break away from the corporate grind and go into business for yourself, schedule a lunch with someone who made a similar move to discover what it takes. You're sure to get an earful of useful input to incorporate in your planning.

TIP

As you interview industry contacts — or people with experience in similar businesses — follow these steps:

- >> **Prepare your questions in advance.** With advance planning, you won't waste time or forget to discuss something really important.

- >> **Explain exactly why you're asking for help.** You can't expect people to be open with you if you aren't honest with them.

>> **Be prepared to listen.** Even if you hear something you don't want to know, listen anyway. Anybody who warns you about potential obstacles is doing you a big favor.

>> **Keep the conversation open-ended.** Always ask whether you should be thinking about other issues or addressing other topics.

>> **Build your network of contacts.** Ask for introductions to others who may be helpful or for suggestions for sources of useful information.

Sharing the load

Identify key people who can help you during the business-planning process. If you're in business on your own chances or you'll shoulder most of the business-planning efforts yourself, advisers or a mentor can offer valuable insight and assistance. If you're in business on your own, chances are you'll shoulder most of the business planning efforts yourself. Still, advisers or a mentor can offer valuable insight and assistance. For one thing, people with different backgrounds have different perspectives that add breadth and depth to your business plan. What's more, by involving team members in the process you ensure that they have a stake in getting results and reaching plan goals.

WARNING

Some large companies hire consultants to handle parts of the planning process. The biggest downside of outsourcing the work is that you may end up with a plan that doesn't really reflect the values or situation of your business. Worse, it may fail to win the commitment of the managers who are ultimately responsible for putting its strategies into action. The remedy is to make sure that those on your senior management team play a central role in the planning process. The marketing team, for example, may be charged with writing the company-strategy section, and the Chief Financial Officer (CFO) is an obvious choice for completing the financial review. And think about asking someone in corporate communications to write a crisp, clear, to-the-point executive summary (but wait until all the other parts of the plan are completed and ready to be summarized).

Staying on track

TIP

To organize your business-planning process, take advantage of Form 1-7, which lists the major components of a typical business plan. If you intend to delegate parts of the planning task, you can use this form to keep track of who's in charge of which component and when it's due. If you're planning all by yourself, you can use the form to track your progress.

TIP

Because business planning involves a lot of brainstorming, discussion, vision, and revision, it generates drafts, redrafts, and edits all along the way. To keep track of it all, name one person, preferably a natural-born organizer to head the team and be the keeper of all the materials related to your plan. (If yours is a one-person business, obviously that person is you.) Plus, consider using collaboration software to consolidate all work in a single document. Dropbox and Google Docs are two of many free tools to help with the task.

The business plan template we introduce in Chapter 16 can help when it's time to assemble your final document. Also, search online for business-planning software — from freeware and shareware programs to full-service commercial software — that can help you through the process.

Forms

Go to www.dummies.com/go/businessplanskit to view and download these forms designed to help you get ready to start the business-planning process:

Form 1-1	**Major Components in a Typical Business Plan**	A checklist of the most common sections found in a typical business plan
Form 1-2	**Typical Business-Planning Situations**	A variety of situations that typically prompt business-planning activity
Form 1-3	**Business-Planning Wish List**	A checklist of your main objectives in writing a business plan
Form 1-4	**Checklist of Common Business Plan Audiences**	Examples of groups and individuals who may have a stake in your business plan
Form 1-5	**Business Plan Target Audiences and Key Messages**	A form for listing the key audiences for your business plan and the messages you want each to receive
Form 1-6	**Business Plan Time Frame Questionnaire**	Questions to help you determine the best time frame to use for your business planning
Form 1-7	**Business Plan Tracker**	A form you can use to keep track of who's in charge of each business plan component and when it's due

Chapter 2

Developing the Idea That Powers Your Plan

Almost all successful businesses begin with a good idea. The idea may be based on a brand new product or service. Or, it may introduce an existing product or service into a new niche. Great business ideas are born when someone figures out a better way to make something or to provide customers what they need or want. Successful business ideas don't have to be world-shaking. But no matter how modest or extensive they are, they have to appeal to customers in order to succeed.

Writing a business plan is one of the most important steps in shaping an idea and putting it to its first test. The process of writing a business plan can help you identify both the strengths and weaknesses of your idea. Doing so can enable you to tweak your idea to make it as strong as possible. Count on the following pages to fuel your idea-generating process with tips and tools for taking stock of your personal resources, asking others for advice, brainstorming ideas alone or in a group, putting your possibilities through a make-it-or-break-it reality check, and, finally, weighing the likelihood that investors, customers, and colleagues will want to buy into your business proposition.

Recognizing the Power of a Good Idea

Facebook started with a good idea. So did Whole Foods. Toyota had a pretty good idea when it developed a hybrid engine. Apple did too, when the company decided to build a touch screen device big enough to read, draw, and write on. Today, Tesla is an engine of innovative ideas. So is Google. Even simple ideas — like creating a website where people with accommodations to rent connect with people who want to rent them — can grow into billion-dollar businesses.

Good ideas aren't limited to major companies. The young couple who decides to open a doggy day care in a town where a lot of people commute to work may have a great idea, too. Or, there's the home brewer who realizes that a small-town ale can make it big. Even the local caterer who decides to take her business on the road in the form of a fleet of food trucks may be able to turn that idea into profit.

TIP

When coming up with a good business idea, keep these five key characteristics in mind:

>> A good business idea meets a real need or desire.

>> It offers something new (or at least a little different).

>> It's grounded in reality, not wishful thinking.

>> It can generate money.

>> It's something you want to do.

Read on to begin the process of developing and fine-tuning your business idea to make sure it can stand up to the harsh realities of the marketplace.

Starting, growing, or pivoting a business

Putting your business idea into words is a no-brainer if you're starting a new company. After all, when you're building something from the ground up, you definitely need a concept and a plan for turning it into reality. But a well-developed idea is just as essential for an established business aiming to grow or planning to pivot in a new strategic direction.

The emphasis of your plan will differ depending on your goal, of course. A business plan for a start-up has to cover all the bases. A plan for growing your business may zero in specifically on customer analysis and marketing strategy. On the other hand, a plan for pivoting a business may focus on how to leverage current resources to make the turn in a new direction. But whether you're aiming to launch, grow, or pivot your business, you need to be clear about the business idea upon which you can build your goals and strategies.

WARNING

Don't assume that defining the idea behind the business plan for growing or pivoting your company is easier than for a start-up. In some ways, it's tougher. An established company with an entrenched way of doing business often has trouble changing its corporate culture quickly and thoroughly enough to make a fleet change in direction. It has to overcome a lot of inertia. A business plan for pivoting to a whole new product or service line, or a new business model, needs to address the obstacles that the business must overcome. As you develop the essential idea behind the new direction, compare it to the idea that launched your business in the first place. Ask these questions:

>> What do your original plan and your new plan have in common?

>> In what ways are they different?

>> What are the key obstacles to changing direction?

Knowing the difference between passion and profitability

Plenty of profitable businesses owe their success to a personal passion. A baker who starts a successful bakery, a musician who opens a recording studio, a teacher who starts a nonprofit tutoring service all have passion in common. That's great. Excitement and confidence are crucial to making a business a success.

So is a good dose of reality.

WARNING

Being excited about what you want to do is no guarantee of success. Businesses that begin with passionate optimism sometimes go belly-up. Personal passion can carry you away, blinding you to the hard realities that any business faces in making it in today's highly competitive world. The bottom line of all for-profit businesses is ultimately — you guessed it — profit. If you're hoping to turn a personal passion into a successful business, you need to ask yourself a simple question: Can it make a profit?

The question may be simple. Answering it isn't always so easy.

TIP

If you're sitting down to write a business plan because you already have a knock-'em-dead idea, now's the good time to give it a test run. Use the questions on Form 2-1. For help, go to www.dummies.com/go/businessplanskit to view and download the Great Business Idea Evaluation form.

BOOST YOUR PERSONAL CREATIVITY QUOTIENT

Where do creative ideas originate? As part of an informal survey, innovative individuals named their top idea-generating activities. The most frequently cited answers lead off the following list:

In the shower	Commuting	Going to sleep
Just waking up	During quiet moments	Actively thinking
Exercising	Meditating	Walking
Talking with friends	While vacationing	During the night
During a business meeting	Reading	Sitting at the desk
While under pressure	Napping	Dreaming
At a business seminar	Lunching with colleagues	In the classroom

Identify the activities that get your creative juices going, and over the next few weeks, devote a little more time to those pursuits. Watch for a boost in your creativity as a result.

Taking a look at ideas behind successful businesses — and some that went bust

Having role models of the kind of business you want to create can offer useful insights into what it takes to succeed. As you develop your idea for a business, think about the ideas that launched the companies you want to emulate.

TIP

Download Form 2-2. After you make a list of businesses powered by ideas that you really like or admire, use this form to zero in on exactly what distinguishes their business ideas and how you can emulate their strengths.

REMEMBER

Evaluating successful business ideas is only one way to begin the process of refining your own idea. Discovering the hard lessons of once-promising ideas that crashed and burned can be just as enlightening.

Recent business history is littered with the wreckage of plenty of ideas that may have seemed like really good ones on paper. Consider Leap Transit, which set out to solve the transportation woes of San Francisco's army of hard-working high-tech commuters. Leap raised $2.5 million to create a fleet that would carry riders around the city in wood-trimmed buses outfitted with black leather seats, Wi-Fi, and individual USB ports — not to mention snack bars with vegan, paleo, and other trendy goodies that could be bought via app. For a brief moment, Leap Transit seemed well on the way to changing the face of commuting. Then, in 2015, the high-flying start-up went belly-up so suddenly that many of its idled buses are still stocked with goodies.

What went wrong? As it turns out, the company made more than its fair share of mistakes. It tried to launch a transit system without getting the necessary licenses from the city, which forced it to temporarily stop service. It also didn't do a good job of creating an image. In a city where the rise of high-tech wealth and privilege has created major tensions, Leap Transit and its vegan snacks came to be seen as the epitome of the silliest self-absorbed aspects of Silicon Valley culture. And it didn't help that Uber and Lyft came along to offer an even more efficient way of getting across the city by the bay. The good idea behind Leap Transit, in other words, wasn't so hot after all.

TIP

Silicon Valley start-ups often crash and burn. Fortunately, the high-tech sector has taken to heart the idea that failures provide valuable lessons that can help spell success the next time around. Luckily, anyone can benefit from those lessons; all you have to do is take time to identify struggling or failing businesses that are in the same marketplace that you hope to enter. Ask these questions:

>> What did they do wrong?

>> What makes the idea behind your business different?

>> What can you do to avoid the same fate?

Searching Out Great Business Ideas

Maybe the idea behind some highly successful businesses began with a flash of inspiration that came out of nowhere. But not many. Most were developed by painstakingly surveying the territory and looking for a new or better product or service, a new way to deliver value to customers, or a new business model. Some great business ideas grow out of a confluence of new technological innovations (think iPad). Some are inspired by regulatory changes (think the solar power industry). Some are born out of passion (think of the artist who opens a gallery). These sections provide tips to assist you in recognizing opportunities that just may lead to an unbeatable business idea.

Tuning in to what customers have to say

The Internet — and specifically online review sites — can be an excellent source of inspiration for new business opportunities. Customers, it turns out, have very strong opinions about what they've bought or what they want, and they're not afraid to voice them. Just look at the reviews on Amazon, Yelp, HomeAway, and other consumer sites. Those reviews, good and bad, can tell you exactly what customers like, what they don't like, and what they'd like to see in products and services. Their input is a gold mine of information.

Say that you're interested in designing and producing a computer program that will make it easier for people to compose their own songs. Several such programs already exist. Go onto the sites that sell them, such as Musician's Friend, and you'll find plenty of chatter from satisfied and unsatisfied customers. Their likes and dislikes can help you decide what your product needs to offer in order to compete with products already in the marketplace.

REMEMBER

The people who write online reviews of products and services are often outliers. Either they loved what they bought or they hated it, which is why they're motivated to take the time to write a review. The bulk of customers falls somewhere in between. Online reviews can give you a good sense of the two ends of the spectrum. Most of your potential customers are likely to lie somewhere in between.

Catching up with marketplace and business world realities

Business planning sometimes addresses specific challenges that an existing company faces: retooling a product or service that isn't working, for example, or addressing a new competitive challenge. Sometimes it aims to seize new market opportunity, such as the surge in interest in microbrews, the quick adoption of wearable fitness devices, or the legalization of marijuana. In some cases, business planning is done on an emergency basis, as in when the company is suddenly bleeding cash and needs major surgery to avoid going under. Sometimes planning is motivated by technological innovations that suddenly change the playing field — and demand a new idea for moving forward. Developing a successful idea depends on taking a clear-eyed look at the opportunity or challenge and coming up with creative solutions backed by an action-based strategic plan. The first step is asking the appropriate questions.

TIP

Use the questions in Form 2-3 to begin the process of brainstorming strategies to meet the pressing challenges your business faces.

Pursuing changes that open up new opportunities

Many fledgling businesses succeed by jumping on new opportunities that arise through technological, social, policy, or other changes. Change can be scary, but it can also open new doors. Spotting that door — and being the first to open it — requires skill and a little daring. For example, when Apple launched the iPad, a whole new industry of apps and accessories sprang into existence, created by designers and developers perceptive and daring enough to plunge into a new technology and a new marketplace.

As Internet bandwidth increased and the potential for streaming video appeared on the horizon, companies like Amazon, Netflix, and Hulu seized the opportunity, establishing themselves as leaders and leaving some competitors — remember Blockbuster video? — in the dust. Today, with baby boomers retiring, a host of companies are looking for ways to strike gold by opening high-end retirement communities, providing healthcare consulting services, or offering products and services that promise to keep people youthful even as they age.

TIP

Any time the government breaks up a monopoly, new arenas for competition arise. Regulatory changes and new tax incentives also open the door to opportunity, if you're smart and agile enough to take advantage. As part of your brainstorming, ask your team to consider ongoing or likely changes that could open up new opportunities.

There are many ways to spell business success. True, many companies succeed by creating a brand-new product or service. But opportunities also materialize for selling existing products or services to new customers or by creating a new business model that makes an existing product or service more appealing to established or new customers.

EXAMPLE

SolarCity has become a major player in the rooftop solar revolution. The company didn't invent a new form of solar panel or a new way of installing panels. Instead, it offered customers a novel way to take advantage of solar without having to pay the steep up-front cost of installing an array of panels. Their innovative solution: SolarCity offers an option wherein it owns and operates the panels. In return for being allowed to put them on your roof, the company agrees to sell you the electricity generated at a guaranteed rate per kilowatt hour over the next 20 years. Customers get the benefit of low up-front costs, no maintenance worries, and the peace of mind that comes from knowing your electricity rate won't climb — not to mention the satisfaction that comes from doing the planet a good turn. SolarCity gets to use your rooftop and take advantage of state and federal incentives for solar. We call that a win-win business model.

These days, many companies prosper by finding clever ways to make people's personal or working lives easier or more efficient. Think no-iron shirts. Think parking garages that offer car washes. Think dictation software that does away with the need to type. Think apps for making restaurant reservations. Evaluate your promising business idea to see whether you can take advantage of new opportunities to improve the efficiency or effectiveness of your customers' lives.

Spotting strategies to grow or pivot existing businesses

Maybe your business is doing okay as it is — but only okay. Sales are lackluster. Your customers seem satisfied, but efforts to expand your customer base haven't exactly taken off. You haven't met the milestones in your existing business plan. Maybe the plan as a whole just isn't working.

Now is the time to brainstorm ideas to put it on a solid path to success. Developing ways to grow or pivot your business is a lot like creating a brand new business, but it's also different in several key ways. You probably already have some ideas about what's working for you and what's not. And you also have employees with skill and knowledge to help you out. Tap into those resources. Put together a team to begin coming up with strategies to grow or pivot your existing business. Start by making a list of what's working in your existing business plan and where you fall short. From there, compile a list of your company's strengths and weaknesses (use the SWOT analysis section in Chapter 5 as your guide). Then, brainstorm ways to leverage your strengths either to grow your business or pivot in a new direction.

Watch for indicators that a pivot may be in the cards, including these signs:

>> One aspect of your business is far outperforming all others and deserves to become the sole or key focus of your business.

>> The customers you set out to target aren't responding to your offerings, your pricing, your distribution channels, or other aspects key to your success, alerting you that that major changes are necessary.

>> The opportunities you set out to seize are overshadowed by new opportunities that change what your business offers or how it produces, presents, prices, and sells established products and services.

If you're contemplating a big shift in how you do business, be prepared for head winds. Chances are some of your employees will welcome change; others won't. Some may be so threatened by change that they resist and even undermine the process. Be alert to how your staff responds — and be prepared to let some people go if they aren't willing to follow the new course you set.

Reimagining your business environment

A survey of 500 of the fastest-growing companies in the United States showed that nearly half grew directly out of the founders' previous work environments. In other words, the founders created these companies after looking around at what they were doing and thinking, "There *has* to be a better way to do this." Solutions to challenges also often come from within. After all, who knows your business and your customers' wants and needs better than you and your employees? With that knowledge, ask: What would you do, what products and services would you offer, and how would you produce and present your products if you were starting from scratch to address the problems and fulfill the desires that your business addresses?

WARNING

As you dream up new business ideas, be aware of potential roadblocks. For example, many companies require employees to sign *noncompete agreements*. These agreements usually prohibit former employees from engaging in competitive businesses for a set period of time. If you've signed one, make sure your new venture doesn't violate its terms.

Also, watch out for tunnel vision. Although people inside the company are an invaluable source of new ideas, we can point to many examples of companies that recognized the challenges they faced but were unable to come up with effective strategies to meet them. The reason: People inside a company who are used to the way things work often have trouble thinking outside the box. Even sole proprietors and small business people run into the same problem. They're so close to the company and its way of doing business that they can't see the forest for the trees.

TIP

One way around the problem of tunnel vision is to invest in the talents of an outside consultant — someone who sees your business and its challenges with fresh, unbiased eyes. Another approach, if you have employees in a variety of positions, is to ask someone from an unrelated part of the business to look at the problem and suggest solutions.

REMEMBER

When considering new business possibilities, keep in mind that 99 percent of all businesses (both old and new) fall into one of three broad categories:

>> **Products for sale:** Consider the range of products that your industry offers.

- Can you think of innovative ways to make them better?
- Can you imagine a product that completely replaces them?
- What new product would knock you out of business if the competition offered it first?

>> **Services for hire:** Consider the services that your industry offers.

- Do you notice problems with consistency?
- What isn't being done that should be?

- What do customers complain about?

- What new services would threaten your business if the competition offered them first?

>> **Distribution and delivery:** Ask yourself similar questions about your distribution and delivery systems.

- What are the most serious bottlenecks?

- Can you think of clever ways to improve distribution?

- Can you envision a radically new delivery system? (Think Amazon and its proposed drone delivery program.)

Adjusting to the digital future

The digital revolution has transformed so many industries and so many markets that the world most people live in today looks very different from what it did just a generation ago. The music business, journalism, retail sales, personal transportation, healthcare, movie-going, and even dating have been turned upside down by the rise of the Internet and mobile devices. The digital era has also changed how people plan and operate businesses. Today, if a business doesn't have a strong website, it may as well be invisible. And that's only the beginning of the transformations that many businesses have undergone.

In some industries and marketplaces, the transformation is still in its early stages. The power of digital technologies is just starting to change the way medicine is practiced, the way home appliances operate, the way people get from here to there, and the way people use energy, to name just a few examples.

WARNING

Every promising business idea must take into account the transformative power of the digital revolution — or risk being buried by it.

As a first step, ask three questions:

>> How important are the Internet and social media to your business idea and how will you employ them in plans for product design and development, research and development, marketing, and customer service, customer retention, and customer loyalty?

>> How could you leverage digital technologies to make a good idea even better, whether through customer and market research, co-creation with customers, team input using web-based collaboration project management and chat tools, or other applications?

>> How can advances in digital technologies — think virtual reality glasses, implantable communication devices, and the *Internet of Things* (the growing network of Internet-connected everyday household and other physical devices), online customer access to goods and services, business access to customer and research data, cloud computing, and more — improve or disrupt your business idea?

TIP

Take the time to come up with as many ideas as you can. Not all of them will turn out to be useful, but pondering the impact and opportunities of digital technology can help you refine your business idea to take into account inevitable changes.

Turning a side gig into a business

Lots of people we know have their day jobs — you know, the work that pays the rent — and then they have the thing they really like to do, whether it's making pottery, volunteering at the animal shelter, or collecting dolls. And most of them would love nothing more than turning their side interests into a profit-making business.

Good for them, we say. But it takes more than passion to start a successful business. Most successful entrepreneurs will tell you that they were surprised to discover what goes into making a business work. Often, the surprise is how little they knew about the nuts and bolts of operating a business. Consider the example of a woman who developed her baking skills at home and then started a highly successful northern California bakery. She knew the craft of baking. She knew the equipment she needed to go from home baking to commercial baking. What she wasn't prepared for was managing a staff. In the first year, personnel problems plagued her bakery and almost scuttled her business.

TIP

If you're thinking of turning something you love to do into a business, take time to ask yourself some basic but important questions. Form 2-4 has some questions you can use to begin the process of exploring what you need to turn passion into profitability.

Inspiring team creativity (with or without donuts or bagels)

The best creative thinking isn't necessarily done alone. Put a few heads together, and you may whip up a mental hurricane. The outcome depends on the nature of the group of individuals you assemble (the more dynamic, inspired, freewheeling, and innovative, the better) and the communication skills that the session leader brings into the room.

Turning a Gig into a Business
Making money by doing something you love to do sounds great. But turning a passion into a business requires a realistic evaluation of your capabilities and the market you hope to serve. Use this form to begin answering the hard questions that will ultimately make the task of turning a gig into a business a little easier.
☐ What is your product or service? (Be as specific as possible.)
☐ How will you make money? (Be as specific and creative as possible.)
☐ How will you reach your customers or clients?
☐ Where will you conduct your business?
☐ Will you need employees? How many? What jobs will they do?
☐ What kinds of equipment will you need to get started?
☐ How much money will you need to get up and running?
☐ What are your monthly operating expenses likely to be?
☐ How much money will you need to earn each month to be successful?
☐ What are your biggest strengths to start this business?
☐ What are your greatest weaknesses?
☐ What can you do to turn those weaknesses into strengths (or at least work around them)?
☐ Who are your competitors? What are their strengths and weaknesses?
☐ What are the potential risks a business like this faces? How can you minimize the risks?

© John Wiley & Sons, Inc.

FORM 2-4: Use this form to explore whether you can turn a passion into a profitable business.

WARNING

The quickest way to kill an idea is to say anything akin to any of the following:

>> It won't work.

>> We're not ready for that.

>> It isn't practical.

>> It's already been done.

>> That's just plain stupid.

The group you assemble needs to remain open to all ideas presented in order to develop a healthy idea–generating environment.

Applying the LCS system to nurture new ideas

To nurture brand–new ideas and allow them to grow, use the three–part *LCS system:*

>> *L* is for *likes,* as in, *"What I like about your idea . . . ."* Begin with some positive comments to encourage people to let loose with every creative idea that comes to mind. Not every idea will work. But even zany ideas can spark more practical and effective ones.

>> *C* is for *concerns,* as in, *"What concerns me about your idea . . . ."* Sharing concerns begins dialogue that opens up and expands the creative process. As you point out a concern, someone else in the group is likely to offer a creative solution.

>> *S* is for *suggestions,* as in, *"I have a few suggestions . . . ."* Offering suggestions moves the brainstorming session along and may lead to the generation of a brand-new set of ideas.

Assembling a brainstorming session

With the LCS system fresh in your minds, your group can take on a brainstorming session following these steps:

1. **Start with a small group of people you trust and admire.**

   You can turn to friends, relatives, professional acquaintances — anyone you think may contribute a new and useful perspective.

2. **Invite a couple of ringers.**

   Consider inviting a few people who can stretch the group's thinking, challenge assumptions, and take the group in new and unexpected directions, even if these individuals may make you feel a bit uncomfortable.

3. **Choose the right time and place.**

   The same old places can lead to the same old thinking, so be inventive. To inspire creativity, change the scene. Larger companies often hold brainstorming sessions at off-site retreats. If you're a small company or sole proprietor, you can still meet in a place that inspires creativity, such as a park or local coffeehouse (as long as it's not too crowded or noisy). Whatever location you choose, be sure to have everything you need for brainstorming — from an old-fashioned scratchpad to an iPad or digital voice recorder — handy.

4. **Establish ground rules.**

   Explain what you want the group to achieve. Introduce the LCS system (see the previous section) so that participants have a tool that allows them to make positive contributions to the session. Emphasize the fact that at this stage in planning, there are no bad ideas. The group should be encouraged to be as freewheeling as possible.

5. **Act as the group's conductor.**

   Keep the process moving without turning into a dictator. Use these tactics:

   - Encourage alternatives: *How else can we do that?*
   - Stimulate visionary thinking: *What if we had no constraints?*
   - Invite new perspectives: *How would a child see this?*
   - Ask for specifics: *What exactly do you mean?*
   - Clarify the next steps: *How should we proceed on that?*

6. **Record the results.**

   Designate a person to take notes throughout the session or record the session to review later. Remember, the best ideas are often side comments, so capture the offbeat comments as well as the mainstream discussion. Every idea, even ones that seem zany, can lead to something useful. Assign someone the task of taking digital pictures of white boards. Sometimes a great idea passes by so quickly that people only later say, "Hey, what was that idea we had?"

7. **Review your notes and thoughts while they're still fresh.**

   Set aside time after the brainstorming session to distill the discussion down to three or four ideas that you want to continue working on.

Narrowing your choices

After some combination of brainstorming, market analysis, and a few random flashes of brilliance, you may accumulate a drawerful of promising business ideas. Following are two guidelines to help you separate the real opportunities from the fluff:

» **Focus on the ideas that you're really excited about.** Your passion is what will keep you motivated on the road to success.

» **Pursue ideas that you can follow through on.** If you feel you don't have the means or the drive to take an idea from the drawing board to the real world, scrap it.

TWEAKING A GOOD IDEA TO MAKE IT EVEN BETTER

A successful business doesn't necessarily require an original idea.

When touch screen phones and tablets came along, a clever entrepreneur created a cool new app that lets people paint digitally with a fingertip. The software wasn't really new; digital art programs for desktops have been around for years. What the innovation did do was make digital art available on mobile devices. The new program was a runaway success — until other app developers came along and began making even better drawing and painting programs for touch screens. By now dozens exist, some more popular among artists than the original app.

Putting your personal stamp on an existing idea can be as bold as designing a better app or as simple as transplanting a successful business concept into your market area, like the couple who started a doggy day care in a town that didn't have one.

Think about the do-it-yourself pottery painting studios that you see practically everywhere these days. The idea migrated from do-it-yourself porcelain painting, which was born out of necessity by a young housewife who reportedly couldn't afford matching china. She decided to paint her own and wanted to help others do the same. Entrepreneurs adapted the idea into a range of do-it-yourself pottery-painting businesses, including hobby shops; ceramics cafes; party businesses; glass, tile, and mosaic studios; and even pottery-painting books and online stores.

TIP

To help you choose among your ideas, use Form 2-7 to complete a Business Opportunity Evaluation Questionnaire for each possibility you're considering. Tally your answers and consider any idea with a score of 24 or higher worthy of serious consideration. The one exception to the scoring: If your promising idea scores high on every question except for number 3 (Is this the kind of business you really want to pursue?), it may be a great idea for someone else — but not for you.

REMEMBER

Use Form 2-7 as a first test for any business idea. If the idea scores high, it still has to pass other hurdles, but at least you know that it's an idea worth pursuing.

After you fill out Form 2-7, separating the promising ideas from all the others, it's a good idea to answer some basic questions that reveal pretty quickly whether or not an idea has what it takes to become a real, live business.

TIP

Use the questions in Form 2-8 to fill in details and to flesh out some of the issues around your preliminary business propositions. If you give your answers some careful thought, they'll reveal to you the likelihood of an idea breaking through as your winning business concept.

If you find yourself struggling to come up with answers to the questions in Form 2-8, your idea may be too sketchy to evaluate. That doesn't mean you have to abandon the idea, but you should take the time to understand the opportunity more fully before taking it to the next stage in the business development process. For example, if you can't easily describe the customer need you're filling or how you plan to make money, you still have homework to do.

Putting a Promising Idea to the Test

Asking questions like "Is this really such a good idea?" and "Who am I kidding, anyway?" doesn't mean you lack confidence. What asking these types of questions does mean is that you've come to the time to step back and make sure that the road you're on is leading you where you want to go. In short, you need a reality check.

TIP

In many ways, writing a business plan is a series of reality checks. By making you carefully think through every aspect of your business — from the product or service you offer to the competitors you face and the customers you serve — the business-planning process brings you face to face with the realities of doing business. Read on for tips on bouncing your ideas around with people who may be able to help refine them, as well as useful ways to appraise your personal strengths and weaknesses when it comes to carrying out your ideas.

Doing your first reality check

After you settle on the idea that can power your business plan, take time out to conduct an honest evaluation. If that sounds easy, think again. Most would-be entrepreneurs are excited by their ideas. Excitement and a can-do spirit help drive success. But a dose of skepticism and honesty are also essential.

Ask these basic questions:

>> Is the idea that will power your business plan clearly stated? (If not, spend a little time refining it. Writing your idea down, and revising what you've written, is one way to get clarity.)

>> Is it doable? (If you have any doubts, rethink the scale of your undertaking, or make a list of what you'll need to make it doable.)

>> What excites you most about the idea?

>> What worries you about the idea?

>> What are the biggest hurdles to implementing your business idea? (A realistic list should probably include at least three items.)

>> How is your idea different from other great ideas out there in the marketplace?

>> Can you tweak the idea to make it even more powerful?

Anticipating disruptive innovations: Opportunities and cautions

Today's blockbuster idea may be next year's bankruptcy if new and unforeseen innovations or business models suddenly disrupt its business arena. Want an example? Remember the Flip video camera? Relatively inexpensive and a snap to use, it gobbled market share from established camcorder companies and soared in valuation. Then suddenly an altogether unanticipated competitor, the smartphone, disrupted the Flip camera. Smartphone cameras came installed, at no additional price, with video capability. As obituaries for Flip put it, the once-popular camera ended up "eating iPhone's dust."

REMEMBER

Disruptive innovations can be a source of both trouble (if you're not prepared) and opportunity (if you know how to seize the moment). The rise of the Internet, for example, spelled the demise of money-making classified ad sections in newspapers; however, it gave birth to Craigslist, eBay, and a host of other online services.

No one can reliably anticipate every disruptive innovation that comes along. Often they seem to come out of nowhere. But in reality signposts are usually along the way. To scan your business arena for possible upheaval, consider opportunities and threats to your idea from the following factors:

>> Changing population demographics, including aging and the impact of immigration as two examples

>> Rising costs, for example, in healthcare, employee benefits, resources, or other factors

>> The impact of wearables, connected devices, and the Internet of Things

>> The sharing economy, also known as *collaborative consumption,* with Uber and Airbnb serving as two leading examples

>> The global economy and how it affects your — and your competitor's — access to customers, resources, labor, and suppliers

>> The changing role of middlemen in everything from accessing legal services to hailing cabs to publishing books and more

>> Social media and how it enables business-to-customer interaction and customer-to-customer sharing, for better or worse

>> Digital technology that can transform industries, for example, driverless cars that alter the auto and fuel industries, cloud computing that affects software sales and business infrastructure and processes, diagnostic apps that replace service providers, and more

To begin to think about how the idea that will power your business plan could be affected by innovations coming through the pipeline:

>> **Make a list of all the technologies involved in the industry you're in or hope to enter.** Among them, identify the technologies that are undergoing — or are likely to undergo — innovative changes. How could those changes affect your business, either as a threat or an opportunity?

>> **Give some thought to your industry or business arena.** Has it undergone sweeping changes in the past? What drove those changes? Are there signs that it could be transformed again? In what ways? How would these scenarios of change affect the idea behind your business?

>> **Make a list of the assumptions that your business idea is founded on.** Question each of these assumptions. What if the founding assumptions behind your idea aren't as solid as you think? What could change? Take the car insurance business, for example. A big underlying assumption is that people like the convenience of owning their own car. But what if they don't? What if more and more people decide that getting a Zipcar or Car2Go is easier than hassling with car ownership? What happens when self-driving cars are a reality and you can hail one via app?

Don't expect to come up with definitive answers here. The idea is to recognize that disruptive changes can come along in almost any industry and marketplace. The more you question your assumptions and assess the implications of technological changes coming along, the better prepared you'll be.

Estimating your runway: How much time does your good idea need?

Most ideas — whether for a start-up or a product launch — require time to take off. A musician who decides to go professional needs to find gigs (and probably music students). An accountant who decides to leave her company and start her own business needs to set up an office and line up clients. An inventor with the next big thing needs to arrange for manufacturing, distribution, and marketing. They all take time. And while the clock ticks, cash goes out — but no or few revenues come in.

The two terms that business planners use to describe the realities of the waiting-to-launch period are

>> **Runway:** The amount of time you have to get your business off the ground and into a profitable position. Put another way, it's the amount of time your funding will last before revenues need to take off.

>> **Burn rate:** The amount of cash required each month to cover the costs of staying in business.

TIP

To calculate the length of your runway, divide the amount of your funding or cash reserves by your monthly burn rate. The result to this equation answers the "how much time do I have" question. If you have a limited amount of cash to get your venture going, knowing your runway is especially important. We've met plenty of entrepreneurs who had great business ideas that might have gone on to achieve success, if only they hadn't run out of runway before they could get airborne.

REMEMBER

The more realistic you are about how much time your idea will take and how much you'll need to spend before revenue kicks in, the better prepared you'll be. Looking ahead, especially with a new venture, requires a fair amount of guesswork, but be as realistic as possible. Detail what you're working to achieve and all the major steps you'll need to take, often referred to as *mileposts* you'll need to pass, in order to succeed. Then establish a timeline for when you'll be able to reach each one. The result? A diagram of the runway for your business or business idea.

Checking out the competition

The saying goes that there's nothing new under the sun. It also applies to most new businesses. Unless it's a totally new and disruptive innovation, chances are a similar business to the one you're planning to launch already exists. One easy way to test your new idea is to check out how other people doing roughly the same thing are faring. In some cases, all you have to do is ask. Unless people perceive you as a competitive threat, they're usually willing to share details about their businesses. If not, you can uncover information in other ways, such as the following:

>> **Check websites of similar businesses for information about products and services, including pricing.** If appropriate, peruse online customer reviews of your competitors, which can provide invaluable tips on how you can do better.

>> **Search the web for business articles about the kind of business you're planning.** Be sure to check publication dates, because business reports can go quickly out of date. If you don't find what you need online, head to your local library to browse the periodical shelves.

>> **Investigate how similar businesses present and market their goods or services.** If you're starting a local business, check out your competitors'

presence in local media and online. If you're going after a national or international market, analyze how other businesses in your arena use major media, their own websites, social media, business partnerships, and collaborations to present their offerings.

>> **Check out local business organizations.** Most cities and even small towns have Chambers of Commerce and economic development organizations with websites you can study. If you don't find what you need there, make a visit to the brick-and-mortar office to talk to a representative about your business sector, its major players, its current conditions, and its untapped opportunities.

>> **Talk to prospective customers.** If you're starting a local business, ask friends and family what they consider important as prospective customers and what wants or needs aren't being addressed. If you're planning a retail business, visit similar stores and observe how customers move through the aisles and what they do and don't buy.

TIP

If your new idea is product-based, your business will face special challenges, such as who will make and distribute the product and what kind of service it will it require. Check out Form 2-7 to begin addressing some of the special considerations involved in product innovation.

Getting a second opinion

To help determine whether or not you're on solid ground, discuss your business idea and preliminary plans with someone outside your company. What you're really seeking is a *mentor* with most or all of the following characteristics:

>> Someone who has experience in the business area you're considering, or at least experience in a similar business

>> Someone with the courage to tell you the truth, whether it's "That's a great idea. Go for it!" or "If I were you, I'd take a little more time to think this over"

>> Someone you respect and admire and from whom you can take candid criticism without feeling defensive

Consider turning to colleagues you've worked with in the past, teachers or professors, friends from college, or other associates.

WARNING

Friends and family members sometimes can offer the advice and perspective you need, but emotional ties can get in the way of absolute honesty and objectivity. If you go this route, set some ground rules in advance. Be specific with your requests. Then, ask for suggestions, comments, and constructive criticism and be prepared to hear both the good and the bad without taking what you hear personally.

In addition to a mentor, consider designating someone to act as the devil's advocate to guarantee that you address the flip side of every issue that you're considering. This person's task is to be critical of each idea on the table — not in a destructive way, but in a skeptical, show-me-the-money, I'll-believe-it-when-I-see-it, how-is-this-new-or-better kind of way. In larger companies, you can accomplish this goal by creating two teams — one to defend the idea and the second to critique it. Ask the opposing team members to think of themselves as a competing firm looking to find weaknesses in the new venture.

Conducting a self-appraisal

Whether your idea will be the genesis for launching or growing a one-person business, a small business, or a business that aspires to be the next Google or Facebook, you still have one very important question to answer: Do you have what it takes to turn this opportunity into a success story?

The CEOs who became multimillionaires before they turned 25 and the entrepreneurs cruising around in sports cars issuing orders on their cellphones while the value of their stock values soar share some common traits: talent *and* hard work. To succeed, you must exhibit both, and to be a high-flyer or, for that matter, to be self-employed, you need discipline, confidence, and the capacity to live with the uncertainty that's part and parcel of being out on your own.

As a first step toward appraising your strengths and weaknesses, download the survey in Form 2-8 and respond to the 20 statements as candidly as you possibly can. There's no such thing as a perfect score. The point of the exercise is to identify your strongest and weakest areas so that you can capitalize and compensate accordingly.

As you review your responses, watch for the following:

>> Areas that receive "poor" ratings represent your weakest areas. Be alert for the need to compensate for these personal shortcomings.

>> Areas that receive "excellent" ratings represent your greatest strengths and the personal resources you can call upon when you start your business venture.

Not all personal strengths and weaknesses will contribute equally as you turn your idea into a business success. For example, if you're planning to be a sole proprietor who works mostly alone, the ability to manage a staff doesn't matter much, but self-motivation is absolutely essential. Or, if your success will depend on face-to-face presentations and individualized service, interpersonal skills will be indispensable.

As you complete Form 2-8, place a star next to the six traits that you think are most important for turning your idea into a business success. For the moment, ignore how you rate yourself in each of those areas. Focus clearly on what it will take to propel your idea into a reality. Next, see how your personal strengths and weaknesses apply to the needs of your proposed business idea. Take the top six traits from Form 2-8 and align them with your personal abilities, using Form 2-9.

REMEMBER

Just because you're personally weak in an important area doesn't mean you don't have what it takes to turn your idea into a business. But it does unveil areas in which you'll either want to develop certain traits or enlist others to add necessary strengths. For example, if you aren't good with details, but details are important to the success of your business idea, this exercise alerts you to the fact that you may need to hire a personal assistant or cajole a colleague into tying up all the loose ends.

TIP

Put a copy of your personal strengths-and-weaknesses grid into your daily organizer or post it near your computer. Having it close by constantly reminds you of who you are, the strengths you can draw on, and the areas you need to bolster as you begin the challenge of planning your business.

Forms

Go to www.dummies.com/go/businessplanskit to view and download these forms that help you develop and refine the idea that will power your business plan.

Form 2-1	Great Business Idea Evaluation Form	Questions to help you begin to evaluate a new business idea
Form 2-2	Ideas Behind Successful Businesses Evaluation Form	Questions to help you understand the ideas that power businesses you admire
Form 2-3	Business Challenges Questionnaire	Questions that help you begin planning to overcome challenges in an existing company
Form 2-4	Turning a Gig into a Business	Questions to help you decide if you can turn something you love to do into a profitable business
Form 2-5	Business Opportunity Evaluation Questionnaire	Questions that help you decide which business ideas are worth pursuing
Form 2-6	Business Opportunity Framework	Questions designed to fill in some important details around your business proposition
Form 2-7	New Product Innovation Questionnaire	Questions to help you evaluate an innovative new product or feature
Form 2-8	Personal Strengths and Weaknesses Survey	A survey designed to provide you with an honest profile of your business abilities and traits
Form 2-9	Personal Strengths and Weaknesses Grid	A tool that allows you to compare your abilities with qualities important to the kind of business you're considering

Chapter 3

Defining Your Business Purpose and Structure

I n any kind of work, you can get buried in the day-to-day demands and so caught up in the details that you miss the bigger picture. That's why the business-planning process is so valuable. Writing a business plan allows you to step back and think about where you've come from and where you want to go. It offers you the chance to ask and answer questions like the following:

>> Why are you in business?

>> What does your business do?

>> What do you want your company to become?

>> What are the competitive challenges you face?

>> How will you make money?

>> How will you get where you want to go?

If you're thinking that these questions are pretty basic, you're right. But that's exactly what makes them so important. We've heard too many sad stories about companies with great promise — and often tons of money to boot — that suddenly falter and fade away. Many of these companies could have avoided a lot of trouble if the people steering the organization had taken the time to address basic issues during the planning process.

To lead your business toward success, start by really focusing on what kind of business you're in and how your business will be structured. Put your business values and vision into words, write a clear and compelling mission statement, and set goals and objectives to turn your mission into reality. This chapter leads the way.

Knowing What Business You're In

The first step in planning for business success is to identify what business you're in. Why do customers want the solution you provide, and why do they choose your business over the competition? One tried-and-true way to begin finding answers is to consider how you would describe your business to a stranger in one sentence.

Here are three related questions to guide you:

>> What basic needs do you fulfill in the marketplace?

>> Beyond specific products and services, why do customers come to you?

>> What are the three nicest things your customers could say about you?

Figure 3-1 shows how a company that provides text-editing services, mainly to marketing and communications departments and mainly over the Internet, answered these questions.

TIP

Go to www.dummies.com/go/businessplanskit to view and download Form 3-1, which you can use to answer the same three questions for your business idea. As you consider each question, jot down whatever comes to mind. Your answers may not go directly into your business plan, but they can influence almost every aspect of your business-planning process.

Basic Business Definition Framework
1. What basic needs do you fulfill in the marketplace?   For each of our corporate clients, we make sure that all printed and Internet text materials are grammatically correct and conform to the company's style requirements.
2. Beyond specific products and services, why do customers come to you?   The reliability and quality of our service. Peace of mind. Not having to worry that the company will look bad in print. Confidence that what's published is correct and understandable.
3. What are the three nicest things your customers could say about you?   That we're thorough and reliable. That we have excellent turnaround. That we're friendly and easy to work with.

FIGURE 3-1:
The three questions on Form 3-1 help you determine the business you're in.

© John Wiley & Sons, Inc.

EXAMPLE

In reviewing their answers, the owners of the text-editing business were struck by the phrase "peace of mind." Those three words helped them realize that in addition to providing a text-editing business, they were also in the insurance business — making sure that embarrassing typos and inconsistencies didn't trip up marketing and communications managers.

In response, the company changed a few of its procedures. The owners put a managing editor in place to oversee the largest projects, and they enhanced their client-service staff to provide more communication throughout the editorial process to reinforce their clients' peace of mind. Within six months, business increased dramatically.

EXAMPLE

Business history is littered with the remains of companies whose founders thought they knew what businesses they were in, only to discover that the industries weren't quite what they seemed. But not all companies rocked by change have faltered. Some have prospered.

>> Consider the railroad industry. During its heyday, railroad tycoons assumed that they were in the railroad business. Along came powerful competitors that had nothing to do with railroads — automobile manufacturers, the interstate highway system, jet aircraft, and regional airports. The tycoons realized that railroads weren't in the railroad business after all; they were in the transportation business. Perhaps if they had seen the big picture sooner, they may have had a rosier future.

>> Eastman Kodak, over its long history, made most of its money processing film — so much money, in fact, that the company came to believe that it was

in the chemical-imaging business. Along came the digital revolution and new ways to record images. In no time, Kodak's customers weren't interested in the photo process, but in capturing memories — on film, video, or computer. Kodak was in the memories business all along.

>> Amazon began as the world's largest bookstore, and it quickly became the most successful Internet-based retail business in the world. Before long, the company expanded to become a shopping mall for virtually anything you need, from kitchen supplies to musical instruments. Its business, though, remained the same: retail sales over the Internet. Then along came the Kindle, Amazon's groundbreaking e-book. In one sense, Amazon remains a bookseller. But it has also become a publisher. The shift from CDs to MP3s has also transformed Amazon into a digital music company. Now the Internet pioneer, like its competitor Apple's iTunes, has its own cloud, offering storage for books, music, and videos.

Choosing the Right Business Structure

Having a clear idea about what kind of business you're in is just the first step. Knowing how you'll make a profit is crucial. If you can't make a profit, after all, you don't have a business — at least not for very long. (Nonprofits are an exception, but even they have to find funding sources.)

Your business model is as much a part of defining your business purpose and structure as is the underlying idea behind your enterprise. All too often, people planning a business don't spend enough time thinking about their business model, by which we mean their bottom line. These sections can help you settle on the best structure to meet your goals.

Identifying your business model

To turn a great idea into a successful business, you need to define and develop a workable *business model*, or a method that your company uses to generate revenue, earn profits, and protect its position in the marketplace. (You can find more information on the topic of business models in Chapter 5.)

Hundreds of different business models exist. The disruptive transformations that have followed in the wake of the digital revolution have spawned brand new models that are still evolving. Something else has changed, too. Once upon a time, companies established a business model and stuck with it for decades. Today the pace of disruptive innovations is so rapid that business models have to be revised and reworked in order to keep up, or they risk being displaced by competitors.

To begin to think about what kind of model is right for you, take a look at how many highly successful companies have modeled themselves:

>> **Auction:** Sales are conducted with bidders competing for a product or service. eBay revolutionized sales on the Internet using a form of online auction. Art auction houses make hundreds of millions in a single sale using this model. Now even individual artists have entered into the game, posting their artwork for sale on Internet sites with bidders competing online.

>> **Bricks and clicks:** This method combines a brick-and-mortar company presence with online sales.

>> **Brick-and-mortar retail:** Stores sell merchandise or services out of a storefront location.

>> **Collective:** Small businesses band together in a collective to leverage their resources. Examples include dairy and wine cooperatives.

>> **Direct sales:** This method, also known as *multilevel marketing,* or MLM, markets and sells directly to customers. The most famous and successful examples of direct sales companies include Avon, Amway, Herbalife, and Tupperware.

>> **Franchise:** A form of chain store in which franchisees pay a fee and a percentage of sales to use the franchise owner's knowledge, processes, and trademarks in the operation of individually owned outlets. Supercuts, Subway, Anytime Fitness, 7-Eleven, and ServPro are examples of franchises.

>> **Freemium:** Under this model, a business offers basic services or products for free, charging for premium versions that include additional features. Many apps for tablets and smartphones offer "lite" versions for free and charge for the fully operational app with all its bells and whistles.

>> **Low-cost:** This model competes by offering the best price on a service or product. Big-box retailers like Costco and Internet sites like Kayak follow this business model.

>> **Online:** All marketing and sales are done online. Amazon is the highest profile example, although a growing number of companies operate exclusively on the Internet.

>> **Person-to-person:** Transactions take place person-to-person. A subcontractor who gets his business by word of mouth thrives on this kind of business model. Internet sites like Craigslist and Etsy put sellers and buyers directly in contact with one another in a way that was never possible before the Internet came along.

>> **Subscription:** Customers pay a weekly, monthly, or yearly rate for a product or service. Magazine subscriptions are the most familiar example. Small farms have begun to sustain themselves by offering subscriptions that offer customers a weekly produce delivery.

This list is just the beginning. Businesses today are built around business models that feature pay-as-you-go programs based on metered service, pay-per-view, or pay-per-use revenue approaches; leasing-versus-sale models; and affiliate sales models that capture or pay commissions (depending on whether your business is the affiliate or the selling business) when website visitors click on links that lead from one website to purchases on another site. Business models, in other words, are constantly evolving.

EXAMPLE

Business models aren't always as straightforward as you may think. Many businesses make money in unexpected ways, such as the following:

» The local movie theater gets revenue from ticket sales, but that's only the beginning. The theater also makes money by projecting billboard-style ads prior to the movie showings and from its concession stand, where it turns a tidy profit selling candy and buckets of popcorn. Lately, some offer, and charge more for, IMAX or 3D versions of movies. For big blockbuster movies, surveys show, some theatergoers attend the same film multiple times, to check out different formats.

» Large fitness-center chains make money on enrollment fees and monthly dues, but they also rake in cash by selling fitness-related supplements, exercise clothes, gym bags, and the services of personal trainers.

» Magazines earn revenue from subscriptions and newsstand sales, but the lion's share of their income results from the sale of advertising space. However, you can find an exception to every business model. *Consumer Reports* declares in its mission that it accepts no advertising. To maintain its independence and impartiality, it supports itself entirely through the sale of information and products, contributions, and noncommercial grants. Some travel magazines *lose* money on subscriptions and newsstand sales. They make their profit by sponsoring travel-related conferences and events — especially important in this era of declining print-media ad purchases.

» Some companies sell their products at a loss — making their money from the sales of related *consumables*. Gillette, for example, doesn't mind selling razors at cost, knowing it will profit from the sale of razor cartridge refills. Inkjet printers are another example.

» Online businesses increasingly work to supplement sales revenue with revenue earned through programs such as Google AdSense (www.google.com/adsense), which allows information-rich websites with reasonable traffic counts to earn revenue by displaying ads on their web pages. Every time someone clicks on the ad, the website gets a little money. Businesses can also make money from their websites by offering affiliated products or premium services, such as expanded content available only with a subscription.

TIP

In this early planning stage, while you're defining your business and its purpose, be as clear as possible about how you expect your business to profit. If your business fits comfortably into a classic business model, include the term in your business plan. If not, don't worry about giving your business model a name. Your job at this stage is to offer a realistic explanation about where your revenues will come from — for the sake of the owners, investors, customers, and employees.

EXAMPLE

Be creative in tracking down potential sources of revenue, which may be more numerous than you first suspect. Many artists who find they can't quite make enough selling their work in galleries, for example, have learned to supplement their income by offering workshops, producing instructional DVDs, and even designing their own lines of art supplies. Additionally, a growing number of restaurants are leveraging their operations by adding catering as an additional revenue source.

Reviewing the advantages and disadvantages of different structures

A variety of different business structures exist, each with its own advantages and disadvantages. Taking the time now to consider the best structure for your business can avoid problems in the future. Especially if you're starting a new venture, your business plan should spell out specifics about your proposed business structure. The most common business structures include

>> **Sole proprietorship:** You, as an individual, are the company.

>> **Cooperative:** A *cooperative* is owned and operated for the benefit of its members. The profits it generates are distributed to those members.

>> **Corporation:** *Corporations,* which are the most complex business structure, are independent legal entities owned by shareholders. Larger companies typically use this structure because corporations are legally and financially complex.

>> **Partnership:** A *partnership* is a business that two or more people own. There are several different kinds of partnerships, each with its own requirements, including general partnerships, limited partnerships, and joint ventures.

>> **Limited Liability Company (LLC):** An *LLC* is a cross between a partnership and a corporation. A single individual or a group of members can own it with all profits passed through to the members.

>> **S Corporation:** *S corporations* are like corporations except that they receive a special designation from the IRS that allows profits and losses to pass through to the individual owners. The shareholders, but not the business itself, must pay taxes.

TIP

For more details about the specific advantages and disadvantages of common business structures, check out Form 3-2. Choose the structure that seems most appropriate for your venture.

MAKING THE WORLD A BETTER PLACE — ONE BUSINESS AT A TIME

The rising influence of socially committed entrepreneurs has spawned a new kind of business model, called a *B corporation,* with the B standing for *benefit.* B Corps, as they're popularly known, are for-profit companies that agree to meet rigorous standards of social and environmental accountability and transparency in order to be certified by the nonprofit organization B Lab. The goal of a B Corp is to align the interests of the business with those of society in order to use business as a force for good. As of 2015, B Lab had certified more than 1,400 B Corps in more than 120 industries. They range from a small apparel maker in Oakland, California, and regional coffee companies to big names like Patagonia and Kickstarter.

If you're considering B Corp status, plan to score well on a survey that covers everything from energy efficiency and employee programs to corporate transparency. Plus, be prepared to include a written commitment to making a positive social and environmental impact in your corporate by-laws.

Why go to the trouble? By joining the B Corp movement, companies go on record committing themselves to social good. In addition, by swelling the ranks and therefore the awareness of B Corp companies, they encourage others to join them as a force for good. And of course, the image of social activism can be good for business with B Corp status attracting interest and support from investors, employees, and customers who share similar goals.

For more information, check out www.bcorporation.net.

Comparing the Most Common Business Structures

Choosing the appropriate business structure is an essential step in planning any new business. The choice you make will have important implications for how the company operates and what its tax obligations will be. Use this form to explore the most common business structures and their advantages and disadvantages.

- **Sole proprietorship:** You, as an individual, are the company.

  Advantages: This is by far the simplest business structure. You don't have to do anything to become a sole proprietorship. As long as you're the sole owner, you're automatically a sole proprietor. You can operate under your own name or use another name for the company. The income from a sole proprietorship is your income — and taxed accordingly.

  Disadvantages: You're responsible for all debts, losses, and other liabilities. And raising substantial amounts of cash for a sole proprietorship is typically difficult.

- **Cooperative:** A cooperative is owned and operated for the benefit of its members. The profits it generates are distributed to those members. A familiar example is a food cooperative, in which individuals join together to buy and distribute food.

  Advantages: Members can come and go and the cooperative remains intact as a business entity. Depending on the nature of the business, cooperatives can sometimes take advantage of grant programs to raise funds.

  Disadvantages: Members must actively participate in all aspects of a cooperative's business. Cooperatives are typically run democratically, which can be good or bad, depending on the individuals involved.

- **Corporation:** The most complex business structure, corporations are independent legal entities owned by shareholders. Because corporations are legally and financially complex, larger companies typically use this structure.

  Advantages: A corporation structure limits the liability of shareholders as far as debts and other responsibilities go. Because corporations are stable, they can generate capital more easily than less formal structures.

  Disadvantages: Corporations are time-consuming and expensive to set up and to operate.

(continued)

FORM 3-2: Each business structure has its own advantages and disadvantages.

- **Partnership:** A partnership is a business owned by two or more people. There are several different kinds of partnerships, each with its own requirements, including general partnerships, limited partnerships, and joint ventures.

    Advantages: Partnerships are easy and inexpensive to form. Partners share in the financial risks and rewards.

    Disadvantages: Owners are personally liable for debts and losses. If partners disagree over crucial business decisions, the result can be conflict and sometimes the end of the partnership.

- **Limited Liability Company (LLC):** An LLC is a cross between a partnership and a corporation. A single individual or a group of members can own it. All profits are passed through to the members. An LLC requires a business name and articles of organization.

    Advantages: LLCs require less record-keeping than corporations and there are fewer restrictions on how the profits are divided up among members.

    Disadvantages: Members of an LLC are considered to be self-employed and must pay self-employment taxes. In some states, an LLC is automatically dissolved if one member leaves, requiring remaining members to start a new business.

- **S Corporation:** S corporations are like corporations except that they receive a special designation from the IRS that allows profits and losses to pass through to the individual owners. The shareholders, but not the business itself, must pay taxes.

    Advantages: If shareholders leave, an S corporation remains intact. Some expenses can be deducted as business expenses.

    Disadvantages: S corporations are complicated to operate, because they require scheduled director and shareholder meetings.

For more detailed information about business structures and which one is right for you and your business, check out the Small Business Administration at www.sba.org.

PAGE 2 OF FORM 3-2.

Getting your business off on the right foot

When you start a new business, try to establish the best business model and business structure right from the get-go. You can save time and money and avoid a lot of hassle that way. At the same time, keep in mind that businesses evolve and change — and in many industries the pace of changing is accelerating. You may have to revise the business model you identify today in the months and years ahead. You may eventually need to adopt a totally different business structure.

EXAMPLE

Consider the example of an antique dealer who opened a small shop just north of Boston. She struggled for a couple of years meeting the rent. Finally, she switched from being a sole proprietor to running the shop as a cooperative made up of small dealers who sublet space in her shop.

Your vision as a company may change over time. Be decisive when you craft a business plan, but then remain flexible and open to change.

Giving Your Company Its Mission

Your *mission statement* defines the purpose of your business and the approach you want to take to achieve success. Crafting a mission statement forces you to take a long, hard look at the key parts of your business, making the process a fundamental part of business planning. If you're still not convinced that writing a mission statement is worth the trouble, consider these factors:

>> **If you're starting a business, a compelling mission statement can convince potential investors that you know who you are and where you want to go.** A great mission statement doesn't make up for a poor business plan, but an ill-defined or uninspired mission statement can make investors think twice about putting money on the table.

>> **If you're a company of one, a clear mission statement keeps you focused on what you do best.** A mission statement helps keep you on track if you run into problems along the way.

>> **If you run a growing business, a strong mission statement can help turn employees into team players.** When everyone pursues the same purpose, your team stays pointed in the right direction.

>> **If your company has run into trouble, a decisive mission statement can help you set the direction you want to take to turn things around.** A mission statement reminds you of what your core business is and why you went into business in the first place. Sometimes that reminder is enough to set the course for a recovery.

>> **If you have to decide between two courses of action, a strong mission statement can help guide you.** Often in business, there is no single right answer. A mission statement can help you evaluate your options when no easy choice exists.

No matter what kind of business you're in, a solid mission statement communicates the purpose of your business to people inside and outside your organization. It tells them who you are and what you do. The following sections help you zero in on exactly what your mission is and how to put it in writing so that it serves as an effective guide for business planning.

Asking basic questions

If you're part of a small organization — which includes a business of one — you can write your own mission statement. Getting an outside perspective never hurts, of course.

If you're part of a medium-size or larger company, enlisting help is essential. You get fresh ideas and insights, and you encourage a sense of ownership in the mission statement, which helps forge a stronger business team.

Whether you move ahead on your own or enlist some outside help, get a head start on the process by jotting down your initial responses to the eight fundamental questions on Form 3-3.

One good way to answer these questions is to assemble a group of creative, energetic people, making sure that the group represents all major areas of your business if you're part of a large company. Schedule several brainstorming sessions (for information on brainstorming, see Chapter 2), following this approach:

>> **Session 1:** Discuss the importance of a mission statement. Ask your team members to answer the Form 3-2 questions. Use a white board or, if some teammates work remotely, an online file-sharing service, so that everyone can see the answers and the ideas as they emerge.

>> **Session 2:** Discuss your answers in a free and open conversation that gives all responses a fair hearing. Begin to build consensus on the best answers to each question.

>> **Session 3:** Using the framework in the following section, begin to outline your company's mission. If your brainstorming group is large, you may want to select a smaller group to work on the mission statement.

>> **Session 4:** Review, revise, and polish the mission statement draft.

Framing your mission

Mission statements come in all shapes and sizes, each reflecting the nature of the company it represents. Some mission statements begin with definitions of company values; others begin with what the companies do; and others begin with descriptions of the customers the companies plan to serve.

In other words, there's no single, perfect way to frame a mission statement.

Your Mission Statement Questionnaire
1. What exactly do you do?
2. What products and services do you offer?
3. Who is your ideal customer?
4. What customer needs do you meet, and what benefits do you provide?
5. What markets and geographic areas do you serve?
6. What sets you apart from your competition?
7. What's the best thing a satisfied customer can say about you?
8. What gets you most excited about the company's future?

FORM 3-3: The eight questions on this form prepare you to write your mission statement.

TIP

A good starting point, however, is to use Form 3-4 to assemble key ideas about what you do, who you serve, and how you plan to distinguish your company from your competitors. Together, these facts link ideas and form a framework for your mission statement. Figure 3-2 illustrates how a company that offers information and referrals for alternative medical treatments completed the form.

Your Mission Statement Framework

OUR PRODUCT OR SERVICE IS holistic health services.

WE PROVIDE reliable advice about alternative therapies
FOR people with chronic illnesses like cancer or diabetes
WHO ARE DISSATISFIED WITH standard medical care.

UNLIKE other referral networks in our area,
WE OFFER both information and referrals to local providers.

FIGURE 3-2:
Fill in the blanks on Form 3-4 to frame a mission statement for your business.

© John Wiley & Sons, Inc.

Crafting your mission

After answering basic questions about your business and evaluating how your answers relate to one another, you're ready to transform your ideas into a mission statement.

Although you don't have any cast-in-stone rules to follow, here are a few guidelines to apply:

>> **Describe who you are, what you do, and what sets you apart.** At the same time, keep your mission statement as short and sweet as possible.

>> **Use plain language.** Your mission statement serves as a guide for people who know your business and people who don't, so make sure that everyone who reads it can understand it. If you can't explain your idea clearly (what's a *multiplatformed B-to-B integration database solution,* anyway?), you aren't clear yourself, or you haven't gotten down to the basics yet.

>> **Be specific.** "We will be a leading provider of software" doesn't say much. In contrast, consider the mission of Intuit, maker of Quicken software: "The company's mission is to create new ways to manage personal finances and small businesses that are so profound and simple, customers cannot imagine going back to the old way." Now that gets down to the nitty-gritty.

>> **Be enthusiastic.** A mission statement is meant to sell your message and inspire your troops, so give it a strong sense of conviction and commitment.

>> **Avoid hype and hyperbole.** The latest buzzwords — from "quantum leap forward" to "a mega-paradigm shift" — don't mean much to most people. Stick to simple, straightforward explanations.

>> **Think ahead.** A mission statement should be grounded in the fundamentals of your business so that it will remain applicable and relevant for years to come.

Your mission statement, like your business plan, must be meaningful to you and everyone in your organization. The mission statement is the core driving principle that guides how you and your employees think of the company and how you approach your work.

Before you finalize your mission statement, take a look at some examples from established companies, both large and small, to see which statements you find impressive, inspiring, or just plain stronger than the others. Start with the examples in Form 3-5. Whether you write your mission statement on your own or as part of a group, take time to respond to each example with a thumbs up or thumbs down, noting what you like about the winners and what you don't like about the losers. Your answers will provide a stronger sense of what you want your mission statement to look like.

Using your favorite mission statements from Form 3-5 as models, shape your own polished version. Enter your refined mission statement into the blank box provided in Form 3-6.

Fixing a weak or ineffective mission statement

A weak or ineffective mission statement may not seem like a big deal, but in fact it can mean trouble if your company finds itself facing challenges that require it to get back to basics.

A strong mission statement describes the heart of your company. From this mission statement flow the goals and objectives that allow you to move forward. If you have a mission statement, take it out and review it. Compare it to the examples in Form 3-5. If it misses the mark — if it fails to capture purpose of your business and how you'll achieve success — scrap it and begin the process of creating a new mission statement. Refer to the previous section for help.

Examples of Real-World Mission Statements

To be the leading global provider of handheld computing products and to provide developers with the industry-standard platform for creating world-class mobile solutions. **(Palm, Inc.)**

☐ Thumbs up   ☐ Thumbs down

Why?

The mission of the Metropolitan Police Department is to prevent crime and the fear of crime, as we work with others to build safe and healthy communities throughout the District of Columbia. **(Washington DC Police Department)**

☐ Thumbs up   ☐ Thumbs down

Why?

Get it there. **(FedEx)**

☐ Thumbs up   ☐ Thumbs down

Why?

To explore, enjoy, and protect the wild places of the earth; to practice and promote the responsible use of the earth's ecosystems and resources; to educate and enlist humanity to protect and restore the quality of the natural and human environment; and to use all lawful means to carry out these objectives. **(Sierra Club)**

☐ Thumbs up   ☐ Thumbs down

Why?

To provide our customers with safe, good value, point-to-point air services. To effect and to offer a consistent and reliable product and fares appealing to leisure and business markets on a range of European routes. To achieve this we will develop our people and establish lasting relationships with our suppliers. **(easyJet.com)**

☐ Thumbs up   ☐ Thumbs down

Why?

The NBA's mission is to be the most respected and successful sports league and sports marketing organization in the world. **(National Basketball Association)**

☐ Thumbs up   ☐ Thumbs down

Why?

To manufacture world-class quality molds to fill our customers' needs, provide satisfying careers for all our employees, and to earn a fair return in order to allow continuous improvement, and thereby enable our customers, and ourselves, to succeed in the future together. **(Stellar Mold & Tool, Inc.)**

☐ Thumbs up   ☐ Thumbs down

Why?

FORM 3-5: This form asks you to rate real-world mission statements to see which examples you find most impressive.

United Community Center is a human service agency providing emergency assistance, daycare, social services and recreational activities for low-income children and families at risk in inner city Atlanta, Georgia. **(United Community Center)**

☐ Thumbs up   ☐ Thumbs down

Why?

To make guests happy. **(Disney World)**

☐ Thumbs up   ☐ Thumbs down

Why?

To create an online community, like no other, encompassing every facet of every municipality in the United States; to aid in online economic revitalization in partnership with local businesses and local, state, and national government agencies; to publish, maintain, and connect a network of community websites designed to entertain, educate, and enlighten the residents of our great nation, while maintaining the highest standards of personal morals, business ethics, and web etiquette. **(A2Z Computing Services)**

☐ Thumbs up   ☐ Thumbs down

Why?

Dell's mission is to be the most successful computer company in the world at delivering the best customer experience in markets we serve. In doing so, Dell will meet customer expectations of:

- **Highest quality**
- **Competitive pricing**
- **Best-in-class service and support**
- **Superior corporate citizenship**

- **Leading technology**
- **Individual and company accountability**
- **Flexible customization capability**
- **Financial stability**

(Dell Computer)

☐ Thumbs up   ☐ Thumbs down

Why?

The YMCA of San Francisco builds strong kids, strong families, and strong communities by enriching the lives of all people in spirit, mind and body. **(YMCA of San Francisco)**

☐ Thumbs up   ☐ Thumbs down

Why?

To connect people to their passions, communities, and the world's knowledge. **(Yahoo!)**

☐ Thumbs up   ☐ Thumbs down

Why?

To organize the world's information and make it universally accessible and useful. **(Google)**

☐ Thumbs up   ☐ Thumbs down

Why?

PAGE 2 OF FORM 3-5.

Putting your mission to work

After you've written a strong, inspiring mission statement, put your words to work. Whether you do business on your own or run a large company, proclaim your mission loud and clear. If you're a company of one, frame and display a copy of your statement to continually inspire yourself, your clients, your suppliers, and friends of your business. If your company is large, include your mission in your employee handbook.

TIP

See to it that everyone in the company knows the statement by heart. Get creative: Print it on the back of business cards, post it on your website's "About Us" page, and include it in company literature. Above all, put the words into action. Ultimately, your mission statement is worth only what you (and everyone around you) make of it.

Exploring Values and Vision

Your mission statement provides a road map that keeps your company moving in the right direction, but a map isn't enough by itself.

You also need a good, reliable compass — something that you can count on to keep you oriented, particularly during rocky times. You need a clear statement of values and a strong vision:

>> A *values statement* is a set of beliefs and principles that exists behind the scenes to guide your business activities and the way you operate.

>> A *vision statement* is a precise set of words that announces to the world what your company hopes to make of itself. The vision statement defines your highest aspirations for your business. It explains why you're doing what you're doing, in terms of the greatest good you hope to achieve.

For detailed information about the roles of values and vision in businesses across a number of industries, check out the latest edition of *Business Plans For Dummies* by Paul Tiffany, Steven Peterson, and Colin Barrow (John Wiley & Sons, Inc.).

Uncovering values you already hold

So, what are the values that you hold for your business? You can probably come up with a list off the top of your head. People tend to take values for granted because they're instinctive — they're the beliefs and principles that serve as a hidden foundation for what you choose to do and how you choose to get things accomplished.

WHY VALUES MATTER

A company's strong sense of values can guide it through troubled times and also improve the bottom line. Studies have shown that companies that recover best from man-made catastrophes and emerge with their reputations intact are the ones with strong values and the ability to recognize their responsibilities to their customers, shareholders, employees, and the public.

Plenty of real-life examples illustrate just how important a strong sense of values can be when a company faces a crisis. Consider a few recent cases:

- When certain chemicals in Coca-Cola products were rumored to have made several hundred people sick in Europe, the governments of France, Belgium, Luxembourg, and the Netherlands ordered Coke products off the shelves. The company, scrambling to define what caused the illnesses while simultaneously working to repair its image, issued an apology that amounted to a values statement: "The Coca-Cola Company's highest priority is the quality of our products. One hundred thirteen years of our success have been based on the trust consumers have in that quality. That trust is sacred to us."

- Over the years, British Petroleum (BP) carefully polished its reputation for protecting the environment through initiatives to cut greenhouse gas emissions. Then, in 2010, a BP-owned oilrig in the Gulf of Mexico exploded, creating a massive oil spill. Many analysts agree that the company's slow and often flat-footed response to the on-going disaster seriously damaged BP's public image. In an effort to repair that damage, the company launched a multimillion dollar TV ad campaign highlighting BP's efforts to clean up the gulf, many of them featuring employees who live and work in the area. Although the campaign has helped win some hearts and minds, industry observers say BP still has a long way to go to win back its former reputation.

- Owners of Amazon's e-book reader were shocked to discover some years back that certain books they had bought for the device had been deleted by the company. The reason: Amazon hadn't properly secured the right to sell the particular titles. (As it happened, the titles included the George Orwell novel *1984*, about Big Brother.) The episode created a public relations nightmare for Amazon. But not for long. The company's founder quickly issued an apology, one that reflects its values. "This is an apology for the way we previously handled illegally sold copies of *1984* and other novels on Kindle. Our 'solution' to the problem was stupid, thoughtless, and painfully out of line with our principles. It is wholly self-inflicted, and we deserve the criticism we've received. We will use the scar tissue from this painful mistake to help make better decisions going forward, ones that match our mission." Notice the words "principle" and "mission." They show how Amazon's strong sense of values helped it respond to a potentially catastrophic mistake.

(continued)

(continued)

- In 2015, Volkswagen shocked the world by admitting that it had placed so-called "defeat devices" — software designed to mislead emissions tests — into millions of its diesel-powered vehicles. The cars, it turned out, were spewing up to 40 times the allowable levels of dangerous pollutants into the air. The admission was all the more shocking because Volkswagen had positioned itself as the manufacturer of fuel-efficient and environmentally friendly cars. Clearly, the company's carefully-burnished image and its fundamental values were at odds. The disconnect cost Volkswagen in many ways. Despite the shocking admission, Volkswagen was slow to acknowledge how many models were involved. And then came revelations that the company's estimates of carbon dioxide emissions were also badly flawed. The carmaker will pay billions in fines and court settlements. Volkswagen will also have to think long and hard about what its real values are — and how it will convince and win back the confidence of its consumers.

These examples involve big companies, which is hardly surprising because, after all, how often does a business like Mary & Pete's Dry-Cleaning Service make the pages of *The Wall Street Journal?* However, values remain important even when you're self-employed or part of a very small company. The following are just two examples:

- A chiropractor resigned from a large medical group, dissatisfied with the way patients were treated in the HMO setting. He opened a small practice, which soon attracted more patients than he could treat. He began to make plans to enlarge his practice, move to a larger facility, and hire two more chiropractors, but then he stopped and took stock.

  The reason he established a private practice — and one of his guiding values — was his belief that patients deserved individualized, personal care. By growing his business, he realized he would spend more time managing staff and less time treating patients. The one thing he valued above all would be diminished, so he decided not to enlarge the practice. Instead, he formed a network with other chiropractors to whom he could refer patients.

- A painting contractor with a large and successful business began to worry about the environmental impact of some of the chemicals used in his paint products. His company valued its role as a local business that contributed to a strong community by offering summer jobs to college students and supporting local sports leagues and events. But that coveted role seemed in jeopardy if the products it used every day posed a danger to its employees and to the community. Reflecting on the company's core values, the CEO decided it was time for a change. He replaced the paint products with alternatives that were more environmentally friendly, despite the fact that they were more expensive and cut into his profit margin. A savvy businessman, he decided to promote the fact that the company had gone green. That gave him an edge over the competition, and in the end his business's bottom line improved.

TIP

One way to uncover some of your core values is to consider how you would respond to a series of hypothetical situations — situations that call on you to make difficult decisions. Read through the scenarios presented in Form 3-7 and check the boxes that best describe what you would do. Remember, these questions don't have right or wrong answers. The whole idea of this survey is for you to get a better handle on the set of values you already hold.

Writing a values statement

Use your responses to the hypothetical situations in Form 3-6 as a guide when you draft a statement of the values you think are most important to your business. The statement doesn't have to be long and fancy. In fact, a simple list, with values written as plainly and clearly as possible, is an ideal form for a values statement. When you finalize your values, record them on Form 3-8.

EXAMPLE

Figure 3-3 presents a values statement created by a young entrepreneur who wants to combine his love of art and his commitment to folk artists into a web-based folk art emporium.

Your Values Statement

Folk Art Bazaar is dedicated to the following values:

- Using the Internet to form a community of artists and collectors
- Encouraging the preservation of folk art tools and methods
- Offering struggling folk artists a means to make a decent living
- Educating collectors about the value and importance of folk art

---

© John Wiley & Sons, Inc.

FIGURE 3-3:
Your values statement can take the form of a checklist.

Writing a vision statement

A vision statement is a short phrase or sentence that describes the enduring purpose of your business. To distinguish the vision statement from the other statements you find in this chapter, remember the following list:

>> Your mission statement defines the purpose of your business and the approach you want to take to achieve success.

>> Your goals and objectives describe what you want to accomplish and the mileposts you want to reach along the way.

» Your values statement summarizes the beliefs and principles that guide your business behaviors and activities.

» Your vision statement expresses the positive impact you intend your business to make in this world and the good work you want it to accomplish. This statement captures the essential reasons why you're in business: The intentions that will remain constant even when strategies and practices — and even your products and services — change in response to a changing world.

EXAMPLE

Return to the business venture started by an entrepreneur whose business values are listed in Figure 3-3. His company's mission statement reads as follows:

> *To create an online marketplace that brings together unique and creative folk artists from around the world with serious collectors from beginner to expert.*

His enduring vision statement reads

> *To promote the continuing production of folk art and the livelihood of folk artists around the world through Internet technology.*

TIP

Form 3-8 presents vision statements that take a range of approaches. Check the ones that really grab you. You can refer to them as you write your vision.

TIP

In 25 words or less, capture the vision you have for your company. Use the examples you like in Form 3-9 as a starting point, and then use Form 3-10 to put your statement in writing. Your vision statement makes its way into your written business plan as part of your company overview.

The vision you have for your company is something you should be very proud of. Make copies for each person you work with. Consider including your vision statement in your company brochure, on your website's "About Us" page, and even on your letterhead or in your email signature to remind everyone of the essential reasons that you're in business.

Aligning your vision with your business model

Your vision and values may seem very different from your bottom line business model. But all these components need to be in sync in order to keep your focus sharp and clear. If your business model diverges too far from your vision and values, everyone involved — from your employees to your customers — may begin to lose a clear sense of what the company is and stands for.

Look back at your values and vision statement and ask yourself three questions to make sure your vision and business model are on the same page.

>> Does your business model support and further the vision of the company?

>> Do the ways you intend to make money reflect your values as a company?

>> Do your values and vision suggest additional ways of reaching customers and boosting your bottom line?

Setting Goals and Objectives

Well-chosen goals and objectives point a new business in the right direction and keep an established company on the right track. Just think about what football would be without end zones or what the Indianapolis 500 would be without a finish line.

The following sections examine goals and objectives more closely and present three ways to approach the task of writing out your goals and objectives. Experiment by using all three approaches. If you come up with more goals than you can handle, the section "Making final choices" later in this chapter can help you sort through your list to choose the most important goals.

When establishing goals and objectives, try to involve everyone who will have the responsibility of achieving those goals and objectives after you lay them out.

Comparing goals and objectives

To help you better understand how you can set goals and objectives, you first need a good foundation for what the two are.

>> *Goals* establish where you intend to go and tell you when you get there. They help improve your overall effectiveness as a company — whether you want to increase your share of the market, for example, or improve your customer service. The more carefully you define your goals, the more likely you are to do the right things and achieve what you wanted to accomplish in the first place.

>> *Objectives* are the specific steps you and your company need to take in order to reach each of your goals. They specify what you must do — and when.

Think of goals and objectives this way:

>> *Goals* tell you where you want to go; *objectives* tell you exactly how to get there.

>> *Goals* can increase your effectiveness; *objectives* back your goals and make you more efficient.

>> *Goals* are typically described in words; *objectives* often come with numbers and specific dates.

EXAMPLE

Suppose that your goal is to double the number of people using your web-conferencing service. Your objectives may be as follows:

>> Gain awareness by placing print ads in four regional markets and by airing radio ads in two major markets (by June 1)

>> Attract first-time customers by offering an online giveaway of $1,000 (by June 10)

>> Cultivate prospects by implementing a permission-based weekly email campaign to 2,500 targeted contacts (by July 10)

>> Convert 10 percent of prospects to clients, using email reminders (beginning July 25)

Together, goals and objectives form the road map for your company's future. Without them, you risk making wrong turns and wasting precious energy.

Approach #1: Tying goals to your mission

The first approach to specifying goals and objectives begins with a review of your company's mission statement. (Don't have one yet? See the section "Giving Your Company Its Mission" earlier in this chapter.) Using key phrases from your mission statement to define your major goals leads into a series of specific business objectives.

EXAMPLE

The connections between goals and your mission are easy to visualize if you use a flowchart, as shown in Figure 3-4. In this example, key phrases in the mission statement lead to major goals, which lead to specific business objectives.

TIP

Use Form 3-11 to create a flowchart of goals and objectives based on your mission statement. If your mission statement doesn't suggest a list of goals, you may want to reevaluate it to see whether it really captures what your business is all about.

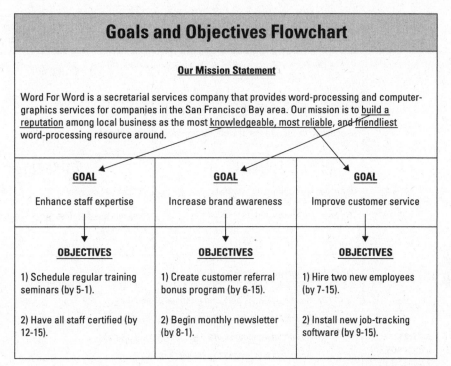

Goals and Objectives Flowchart

Our Mission Statement

Word For Word is a secretarial services company that provides word-processing and computer-graphics services for companies in the San Francisco Bay area. Our mission is to <u>build a reputation</u> among local business as the most <u>knowledgeable, most reliable, and friendliest</u> word-processing resource around.

GOAL	GOAL	GOAL
Enhance staff expertise	Increase brand awareness	Improve customer service
OBJECTIVES	**OBJECTIVES**	**OBJECTIVES**
1) Schedule regular training seminars (by 5-1).	1) Create customer referral bonus program (by 6-15).	1) Hire two new employees (by 7-15).
2) Have all staff certified (by 12-15).	2) Begin monthly newsletter (by 8-1).	2) Install new job-tracking software (by 9-15).

© John Wiley & Sons, Inc.

FIGURE 3-4: Use Form 3-11 and follow this example to create goals and objectives tied directly to your company mission.

TIP

Make sure your goals are always measurable. By establishing metrics goals, you can gauge your progress and recognize immediately when your efforts are going off track.

Approach #2: Using goal-setting ACES

Most goals define positive outcomes that you want your business to achieve, but sometimes you also want to set goals to avoid pitfalls and to eliminate a few weaknesses. To help develop goals that cover all the bases, use the acronym ACES as you tick through the following key questions:

>> **A**chieve: What do you want to attain in the future?

>> **C**onserve: What do you want to hang on to?

>> **E**liminate: What do you want to get rid of?

>> **S**teer clear: What do you want to avoid?

EXAMPLE

Figure 3-5 shows how an online shopping emporium, a small start-up company with big dreams, applied the ACES questions when creating a set of business goals.

Goals and Objectives Based on "ACES"

ACHIEVE	CONSERVE
Website up and running with at least 25 different "storefronts"	Strong sense of employee morale and enthusiasm
Successful second round of venture capital	Staff expertise

ELIMINATE	STEER CLEAR OF
Unnecessary duplication of efforts	A financial crunch
The competition (ha, ha)	Losing valued staff to other dot-com companies

SET OF BUSINESS GOALS:

- Revise business plan and financial projections.
- Review storefront vendor acquisition strategy.
- Streamline management decision-making process.
- Redesign employee benefits packages.
- Develop a new-hire training curriculum.

FIGURE 3-5:
The four ACES questions lead to establishing business goals.

© John Wiley & Sons, Inc.

TIP

Use Form 3-12 to apply the ACES questions to your business situation. Fill in the grid with the first thoughts that come to mind; you can revisit your responses later to see if they lead to a clear set of business goals.

Approach #3: Covering all the bases

One more way to think about business goals is to consider each of the four categories into which most goals fall:

>> *Day-to-day work goals* are directed at increasing your company's everyday effectiveness. They may involve things like order tracking, office management, or customer follow-up. As a start, name at least one change that you can make in your day-to-day operations that will make a difference in your overall effectiveness. Write it down in the form of a business goal.

>> *Problem-solving goals* address specific challenges that confront your business, such as low employee morale or quality of service issues. List the two biggest problems that your company faces, and then write goals that can solve them.

>> *Development goals* encourage the acquisition of new skills and expertise, whether for your employees or for yourself, and whether you run a large company or operate as a freelancer or an independent contractor. So, how about formulating at least one development goal for yourself or your company?

>> *Innovation goals* help you find new ways to improve the following: the products or services that your company offers, how you market your company, and how you distribute and deliver what your company sells. Can you identify any innovative approaches that could make your business more effective in the future? If so, formulate an appropriate goal.

>> *Profitability goals* set your sights on where you want your bottom line to be. When all is said and done, profit is the No. 1 goal for profit-making companies. For nonprofit companies, this goal may take the form of how many dollars in contributions you plan to raise or a goal for increasing the company's endowment.

TIP

Use Form 3-13 to review common business goals. Check off any that ring true for your company and add them to your list of goals.

Checklist of Common Business Goals
☐ **Improve customer satisfaction**
☐ **Establish or increase brand awareness**
☐ **Find new markets for products or services**
☐ **Expand product or service lines**
☐ **Decrease time to market**
☐ **Improve employee satisfaction**
☐ **Increase management communication**
☐ **Reduce operational costs**
☐ **Generate new sources of revenue**
☐ **Become more entrepreneurial**
☐ **Increase networking with partners**

© *John Wiley & Sons, Inc.*

FORM 3-13: Sift through the common business goals listed on this form to trigger your goal-oriented thinking.

Making final choices

The three goal-setting approaches in the previous sections lead to a respectable list of goals — maybe more goals than is practical for one business plan. Select the five goals that you think are absolutely, positively essential to your business success. (If you come up with only four, don't worry. If you can't get away with fewer than six or seven, that's okay, too. Just be sure you establish a list of goals long enough to drive your success, but don't overwhelm your ability to focus on each one.)

TIP

After you decide on your list, fine-tune each goal, using these guidelines:

>> Keep each goal clear and simple.

>> Be specific.

>> Be realistic.

>> Don't be afraid to push yourself and think big.

>> Make sure that your goals are in sync with your mission.

TIP

Tie your goals to objectives, using the goals and objectives flowchart in Form 3-14.

REMEMBER

Your goals become part of your written business plan. Long-range goals are wrapped into your business strategy, and immediate goals drive your short-term action plans.

Putting Your Principles into Practice

Companies that remain devoted to nothing more than the bottom line will always exist. But, increasingly, business leaders are realizing that strong values contribute to strong businesses, and they craft their business plans accordingly. Many are creating detailed ethics guidelines that articulate exactly what they stand for and how they intend to act. Companies often post those guidelines on their websites so that both customers and employees can see them. They help guide employees in their everyday working lives. These guidelines also reassure customers that the company intends to act in an ethical way.

Use your mission, vision, and values to guide the way that your business functions as a socially responsible contributor to the world around you — to your employees, your clients, your industry, and your community. And use your business plan to design strategies that uphold your company values and what they mean to all who deal with your business.

EXAMPLE

Williams-Sonoma, which sells kitchen and home products, proudly posts its corporate values on its website. "We are here to please our customers — without them, nothing else matters," the document declares. Almost any company would say the same thing. But with the growth of online reviews, social media, and increased emphasis on business transparency, Williams-Sonoma and companies like it are committing themselves more publicly to social and environmental responsibility. Indeed, Williams-Sonoma asks all the companies that make the products it sells to sign a code of conduct that includes offering safe working conditions and fair wages. That code reflects its deepest values. More than that, it puts those values into action.

REMEMBER

Consider incorporating similar principles about trust, loyalty, ethics, and contribution in your values statement and then create a plan for translating the words into actions whenever the need arises, following these steps:

1. **Whenever you encounter a difficult business or ethical situation, assess your options in light of your values.**

2. **Analyze the consequences of the various actions you can take, considering who will benefit and who will be hurt or damaged by each response.**

3. **Weigh whether your response is honest and fair.**

4. **When you're confident that your response to a difficult decision is consistent with your values and that your actions will be fair and honest, proceed with confidence.**

By knowing and remaining true to your values, when and if you encounter an ethical dilemma, you'll have a strong foundation upon which to build.

And now you know how you put your values to work.

Forms

Go to www.dummies.com/go/businessplanskit to view and download the following forms if you need help setting up the ground rules for your business:

Form 3-1	Basic Business Definition Framework	Questions to help you determine which business you're really in
Form 3-2	Comparing the Most Common Business Structures	A form that allows you to compare and contrast a variety of business structures
Form 3-3	Your Mission Statement Questionnaire	Questions designed to generate ideas about your company's mission
Form 3-4	Your Mission Statement Framework	A form to help you bring ideas together into a statement of mission
Form 3-5	Examples of Real-World Mission Statements	Actual company mission statements along with space to record your impressions
Form 3-6	Your Mission Statement	A form on which you can record the final version of your company's mission statement
Form 3-7	Values Questionnaire	Situations designed to help you identify the values you already hold
Form 3-8	Your Values Statement	A form on which to record your values statement
Form 3-9	Examples of Real-World Vision Statements	A selection of actual vision statements with space to check off which ones you like
Form 3-10	Your Vision Statement	A form on which to record your vision statement
Form 3-11	Goals and Objectives Flowchart	A form to capture your company's goals and objectives as they relate to your mission statement
Form 3-12	Goals and Objectives based on ACES	A form to capture your goals and objectives based on things you want to achieve, conserve, eliminate, and avoid
Form 3-13	Checklist of Common Business Goals	A checklist of common business goals of many companies
Form 3-14	Your Major Business Goals	A form to record your goals

2
Developing Your Plan's Components

Chapter 4

Understanding Changing Conditions, Customers, and Competition

B usiness gurus love to toss around fancy-sounding jargon — terms like interfunctional coordination and matrix-based portfolio analysis. But when it comes down to running a successful business, the basics are pretty simple. Call them the three Cs: conditions, customers, and competition. You already know what customers and competition mean. *Conditions* refers to the environment you're doing business in and the forces that will affect your marketplace, such as economic outlook, regulations, technologies, and other factors. This chapter offers a road map for exploring the three Cs as part of your business planning process.

Along the way, you're going to see another C word, *change*, more than a few times. Here's why. Not all that long ago, business planners could scan the landscape and be fairly confident about what the future held. Today, change is the constant. Changes in financial, environmental, social, technological, communication, and regulatory conditions have shifted the landscapes of entire industries, dramatically altering how businesses operate and how customers buy.

Use this chapter as you analyze your business environment, your customers and prospective customers, your competition, and the economic conditions you face, all with an eye to how they affect your business success — and your business plan.

Zooming In on Your Industry

Your business may be one-of-a-kind, but it's also part of a larger industry: retail, telecommunications, entertainment, travel, publishing, nonprofit — or any of a hundred others. What's more, regardless of your field, your industry is likely facing changes of one sort or another. Environmental concerns are driving change in some industries. Demographic changes are roiling others. Technologies keep advancing at quantum speed, changing how people shop, entertain themselves, stay in touch, keep healthy, and do virtually everything people do.

These sections help you gain a clear sense of the conditions your industry faces and assess how well your business is configured to succeed.

Analyzing your industry's big picture

To understand the larger forces at work in your industry, ask yourself these questions:

>> What are the immediate and long-term product and pricing trends in your industry?

>> Is market demand for your industry's offerings growing, shrinking, or holding steady?

>> Is it easy or difficult for new competitors to enter your industry?

>> How fast are technologies, regulations, or other fundamentals of your industry changing?

>> How will your business address the disruptions it already faces or the changes you see on the horizon?

Answers to questions like the preceding ones are key to creating a successful business plan. By compiling a good overview of your industry, you gain a better sense of how and where your business fits in and what it will need to do to become and stay competitive — insights that will help you sidestep trouble and chart a steadier course.

TIP

Go to www.dummies.com/go/businessplanskit to find the Form 4-1 questionnaire, which you can use to summarize what you know about your industry and, even more important, what you still need to find out.

WARNING

What you don't know *can* hurt your business, so instead of leaving questions in Form 4-1 unanswered, take the time to do some research in order to come up with answers. For example, if a few suppliers control most of your industry's material costs, you can make sound decisions based on that knowledge — or you can overlook that fact and have it come back to haunt you later.

After you complete the questionnaire, look over your answers and single out areas that are most apt to influence your future:

>> Who really drives change in your industry: customers, distributors, or suppliers?

>> Will you be able to ride the rising tide of an expanding industry, or will you have to find ways to succeed in spite of a general industry slowdown?

>> Do you anticipate major transformations — in technology, production processes, global influences, or customer buying patterns — that could affect your industry and your competitive position and profitability? What are they? How will you respond?

Any one of the industry forces, trends, or issues you identify may be the one that presents a threat to plan around or an opportunity to leverage.

Anticipating major industry changes and disruptions

Businesses have always had to adapt to change. An innovation makes a widget a little smaller or a whirligig a little faster. New competitors enter the market. Changes like these are sometimes dubbed *evolutionary.* In the 1990s, business strategists started talking about *disruptive changes* — innovations or new business models so dramatic that they transform the very nature of an industry, turning everything people thought they knew upside down, fast.

EXAMPLE

Consider map makers. Not all that long ago, the business of making and printing maps looked pretty secure. Then along came GPS, and now most people turn to their smartphones or car navigation systems to figure out where they are and how to get from here to there.

Until recently, electric power companies were feeling pretty comfortable, too. They generated power and delivered it to people's homes, sending a monthly bill.

Then rooftop solar panels became efficient enough to make economic sense, and suddenly homeowners who were customers of the electric utility became competitors, generating their own power.

Now's a good time to ponder how your business and the larger industry you're part of could be turned upside down. Ask

>> Could the product or service you offer be delivered in a totally different way?

>> Could your customers find a completely new way to get what they want or need, bypassing you completely?

>> Could technological innovation upend your business model?

WARNING

With so many examples of disruptive change — from apps by which doctors deliver healthcare to self-driving cars — you easily can assume that almost any dramatic new technology will turn the business arena upside down. But not every innovation turns out to be as transformative as hyped. For example, many analysts figured that the rise of e-books would put print publishing and brick-and-mortar bookstores out of business. Certainly, e-books posed a threat. But the latest statistics suggest that the e-book business has leveled off, while print publishing is growing. Turns out lots of people like to hold a good old-fashioned book in their hands. The lesson? Overreacting to technological changes can be as risky for a business as failing to react. Your task as a planner is to evaluate changes out there on the horizon and decide how important they are, either as a threat or an opportunity. Check out Chapter 15 for more on planning in a transformed world.

TIP

Summarize the findings from your industry analysis and include your overview in the business environment section of your written business plan.

Recognizing — and leveraging — barriers to entry

An important step in assessing your business environment is to understand what kinds of obstacles — known as *entry barriers* — challenge new contenders in your industry. If the barriers are low, almost anyone can join the fray and compete for business. If the walls are high, entry is harder and fewer competitors make the plunge. As part of the business planning process, you need to recognize barriers that challenge your success while also devising how to build or strengthen barriers that deter competitors from entering your arena.

EXAMPLE

Consider the following examples:

>> Suppose that you're starting a catering business. One entry barrier is the capital cost associated with acquiring kitchen, delivery, and serving supplies

and equipment. To overcome the barrier, rent use of a commercial kitchen, tables, linens, and place settings and glassware, and lease a delivery van until you get up to full speed.

>> If you're planning a clothing shop, it will have to compete with chain and online stores that enjoy the competitive advantage of a built-in *economy of scale.* Simply put, large retailers can buy inventory at a lower cost because they buy so much of it at a time. To overcome the barrier, compete on attributes other than price: the quality of inventory, for example, or special services or unique fashions.

>> If you're thinking of starting a health-related blog, publishing costs almost nothing. Anyone with a computer and Internet connection can do it, which is part of the challenge. The hurdle is setting yourself apart and gaining a devoted readership — not to mention figuring out a business model that assures you get paid for all the hours you put in developing content.

TIP

Form 4-2 presents typical entry barriers that challenge new competitors in a variety of industries. Check the ones that apply to your industry and marketplace. Use the space at the end of the form to add barriers unique to your business situation.

TIP

On a scale of 1 to 10, with 1 being the most significant impediment to success, rank the entry barriers that new competitors in your industry encounter and, if you're launching a business, the top three barriers you'll face. In your plan, summarize how you'll build entry barriers to win competitive advantage. Also detail how you plan to overcome the obstacles represented by the top barriers your business faces.

BUILDING ENTRY BARRIERS

If your business is entering a new (to you) industry or market area, expect to face some barriers as you seek to compete profitably with already-established businesses. At the same time, think about building some barriers of your own in an effort to up the ante for competitors seeking to follow you into your business arena or market area.

Entry barriers come in a wide range of forms, including

- **Intellectual property:** By protecting your idea and production process, you can block others from legally using your approach for a number of years. Visit the website of the US Patent and Trademark Office at www.uspto.gov for information.

(continued)

(continued)

- **Cost and pricing advantages:** Consider building a cash reserve to allow your business to cut prices or enhance promotions, if necessary, to force new competitors to operate at an unsustainable loss. Also, consider volume-purchase commitments with key suppliers in return for lower costs that result in product pricing that competitors will find hard to match, as well as contracts and relationships that deter customers from switching to competitors.

- **Credibility advantages:** By securing specific accreditation or certification, exclusive distribution or licensing agreements, industry endorsements or other differentiating associations, or credentials, your business can develop marketable attributes that are difficult for competitors to match.

- **Branding advantages:** Especially if you're the first in your market with a particular product or service, invest upfront to quickly build market awareness and a strong brand that will make future marketing efforts both more manageable and less costly. (Chapter 7 focuses on the topic of marketing.) The faster you establish your product or service as the preferred choice, the more expensive unseating you in the marketplace becomes for newcomers.

- **Regulations and trade restrictions:** Tariffs and quotas work as entry barriers to international and some domestic markets. If your industry is subject to trade restrictions, join industry associations, attend industry conferences, and follow industry news to keep up on the rules under which your business needs to operate. You should also participate in efforts to protect your markets from those who aren't authorized to participate.

- **Economic factors:** The price of equipment, licensing, research and development, or other mandatory expenses involved in setting up shop deter other competitors from entering your arena. As you establish your business, think in preemptive terms, selecting equipment and processes around which you can build a distinct and impenetrable advantage.

Defining Your Customers

The more you know about your customers, the more you know about where to find others just like them, how to reach them with media or other marketing communications, and what kinds of messages, offers, and incentives will entice them to plunk down their hard-earned cash. These days, understanding and serving customers is a bigger challenge than ever. The Internet and social media have created what business experts call "the empowered customer." Customers can shop around for the best deal with a few taps on a smartphone or tablet. They can read what other customers think of a product or service and write their own reviews. In online communities, people who share an interest can chat about everything from the best this to the cheapest that. Talk about power!

But the rise of the empowered customer also gives companies unprecedented tools to see not only what customers buy but also what they look at, what their interests are, and what they like or don't like about competitors' offerings. The upcoming sections guide you through the process of researching and compiling customer information so that you can focus your business efforts not just on prospective customers, but on ideal customers for each of the product lines your business offers. If yours is a business-to-business company, be sure to check out "Doing business with business customers," later in this section.

Developing your customer profile

No business can be all things to all people. In fact, one of the keys to success is knowing who is and isn't a good prospective customer. Defining your customers by location, lifestyle characteristics, purchase interest and ability, and shopping and buying behaviors allows you to compile the information necessary for targeting your business efforts to and only to the precise, intended audience. As you profile your customers, four terms apply:

>> **Geographics:** This term describes *where* your customers and your potential customers — or prospects — reside. When you know this information, you can target your marketing efforts into specific regions, counties, states, countries, or zip codes.

>> **Demographics:** This term describes *who* your prospects are in factual terms, such as age, gender, ethnicity, education level, marital status, sexual orientation, income level, and household size.

>> **Psychographics:** This term describes *lifestyle characteristics,* including attitudes, beliefs, and opinions that affect customer-purchasing patterns.

>> **Behavioral patterns:** This term describes *how* customers buy, including when, why, how much, and how often they buy, their level of loyalty, their purchase occasions and timing, and whether they make buying decisions based on price or quality, on impulse or after careful consideration, based on personal decisions or on the recommendation of others, and other such behavioral patterns.

Another term worth noting is *geodemographics,* also called *cluster marketing* or *lifestyle marketing.* It combines facts about geographics, demographics, and psychographics to locate geographic areas where residents share the age, income, lifestyle characteristics, and buying patterns of your target customers, therefore that make them good prospective target market areas.

TIP

Use Form 4-3 to develop your customer profile. If yours is an existing business, create a profile of your current customers. If you're planning for a new business, describe the person most apt to purchase your offering.

Conducting customer research

You may need to do some research in order to gain a clear picture of your customers. You can survey your clientele yourself, or you can use available market analyses, called *secondary research*, which you can apply to your particular business situation. The goal is to know exactly who is apt to buy from your business, how to reach those people, and what to say when you have their attention.

Compiling an analysis of your customer

Large companies commit huge budgets to conduct customized market research. Fortunately, simpler and cheaper ways to obtain a picture of your customers are available. Consider the following ideas:

>> **Stop, look, and listen.** You can discover plenty simply by observing customers. If you deal with customers in person, note how they arrive, what they wear, whether they arrive alone or with others who share in or influence their decisions, how long they stay, and what interests them and motivates their purchases. If you're in the retail business, watch where they go inside your store and what products they linger over the longest. At industry trade shows, watch which exhibits attract the biggest crowds. In any setting, conduct informal surveys by asking prospects about their reactions to various products, services, and features.

>> **Create a dialogue.** If you're thinking about improving a product or developing a service, invite your best customers or most likely prospects into the creative process. Ask what they like and don't like about existing offerings. What would they change? What features would they add?

  Additionally, use your website, social media pages, or online survey services such as SurveyMonkey to request input.

>> **Go virtual.** If your customers are far-flung, consider a virtual focus group by arranging for selected customers to meet in an online chat room or web conference to discuss a particular aspect of your product or service. Your social media networks are a good place to issue invitations. As in a traditional focus group, involve a moderator and offer participants some token of thanks for their time and ideas.

Casting a wider net

Supplement your customer and prospect knowledge with secondary research:

>> **Contact your industry association and the major media groups that serve your industry to obtain their analyses of the consumers in your**

market arena. Also, inquire within your industry about other research reports that reveal customer and business trends in your business arena.

>> **Search the Internet for purchasing trends in your business arena.** Publishers and authors can track which books are selling well. Winemakers can follow which vintages customers are snapping up. Consultants can research the hottest business topics. Digital gadget makers can survey customer reaction to cutting-edge technologies.

To tap into a wealth of consumer opinion, visit review sites used by customers in your arena and read the range of rants and raves to discover what people love and hate about offerings like yours. If you aren't sure which sites to study, enter the generic term for your business, along with the word "ratings" or "reviews" (example, hair salon ratings or reviews). When you find sites where customers post opinions, visit regularly for useful information.

TIP

>> **Put the Google Adwords keyword planner tool to work.** Go to a keyword tool such as the one at http://adwords.google.com/keywordplanner to see which terms related to your products and services people are searching for. For example, you may discover that 190,000 people recently searched for "red Mercedes convertibles" and only 1,100 people searched for "blue Mercedes trucks." By discovering what people are looking for you can better identify your customer interests.

TIP

>> **Visit the reference area of your public or university library.** It most likely has copies of the otherwise costly *SRDS Lifestyle Market Analyst* and the *CACI Sourcebook of ZIP Code Demographics.* Both resources can help you locate geographic areas with concentrations of residents who match your customer profile, helping you pinpoint regions for business expansion.

Getting research assistance

If your research requires questionnaires, focus groups, or interviews, consider bringing in specialists to help you maintain objectivity and convey professionalism throughout the process. Contact research firms, marketing firms, and public-relations companies for help.

Another good resource is your Small Business Development Center. To find a nearby center, visit the Local Resources listing of the Small Business Association website at www.sba.gov/sbdc.

TIP

For help identifying the approaches, advantages, and challenges of various research methods, see Table 4-1.

TABLE 4-1   ## Customer Research Approaches

Method	Purpose	Advantages	Challenges
Questionnaires and surveys	Obtain general information	Anonymous, inexpensive, easy to analyze, and easy to format and conduct in person or online	Impersonal, feedback may not be accurate, and wording can skew results
Interviews	Obtain information and probe answers	Develop customer relationships, adapt to each situation, and access fuller range of information	Time consuming, reliant on good interviewers, and difficult to analyze
Observation	Document actual buyer behavior	Anonymous, immediate findings, and relatively easy to implement	Can be difficult to interpret findings and to target which behaviors to monitor
Documentation review	Study factual history of clients and transactions	Readily available, not disruptive to operations, not subject to interpretation	Research is limited to previously collected data
Focus groups	Find out about and compare customer experiences and reactions	Convey information to customers, collect customer impressions	Requires expert facilitation and advance scheduling; difficult to analyze findings

Establishing your customer intelligence game plan

Don't consider your research efforts over until you enrich your findings with insights about how customers actually reach, shop for, purchase, and interact with your offerings or with offerings like those you'll be introducing.

The method you use depends on whether you're starting up, in which case you'll study likely customers, or whether you're up and running, in which case you'll gather information from established customers.

TIP

Make customer intelligence an ongoing effort. If yours is an online business, for example, you can follow each sale with an email questionnaire. If you deliver purchases, you can include a customer survey with each order. Many businesses find that customers appreciate a telephone follow-up, which offers an ideal time to do some intelligence gathering. Whatever strategy you use to communicate with your customers, be sure to ask these questions:

» How did you hear about us?

» What attracted you to our business?

» What do you like best about what we offer?

>> What would you suggest that we do differently?

>> How can we better serve you in the future?

Customer knowledge leads to product, marketing, and service improvements that build not only business but also loyalty.

TIP

Use the customer intelligence checklist in Form 4-4 to create an agenda for times, places, and ways to get closer to your customers.

Putting your customer description into words

When planning and directing your company's business activities, customer knowledge equals business power.

To be sure that everyone in your business — and everyone reading your business plan — understands the profile of the customer your business serves, create a detailed customer description.

TIP

Use Form 4-5 to condense everything you know about your clientele into a clearly worded customer snapshot that describes the person most likely to buy from your business, where that person resides, what that person is looking for, how you're most likely to reach that person, and what will prompt that person to select your business over the competing options.

TIP

Make the description of your customer part of your business plan. Doing so keeps your business and its marketing efforts focused and effective.

Getting to know your ideal customer

Every customer is important to your business, but some are more important than others, and a precious few are most important of all.

The difference between good and great customers is huge. If you're already in business, you know that some customers are more profitable, more pleasant, more apt to buy frequently, and most likely to spread good words about your business. Those customers are the ones you want to focus on and increase in number.

Separating the good from the best

Make sure you know which customers are most valuable to your business so you can focus your attention on strengthening relationships with them — and reaching more just like them.

Your best customers

>> Want the products or services that you're particularly good at providing.

>> Appreciate what you do and are willing to pay the price that you ask.

>> Make reasonable requests that lead to improvement and expansion of your skills and services.

>> Inspire your business to move in new and profitable directions.

Great customers inspire and deserve utmost attention. Heap on the special services, pile on the appreciation, and do what you can to keep them loyal to your business. You'll be doubly rewarded with repeat purchases and invaluable word of mouth.

Good customers appreciate your offerings, buy your products, and pay on time. But they can be transitory — here today, and gone tomorrow. And what often lures them away is a better offer. They may never become loyal patrons because they value special deals more than they value long-term business relationships.

Your *most troublesome customers* are mismatched to your offerings. They're unreasonably demanding and may even be a drain on your staff and your business systems. Here's what to watch out for:

>> They consume considerable time and attention yet buy very little.

>> They demand unreasonable concessions on pricing, service, or product alterations.

>> They demoralize your staff.

>> They refuse to pay your fair price for your offering or refuse to comply with your billing and service standards.

>> They act dissatisfied no matter what you do for them.

Great, good, and troublesome customers affect your business in very different but predictable ways, following the 80/20 rule, which is also called the *Pareto Principle* or the *law of maldistribution*. In most businesses, roughly 20 percent of customers account for 80 percent of the customer service efforts. But keep in mind that the same 80/20 rule applies to your profits as well: 20 percent of customers will account for 80 percent of your profits. By identifying which customers fit into which group, you can spend more time with your best customers to greatly increase your profits.

Defining perfection

Indulge in a little fantasy. Conjure up an image of your ideal customer, whether that customer is an individual buyer or a business client (see "Doing business with business customers," later in this chapter). Imagine the sort of person who eagerly buys your products or services, raves about you to friends and colleagues, and returns to purchase from your business on a regular basis.

TIP

Get specific. Use the Form 4-6 questionnaire to detail aspects that differentiate your ideal customers from all others. Then use Form 4-7 to list the top traits that distinguish best and all other customers.

Segmenting customers into buyer groups

By determining which customers share similar interests and buying habits, you can target offerings to groups of people who respond in similar ways.

EXAMPLE

Consider the example of an urban apartment complex renting to affluent city residents. After gathering customer data, the complex managers found that renters from the immediate market area chose the complex for its quality accommodations, but even more so for its pet-friendly policy. Renters moving from more distant locations chose the complex for the quality of its interiors, terraces, and views.

Studying further, the managers learned that tenants moving from out of area fell into two categories: those seeking small apartments with short-term leases, either because they were moving for temporary jobs or because they were renting while searching for a home purchase, and those seeking larger apartments with longer-term leases, which they would make their primary residences for the foreseeable future.

Armed with this information, the managers used ads and social media posts to reach local residents with a pet-friendly message, distributed flyers through employers and real estate agents to reach people seeking short-term, small-unit accommodations, and hosted events and test-drive overnight stays to reach those considering the apartments as long-term homes.

TIP

Use Form 4-8 to analyze how your customers segment into groups and how various groups seek different products and purchase offers. Then use Form 4-9 to automatically calculate the distribution channels through which your customers purchase. Finally, use Form 4-10 to analyze how your sales or sales forecasts are allocated geographically, by product type, by season, and by distribution channel.

REMEMBER

Include a summary of your market segmentation analysis in the business environment section of your written business plan.

Shaping a strategy to ensure customer loyalty

Reeling in new customers keeps your business growing, but you need to retain those customers in order to leverage marketing costs and build a solid customer base. Providing a great product or service at the right price is crucial. So is individualized and outstanding customer service. Those are fundamentals. Without them, loyalty will never be achieved. But as part of your business plan, consider outlining a formal customer loyalty program.

Most loyalty programs follow one of these formats:

>> **Buy-ahead discounts** provide an immediate reward with discounts on future purchases.

>> **Purchase-level rewards** offer gifts, discounts, or services when spending levels are reached.

>> **Rebates against accumulated purchases** reward for purchases made, usually in the form of a year-end check.

>> **VIP member offers** reward customers who join a loyalty club or program, usually by paying a fee. Benefits range from free shipping on all orders to redeemable points for travel or other purchases.

>> **Shared-value programs** develop loyalty by supporting issues of value to customers. For example, a children's clothing manufacturer can offer discounts to purchasers who return used clothes for distribution to those in need.

>> *Gamification* **programs** employ game actions (for example, stars, badges, leaderboards) to motivate customers with rewards for purchases, referrals, customer-to-business engagement, or other desired activities.

>> **Upgrades and special treatments** offer customers something beyond the specific product or service being sold. That something could be as simple as a "happy birthday" gift, or a spontaneous "this one's on us" surprise.

Whatever form they take, loyalty programs aim to increase customer commitment and inspire future purchases. Most programs also collect customer information, which assists in refining knowledge of customer buying patterns. Even businesses without a formal loyalty program need to plan efforts to cement loyalty through repeat-purchase offers or loyalty-building events.

EXAMPLE

Consider the example of an art supply company in northern California that struggled to compete against big online suppliers, which can offer deeper discounts because of economies of scale. The staff and management got together to brainstorm about what they, as a small business, could offer that the big guys couldn't.

Their answer: expert advice and inspiration. To win customer loyalty, the art supply company offered weekend classes, run by local artists and artisans. Customers who bought $50 or more in supplies got a free coupon to attend a class of their choice. Customers who attended classes got discounts on supplies specific to that class (watercolor paints, for instance, or printmaking inks). The store mounted artwork from various classes on the walls, encouraging more customers to participate. Artists loved it. The buzz brought in new customers. Before long the store had waiting lists for most of its classes. And sales boomed.

TIP

If customer loyalty will be key to your business success, include details about the strategies you expect to use in your business plan.

Doing business with business customers

B2B is shorthand for businesses that sell to other businesses rather than to individual consumers.

Business and individual customers share concerns about price, quality, convenience, service, reliability, and expertise. But you can also expect some important distinctions in how business customers buy:

>> They rarely buy on impulse.

>> The buying patterns of their customers and what's happening in their industries affect their buying behavior.

>> Their buying decisions often rely on approval from managers, owners, financial consultants, or others.

TIP

For success selling to businesses, you need to get organized. Use Form 4-11 to create a profile for each of your business clients and major prospects and then circle the characteristics all have in common. Use these common traits to create an ideal business customer snapshot — two or three paragraphs describing the kinds of clients you want to target. For assistance, use Form 4-5 (Customer Snapshot).

TIP

If you have a business-to-business company, include a detailed description of the ideal client in your business plan.

Defining and Addressing Market Shifts

Every business faces a business environment in flux — the result of changing demographics, technical innovations, economic shifts, and other changes that transform the marketplace. To plan for the future, use these sections to figure out whether your market is growing or shrinking and whether your customers' tastes, needs, and buying patterns are changing in ways that could affect your business.

Charting target market growth patterns

If the population you serve is growing in size and consuming more products or services like the ones you sell, your business plan can include approaches for seizing growth opportunity. If your market is shrinking or customers are buying less often or differently, your business plan needs to address how you'll overcome growth challenges. To assess how your market area — and particularly the segment of the population you serve within your market area — is growing or changing, take these steps:

If your business serves one or several geographic market areas, compile marketplace data using these resources:

1. **Go to** www.census.gov/mycd/ **for population, resident, and business characteristics for the US communities you serve.**

2. **Visit** www.makeuseof.com/tag/zipskinny/ **for quick access to US Census data on specific zip code areas.**

3. **Obtain population statistics and trends from your state's economic development department, regional business development offices, local chamber of commerce, small business development center, and the advertising departments of media outlets that serve your market area.**

    Study how market area population has changed over recent years — both in your overall market area and in demographic groups within your market — to gain a sense of the growth trend that will affect your business future.

If your business serves customers with similar interests anywhere in the world, compile market information using these resources:

1. **Obtain information on the dynamics and trends of your market from websites for associations that serve your industry or business arena.**

    To find associations, search online by entering a word that describes the focus of your business, plus the word association.

2. **Search online for available research studies in your business arena.**

    For example, if you search for "golf industry statistics," results will include studies of the golf market size, composition, and growth trends.

3. **Study statistics compiled by publications that serve your industry.**

    Most publications post online versions of their media kits, which provide trends and forecasts of how the market is growing or changing.

TIP

In your business plan, summarize the extent to which your market area and target-customer group are growing or shrinking. Then describe the steps you'll take to capitalize on market growth or, if the market you serve is shrinking, how you plan to maintain sales momentum.

Tracking changes in buyer tastes and trends

In addition to defining market growth trends, your business plan also needs to address how you'll deal with changes in the way customers choose, value, and buy products.

If your business serves individual customers, answer each of the following questions three times — once for how customers have typically acted in the recent past, once for how they're acting under current market conditions, and once for how you believe they'll act in the near future.

>> Do customers make purchase decisions on their own or upon the advice of others?

>> Do they buy on impulse or after careful study and consideration?

>> Do they pay cash or use credit or payment plans?

>> Do they seem to place higher value on the prices or the level of your product or service quality?

>> How frequently do they buy from you, and what is the typical size of their purchases?

>> Of the products you offer, which ones are in highest demand and why?

If your business serves business clients, answer each of the following questions three times — once for how clients have typically acted in the recent past, once for how they're acting under current market conditions, and once for how you believe they'll act in the near future.

>> Are purchase decisions made by owners, or by operations, finance, technical or marketing managers? Are they made through a central office?

>> Do purchases require several levels of approval, and how long does the approval process take?

>> Do clients work exclusively with a single vendor, or do they use multiple suppliers to purchase products like the ones you offer?

> » Do clients put their purchase orders out for competitive bids, and if so, do they base selections on price, quality, speed, or other factors?
>
> » Do clients pay upon delivery or upon invoice, and how long is the typical payment cycle?

REMEMBER

In your business plan, summarize how your customers' purchase habits have and will continue to change and how those changes affect your products, pricing, marketing, sales, and operations.

Sizing Up Your Competition

Except for government agencies and communist states, everyone has competition. Even if your business idea launches a brand-new industry, you can expect a throng of new competitors to rush in, each fighting to grab its slice of the market pie. Your success depends largely on how well you understand your competitors and how successful you are at distinguishing yourself from the alternatives that exist in the minds of your potential customers.

Competition isn't necessarily a bad thing — as long as you know exactly who and what you're up against. The upcoming sections offer tips on how to search and sleuth your way to competitive knowledge. With good intelligence, competitors better your business by forcing you to distinguish yourself from the crowd.

TIP

Identify your five most significant competitors — those businesses that are most likely to take business away from you if you're not careful. Can't come up with five? Name as many as you can and record your list on Form 4-12.

Using cloak-and-dagger methods

If your plan is to open or expand a gift shop on Main Street, scoping out your competition isn't difficult. Browse through neighboring shops that cater to the same kinds of customers you hope to attract. Then inquire around — talking to your banker, other retailers, business leaders, clerks at your city hall or county courthouse, those in business networking groups, local media including business blogs, and others — to find out what businesses are planning to open in the near future. Finally, uncover stealth competitors (see the following section), including online and other less apparent businesses that can take a bite out of your market.

For many businesses, however, competitive research is more complicated. You have to work harder to discover the following about distant or corporate competitors:

>> What products or services they offer

>> Who their customers are

>> What their strengths are

>> Where their weaknesses are

Corporate strategists call this information-gathering effort *competitive intelligence*, or CI. Fortunately, the Internet provides a great starting point:

1. **Begin with your competitors' websites.**

   You'll likely see everything from product specifications to client lists to news-release archives containing information about future strategies and plans. Study every word, while paying extra attention to marketing messages and calls to action.

TIP

2. **Put search engines to work, entering competitors' names and scouring the results.**

   In addition to links to competitor-controlled sites, also study news, blog posts and comments, social media mentions, and information about joint ventures with other companies.

3. **Find your competitors in ratings and review sites.**

   You can discover what their customers like and dislike, giving you valuable information upon which to build better solutions.

TIP

Use the competitive intelligence checklist in Form 4-13 as you assemble information on your primary competitors.

Identifying your stealth competitors

You can usually spot direct competitors pretty easily. They look a lot like your business, offer similar products or services, and go after the same customers and market areas. But you have to watch out for less obvious competitors — known as *stealth competitors* — who serve the same customers you do, but in different, sometimes unexpected, ways.

EXAMPLE

Competition is almost always more than immediately meets the eye. Suppose that you're starting a bakery. Your direct competitors are other bakeries within, say, a 10-mile radius. But under-the-radar threats lurk. Most obvious are the bakery sections of grocery stores and restaurants. A little more obscure are bakeries tucked in brewpubs, coffee shops, and health-conscious businesses, or home-based operations selling at farmer's markets. Competition also hides in grocery aisles, where consumers can buy bake-it-yourself mixes. Plus, weight-loss programs offer bakery-product alternatives. Dieticians work to curb bakery-product cravings. Even the fresh-fruit industry arises as a healthy option to your bakery offerings.

TIP

To understand all you're up against, imagine yourself in your customers' shoes and consider every possible alternative — near or far — to the solution your business offers. Here are a few examples:

>> The bookstore that used to compete with the bookstore around the corner now goes head-to-head with online booksellers and e-books.

>> The local travel agent now competes with online sites that allow travelers to book hotels, flights, car rentals — even ski equipment — on their own, often with bonus benefits. Suddenly, travel agencies are lonely places, except for forward-thinking agents who read the competitive tea leaves and focused their efforts on particular market segments and services, such as group sales or customized tour packages.

When unmasking stealth competitors, don't limit your thinking to Internet offerings. Here's an example of a business blindsided by the impact of a research breakthrough: Makers of flea collars and flea shampoos are slowly fading away because of once-a-month wonder drugs that wipe out fleas.

TIP

Use the questionnaire in Form 4-14 to identify stealth competitors. After you uncover your stealth competitors, keep track of them, along with all your other competitors, whether stealth, direct, or indirect. Use Form 4-15 to detail the full array of competition you face, including the level of threat each competitor presents today and how you anticipate the threat to grow or recede in the future.

Staying a step ahead

Most likely, your competitors' next moves will build on their strongest capabilities. For example, a competitor whose strength is in research and development may be planning to develop and introduce a new product or a competitor strong in marketing and sales may have plans to undertake a market expansion.

REMEMBER

More often than not, companies compete in the following ways:

>> Lower prices

>> Better service

>> Highly targeted customer focus and interaction

>> Unique and attention-getting products or services

As you create your business plan, keep in mind the strongest competitive advantage held by your business and by each of your major competitors. Then, to compete in today's environment, plan to build upon your established area of strength while boosting additional strengths to win and keep customers.

For example, become known for price *plus* service, for service *plus* expanded customer focus, for tailored customer solutions *plus* competitive pricing. As examples of well-known businesses that are adding to their competitive strengths, look at the recent strategies of McDonald's, which added customer-responsive coffee shop and wine bar offerings, and Walmart, which added a new focus on green products to its established low-price position.

Use Form 4-16 to describe each major competitor's strongest suit or key capability — along with the strategic move you think each competitor is likely to make in the next year or so. (If you haven't done so already, use Form 4-12 to list the names of your top five competitors.) By thinking through the possibilities, you can fine-tune your business plan and prepare yourself for the competitive challenges ahead.

Then use Form 4-17 to assess how each competitor stacks up against your business and how you might develop strategies to improve your competitive advantage. These findings can help as you develop your business plan strategies in Chapter 5.

In your business plan, include a description of your competitive environment, including the strengths, capabilities, and likely moves of major competing businesses. This information will influence all your other business planning.

Reimagining How to Do Business in Today's Environment

Mobile digital devices and other disruptive technologies have transformed not only the way companies interact with customers but also the way they run their operations and conduct business. More changes will come. As you draw up your business plan, give serious thought to how changes in your industry could alter how you conduct your business. You don't have to predict the future accurately. All you have to do is be aware of trends and developments that could change the way you and your competitors reach and serve customers. Chapter 15 can help.

The most pressing changes on your business horizon depend on the kind of business you're in. Read on to explore two issues that we think are likely to affect most businesses as they compete in today's changing environment.

Meeting the challenge of hiring and retaining top-quality people

The No. 1 factor in staying competitive these days is hiring — and retaining — top-notch employees. There's a good reason that many high-profile tech companies offer employees all kinds of deluxe perks, from gourmet company restaurants to meditation rooms (not to mention competitive salaries). They know that if a software engineer or creative type isn't happy, he or she can jump ship and join any of dozens of other tech businesses. Especially in highly technical and creative fields, attracting and keeping talent is important. But even in less glitzy industries, hiring and retaining the best employees is critical to competitive success.

EXAMPLE

As the housing market recovered and the local economy boomed, a New York construction company began to land big ticket contracts to build luxury homes. Suddenly it faced an unexpected problem: hiring enough skilled carpenters, dry wall installers, stone masons, and other construction tradespeople. Competing for customers wasn't as much of a challenge as competing for skilled employees — people who could meet the exacting standards of high-end clients. To jump-start its hiring efforts, the business offered current employees a bonus for referring qualified tradespeople. The company also asked its current employees what perks would be most likely to win their loyalty. Forget gourmet lunches and meditation rooms. What current employees most wanted was a little more flexibility in their schedules. Many of them had young children and a spouse who worked, so dropping the kids off and picking them up at childcare or school was a constant scheduling hassle. The company offered flextime — and to sweeten the deal, also arranged for food trucks to visit the major construction sites at lunchtime. Before long, they had tradespeople knocking at their door.

TIP

If hiring and retaining skilled employees are key to your business success, include the strategies you will use in your written plan.

Greening your business

Before concluding the assessment of your industry, customers, and competition, analyze the importance of environmental stewardship to your business success. Include the following considerations:

>> **How going green provides a competitive advantage in your field:** For example, building owners and operators increasingly consider LEED Green Building ratings important to leasing or sales success. Likewise, businesses from the Fortune 500 to the smallest Main Street are finding that environmental improvements attract customers and deliver market share growth.

>> **How environmental actions can improve efficiencies or lower costs in your business:** You can do so through reduced energy usage, cleaner technology, reduced consumption of supplies, or other positive impacts.

>> **How greater sustainability contributes to a cleaner, healthier, more positive work environment:** Beyond the financial impact, assess how going green enhances morale and loyalty in your field of business, both among employees and customers.

>> **How environmental regulations affect your business:** Stay abreast of how regulations are likely to affect your business, what actions will be necessary to stay abreast of the laws, and how you can get involved in industry efforts to address the issues with positive solutions.

>> **How other businesses have implemented ecofriendly practices in your industry:** Check how their actions have improved their images, competitive positions, and profitability.

TIP

In your business plan, include a section assessing the environmental impact of your business and industry, followed by steps to take to further green your business while also enhancing your competitive position, operational policies, workplace, community relations, and, often, your bottom line as well.

Forms

To help you assess the business environment you're likely to face, check out the following forms, which you can download at www.dummies.com/go/business planskit:

Form 4-1	Industry Analysis Questionnaire	A list of questions designed to unveil what you know and what you don't know about your industry
Form 4-2	Barriers to Entry Checklist	A checklist of the hurdles new competitors face in a variety of industries
Form 4-3	Customer Profile Questionnaire	A list of questions to ask and answer when creating your customer profile

(continued)

(continued)

Form 4-4	**Customer Intelligence Checklist**	A form for collecting customer input on an ongoing basis
Form 4-5	**Customer Snapshot**	A framework for creating your customer description
Form 4-6	**Ideal Customer Questionnaire**	Questions that help you define your ideal customer
Form 4-7	**Distinguishing Traits of Ideal Customers**	A form for making side-by-side comparisons between your best customers and all the others
Form 4-8	**Basic Market Segmentation Framework**	Questions that help you group customers into market segments
Form 4-9	**Channel Distribution Analysis**	An Excel worksheet that helps you determine sales volume by distribution channel
Form 4-10	**Market Segmentation Analysis Worksheet**	An Excel worksheet that helps you determine sales volume by geographic market area
Form 4-11	**Business Customer Profile**	A questionnaire to help you create a profile of your business customers
Form 4-12	**Our Biggest Competitors**	A form to record the list of your top five competitors
Form 4-13	**Competitive Intelligence Checklist**	A form to keep track of information on each of your biggest competitors
Form 4-14	**Potential Stealth Competitors Questionnaire**	Questions to help you identify potential competitors before they become threats
Form 4-15	**Competitor Tracking Form**	A form for keeping track of direct, indirect, and stealth competitors, including the degree of threat each presents
Form 4-16	**Our Biggest Competitors and Their Likely Moves**	A form to keep track of large competitors and their likely strategic moves
Form 4-17	**Competitive Analysis Worksheet**	A form for analyzing competitive information and opportunities

Chapter 5

Charting Your Strategic Direction

I f you've worked your way through the last few chapters, you may feel like a juggler. On the one hand, you're evaluating the industry that you're in. On the other hand, you're getting to know your customers better. All the while, you're keeping both eyes on the competition. (Chapter 4 helps you on all three fronts.)

But wait; you still have more to track. You need to watch what's happening *inside* your business. Whether your business is up and running or in the planning stages, how do you assess its strengths — and its weaknesses? What opportunities — and what threats — are on the horizon? Amidst all the marketplace change and challenge, how do you plan to compete and win? How will you make money? What's your long-term strategy? How will you expand and develop your business? And when the time comes to retire or move on to other ventures, what exit strategy will you follow?

The answers to these questions are essential to your business planning, and they're what this chapter is all about.

Matching Your Capabilities to Business Opportunities and Threats

Especially in the turmoil of today's business world, companies with their heads in the sand are headed toward extinction. While they cling to the past or hunker down in the moment, companies with visionary leaders are moving into the passing lane by adapting their plans to steer clear of trouble and seize the opportunities they see on the horizon.

So how do you put your business in the fast lane? For starters, take an eye-opening look at your business situation by conducting a *SWOT analysis.* In business school lingo, *SWOT* is an acronym for strengths, weaknesses, opportunities, and threats. Strengths and weaknesses are internal issues to address, while opportunities and threats are external forces to deal with. A SWOT analysis is an important tool in business planning for one simple reason: It works.

Before you can carry out a SWOT analysis, you need to look at each of the pieces of the process separately, first by sizing up your business strengths and weaknesses and then by looking at your opportunities and threats.

Sizing up your strengths and weaknesses

In business, strengths and weaknesses come in the form of eight key *capabilities* that make up the essential elements of success:

>> **Research and development (R&D):** Your ability to design and develop new products, services, or technologies

>> **Operations:** Having the resources and systems necessary to produce the highest-quality products or services in the most efficient ways possible

>> **Marketing:** How well you get your products or services into the marketplace, onto customer radar screens, and through the sales process

>> **Distribution and delivery:** The ability to get your products into customers' hands

>> **Customer service:** Everything you do to create a loyal clientele that supports you with purchases, repeat purchases, and praise

>> **Management and leadership:** How you provide direction and a vision for your company

>> **Organization:** The procedures, people, and business structures that enable you to make the most of your resources and business opportunity

>> **Financial condition:** The financial health of your business

Not all capabilities are equally important to every business. (For a more complete description of each, see Chapter 6.) For example, a state-of-the-art distribution and delivery system may be essential to the success of one firm but not particularly important to another. R&D may be crucial for a computer manufacturer, but of little impact to a massage business. And, to a one-person business, management capabilities — at least as they apply to staffing issues — may be largely irrelevant.

WARNING

Don't jump to conclusions, however. Chances are good that, in some way, shape, or form, each of the key capabilities contributes in some way to your company's ability to compete and succeed.

Grading your capabilities

TIP

To rank the importance of each capability to your company's success, use Form 5-1 (see Figure 5-1), which you can find at www.dummies.com/go/business planskit. Be honest, circling Excellent in each area where you know that your business excels, and giving lower ratings where you think your business falls short.

Figure 5-1 shows how the owners of Soup's On, a gourmet catering company with plans to expand from a single outlet into a small chain, graded the company.

Company Strengths and Weaknesses Survey						
Capability	**Importance to Business**			**How Does the Company Rate?**			
Research and development	Low	(Medium)	High	(Poor)	Fair	Good	Excellent
Operations	Low	Medium	(High)	Poor	Fair	Good	(Excellent)
Sales and marketing	Low	Medium	(High)	(Poor)	Fair	Good	Excellent
Distribution and delivery	Low	Medium	(High)	Poor	Fair	Good	(Excellent)
Customer service	Low	Medium	(High)	Poor	Fair	(Good)	Excellent
Management	Low	Medium	(High)	Poor	(Fair)	Good	Excellent
Organization	Low	(Medium)	High	Poor	Fair	(Good)	Excellent
Financial condition	Low	Medium	(High)	Poor	(Fair)	Good	Excellent

FIGURE 5-1: Rank the importance of key capabilities to your business success. Use Form 5-1 to assess how your company rates in each area.

© John Wiley & Sons, Inc.

Here's a little background about what went into their thinking. R&D may not seem important to the success of a catering firm, but the Soup's On expansion strategy called for a website where customers could view the current selection of dishes, create personalized menus, place orders, and schedule catered events. To support this Internet strategy, the owners knew that they needed to beef up their web presence, so they gave R&D a ranking of medium importance. They gave operational ability a ranking of high importance after deciding that their ability to accurately fill orders and prepare meals was fundamental to their success. They also gave a high ranking to distribution and delivery, which they defined as their ability to transport food to events and to supervise setup, serving, and cleanup.

Matching your capabilities to the task at hand

TIP

After you rank and assess your company's capabilities, use your findings to complete Form 5-2, the Strengths and Weaknesses Grid. This form shows you, at a glance, how your business strengths and weaknesses align with the capabilities most necessary to your success.

Figure 5-2 shows how the owners of the catering company completed the grid. On the plus side, the caterers gave themselves excellent rankings in the crucial areas of operations and distribution and delivery. And they rated their customer service as good — an adequate position upon which they can build.

Company Strengths and Weaknesses Grid

How Does the Company Rate?	Importance to Business		
	High	Medium	Low
Excellent	• Operations • Distribution and delivery		
Good	• Customer service	• Organization	
Fair	• Management • Financial condition		
Poor	• Sales and marketing	• Research and development	

STRENGTHS

WEAKNESSES

FIGURE 5-2: The grid provided in Form 5-2 helps you match your business expertise with the capabilities most important to your success.

© John Wiley & Sons, Inc.

But then red flags really begin to flutter. The caterers ranked the areas of management and financial condition as highly important but gave their business only fair grades in those areas. They found more trouble in the area of marketing. Their plan called for expansion into new geographic areas, but current sales come almost entirely from repeat business and word of mouth. In all honesty, they had to rate their marketing capability as poor. They also decided that they were no better at R&D. No one on staff had expertise to match the aspirations of their Internet strategy.

Based on their findings, the caterers called a timeout to boost capabilities in key areas before proceeding with their expansion plans.

TIP

As you study your strengths and weaknesses grid, keep the following thoughts in mind:

>> Capabilities listed in the top left of the grid are essential capabilities and areas where you possess strong expertise — a great combination.

>> Capabilities at the bottom left of the grid are essential to your success, but your company is weak in these areas and, therefore, vulnerable until you beef up strengths.

>> Capabilities in the middle row of the grid are of medium importance to your success. The capabilities listed in the right-hand column are of minor importance. Any poor rating is cause for concern, but when your business is weak in an area of minor importance, the deficiency is of lesser concern — at least for now.

Capitalizing on strengths and overcoming weaknesses

After you know where your business stands on key capabilities — and which capabilities matter most to your business success — you're in position to build on strengths and work on weaknesses.

REMEMBER

As you write your business plan, don't be afraid to shine a spotlight on important company strengths. After all, these strengths provide evidence that you have what it takes to succeed in your field. At the same time, acknowledge deficiencies by detailing your strategy for turning those company weaknesses around.

TIP

One more word of advice: Because your company's strengths and weaknesses are likely to change over time, return to the grid in Form 5-2 on a regular basis to take a fresh look at where you stand.

WHEN YOU'RE THE ONE AND ONLY

If you're the boss and entire staff of a one-person company, you may wonder what all this talk about capabilities has to do with your success. The answer: Plenty. The same issues that confront big companies apply to your business — just on a smaller scale. Here's how a freelance web designer adapted the descriptions of each capability to fit her situation:

- **Research and development:** This capability involves staying current with new software, hardware, and design technologies by completing training and certification programs.
- **Operations:** This capability involves billing, accounting, scheduling, client service, back-up arrangements for fielding calls, and helping suppliers, subcontractors, and others in emergency situations.
- **Marketing:** This capability includes a strong identity and reputation, good marketing materials, and a website and online presence that's competitive and current. It also includes the ability to promote services, network, and make calls and presentations to prospective clients.
- **Distribution and delivery:** This capability includes getting to and from client meetings with the right equipment, software, and file access in the right place at the right time, as well as ability to serve customers remotely as appropriate.
- **Customer service:** This capability involves establishing working relationships with clients who have information technology needs and creating loyalty through excellent service, especially in emergency situations.
- **Management:** This capability includes the ability to set and reach goals and objectives, to maintain a sense of direction and vision, and to establish and run the practice like a business that earns and deserves a great reputation.
- **Organization:** This capability involves contracting for accounting, secretarial, subcontractor, and other support services.
- **Financial condition:** This capability means having funds for computer hardware, software, and testing equipment, cash to stay afloat until invoices are paid, a financial cushion, and a satisfactory salary and benefits.

Identifying opportunities and threats

After assessing the strengths and weaknesses of your business, look for external forces that can affect its destiny. These changes include

>> The appearance of new or stronger competitors

>> The emergence of unique technologies

>> Shifts in the size or demographic composition of your market area

>> Changes in the economy that affect customer buying habits

>> Changes in customer preferences that affect buying habits

>> Changes that alter the way customers access your business

>> Changes in politics, policies, and regulations

>> Fads and fashion crazes

For more details on planning in the midst of turbulent change, check out Chapter 15.

TIP

Using Form 5-3, list the threats and opportunities facing your business, and follow these guidelines:

>> When listing opportunities, consider emerging technologies, availability of new materials, new customer categories, changing customer tastes, market growth, new uses for old products (think about how mobile phones and even eyeglasses now double as cameras and computers), new distribution or location opportunities, positive changes in your competitive environment, and other forces that can affect your success.

>> When listing threats, consider the impact of shrinking markets, altered consumer tastes and purchase tendencies, raw material shortages, economic downturns, new regulations, changes that affect access to your business, and competitive threats, including new competing businesses and competitive mergers and alliances. Also think about the impact of expiring patents, labor issues, global issues, and new products that may make your offering outdated or unnecessary.

TIP

If you're having a tough time getting specific, go back to the strengths and weaknesses survey in Form 5-1, but this time use it to list strengths and weaknesses of your leading competitor. You won't know as much about your competitor's capabilities as you know about your own, but you probably know enough to flag areas of strength and weakness. Your competitor's strengths are potential threats to your business, and its weaknesses present potential opportunities.

EXAMPLE

When the catering company mentioned in the previous sections began planning to expand into a small chain, the owners held a retreat to consider potential threats and opportunities. Figure 5-3 shows their findings.

Company Opportunities and Threats	
Possible Opportunities	**Potential Threats**
• Increasing number of working couples who don't have time to cook meals • Growing interest in healthy, organic ingredients • Growing number of consumers opting to eat in rather than incur restaurant expenses • Growing demand for high-quality takeout food • Increased demand for in-business catered events rather than more costly off-premise dining • Acceptance of the Internet as a marketing and customer service medium	• Difficulty convincing cost-conscious consumers to spend on quality in-home catered meals • Growing cost of employee benefits, which contributes to increased product prices • Competition from restaurants offering home or business delivery by "waiters on wheels" as a way to compensate for reduced in-restaurant business • Indirect competition from expanded takeout sections at local grocery stores

© John Wiley & Sons, Inc.

FIGURE 5-3:
Use Form 5-3 to list external forces that could present your business with opportunities and threats.

Looking over the list, the caterers were encouraged. Their opportunities outnumbered their threats. What's more, they were convinced that they had the capabilities to capitalize on the pluses and counter the negatives.

Conducting a SWOT analysis

In order to plan to seize business opportunities and sidestep potential threats, you start by conducting a SWOT (strengths, weaknesses, opportunities, threats) analysis.

A SWOT analysis helps you analyze your company's capabilities against the realities of your business environment so you can direct your business toward areas where your capabilities are strong and your opportunities are great.

TIP

To conduct a SWOT analysis, follow these steps:

1. **List your company's strengths and weaknesses (see Form 5-2) and its opportunities and threats (see Form 5-3).**

2. **Divide your strengths into two groups:**

   Those that can help you take advantage of opportunities facing your business

   Those that can help you head off potential threats

3. **Divide your weaknesses into two groups:**

Those that require improvement before you can take advantage of opportunities

Those that you need to completely and quickly overhaul and convert into strengths in order to avert potential threats to your business

4. **Use your lists as you make decisions that contribute to your business plan.**

Develop strategies and actions for capitalizing on opportunities and create plans for addressing threats and weaknesses that could threaten the future of your business.

TIP

Use Form 5-4 to record the findings of your SWOT analysis. Figure 5-4 shows how the owners of the Soup's On catering business completed the grid for their company.

Company SWOT Analysis Grid

	Opportunities	Threats
Strengths	Use superior operations and delivery to go after increasingly sophisticated high-end takeout and catering markets CAPITALIZE ON THESE	We depend on our high quality and service, but it's harder to attract and keep good people MONITOR THESE
Weaknesses	Big growth in catered events market, but we're weak in marketing Promise of the Internet, but we have no R&D IMPROVE THESE	Our poor marketing and precarious financial condition are dangerous, given the increased competition we face ELIMINATE THESE

© *John Wiley & Sons, Inc.*

FIGURE 5-4:
Fill in the SWOT Analysis Grid on Form 5-4 to analyze your company against your business environment.

Based on the outcome of the caterers' SWOT analysis, they made some significant business decisions: They hired a marketing consultant with experience developing restaurant chains; they conducted research to get a sense of the resources required to achieve competitive Internet presence; they strengthened their management structure to prepare for growth; and they recruited two investors to improve their company's financial condition.

As a result, Soup's On is ready to grow into a small chain. The owners expect increased competition for catering and takeout services, but they project that growing demand will support a number of catering companies. What's more, they're confident that by focusing on quality, consistency, and sophisticated menus, they can compete successfully. By investing time upfront to understand their strengths and weaknesses — and by dealing with their opportunities and threats — the caterers increased their chances of success.

REMEMBER

Include findings from your SWOT analysis in your business plan, addressing how you intend to

>> Seize business opportunities by capitalizing on business strengths

>> Overcome weaknesses to take advantage of business opportunities

>> Monitor potentially threatening outside forces while maintaining or developing internal capabilities so that you're prepared to respond from a position of strength if a threat arises

>> Eliminate weaknesses to protect your business from threats

TIP

Revisit your SWOT analysis on a regular basis — at least annually and more frequently if your business is facing major changes in marketplace or competitive conditions, experiencing growth problems, or failing to meet goals and objectives — to see how the balance of strengths, weaknesses, opportunities, and threats may have shifted. Your business environment is constantly in flux, so you want to be sure that your business plan reflects the world around you as it *is*, not the way it *was*.

Defining Your Business Model

When management-types ask "So, what's your business model?" they really want an answer to a much more basic question: "How do you plan to make money?"

Behind that question is a lineup of other questions:

>> What, exactly, will you sell?

>> How will you deliver your products, for example through retail outlets, online, through franchises, by selling a product along with an ongoing service or supply agreement, through a free or low-cost offering with upgrade options, or through a combination of delivery approaches?

>> How much will you charge?

>> How will you reach, acquire, and keep customers?

>> How will you define your offering and differentiate it from similar offerings available to your customers?

>> What's your cost structure? In people language, how much does it cost to produce, market, and sell your offering, and where and when are those costs incurred?

>> What's your profit margin after subtracting all the anticipated costs from the revenue you expect to generate?

>> Will customers make one-time purchases, repeat purchases, or sign contracts or purchase agreements that deliver recurring revenue?

>> How much revenue and profit do you expect to generate?

In plain English, a *business model* basically is how you'll generate revenue and turn a profit. Bankers and funding partners will ask about your business model because they'll want to know your business can and will make money — soon and over the long-haul. Use these next sections as you prepare your answer.

Checking out traditional and digital-era business models

Some business models, like retail sales, have been around for as long as people have bought and sold stuff. Others, like *crowdsourcing* (calling on people for product development, on-demand talent, funding, or other business needs and transactions), are newer and still being tested and refined.

The digital revolution and the rise of the Internet have spawned all kinds of variations on the basic theme of connecting buyers and sellers. Auctions have been around for centuries; for example, eBay came along and transformed the traditional model into a digital worldwide marketplace. Electric, gas, and water companies have always sold their product using meters to measure how much consumers use. The Internet has expanded that concept to allow lawyers, IT professionals, editors, and even business consultants to offer metered services, where clients can turn to them as needed.

In another example, like-minded people — farmers in the grange hall, for example — have often banded together to buy stuff as a group. The rise of vast user groups means marketers can go after a discrete group of people with similar interests. If you offer something of value to a group of people with a shared interest, you may find that they begin to do your marketing for you, sharing information with others in the group on their own.

Business gurus love to come up with all kinds of names for different business models, from pay-per-view to affinity club sales. You can find lists with names like the 7 basic business models, 10 essential business models, and even 25 knock-'em-dead business models. Instead of wasting a lot of time poring over lists, we recommend that you take a close look at businesses out there that are already doing roughly what you want to do. First, make a list of five or six. Then, ask these questions about each one:

>> How does the business generate revenue?

>> Will the same business model work for you?

>> How can you adapt the business model to be even more competitive?

>> How may your business model change over time?

WARNING

Just having a cool idea for a business doesn't mean you have a viable business model. The truth is that some high profile and seemingly successful companies are still trying to figure out a sustainable way to make money. Take Twitter. Everyone knows the company. Millions of people around the world use it. But Twitter is still trying to figure out how to generate sustainable revenues.

You can watch some businesses in the struggle to find a business model. Consider the example of apps designed to let people paint on touch screens. To stay competitive in this crowded niche, developers can only charge a few bucks to download the apps. What's more, consumers expect the apps to be upgraded frequently to keep up with new operating systems. To try to bring in much-needed revenue, some apps offer specialized digital brushes — at an extra charge, of course. Some offer platinum versions of the standard painting app. Many now incorporate ads, so that they can at least earn a little pocket change while working to build revenue from app and accessory sales.

Following the money

Sooner rather than later in the business-planning process, you need to delve into the nitty-gritty details of your company's finances — your income statements, balance sheets, cash flow, budgets, and all the details that can make or break your company's future. (Chapter 9 makes poring over the numbers as pain free as possible.) At this point, however, your assignment is more basic: Figure out where your business revenues will come from. Who will pay? How much? How often? And what portion of every sale will make its way to your bottom line in the form of — here's the magic word — *profit*.

Following are terms you'll hear on your journey to profitability:

>> **In the black:** If your revenues exceed your costs, you're *in the black.*

>> **Red ink:** If you're not in the black you're losing money. The negative difference between your revenues and your costs is called *red ink.*

>> **Fixed costs:** Some business costs — rent or salaries, for example — don't change often and must be paid on a regular basis, no matter how many sales your business is (or isn't) making. These are called fixed costs or *overhead.*

>> **Variable costs:** Other costs, called *variable costs,* fluctuate with your sales volume. They include the materials that go into producing and marketing your product or service.

To keep out of red ink, you need enough revenue coming in to cover all your costs. But to break into the black, you need to price your goods and services to cover your costs *plus* a little (or more than a little) for your bottom line. That's called *profit.* Don't leave your business plan without it!

TIP

The first step toward profitability is to create a financial projection for your business. Use Form 5-5 as you estimate costs and revenues.

EXAMPLE

Figure 5-5 shows financial projections for a restaurant with plans to open in Chicago. The owners are looking for investors, so they want to present a convincing business model as a part of their business plan, and they want to show that revenues will exceed costs and deliver a profit.

BUSINESS MODELS ARE ESSENTIAL FOR NONPROFITS, TOO

If you're running a nonprofit organization, you may think you can skim past information on business models, but think again. Even though generating a profit isn't your motivator, generating social value is, and to do that you need a funding model sufficient to generate the money — through grants, donations, and other revenue sources — necessary to achieve your goals.

Chapter 14 contains advice on planning for nonprofits, but spend time in this chapter as well so that you're clear about the environment you're operating in, the funds you need to generate, where you think those funds will come from, and how you'll compel donors to open their billfolds on behalf of your cause.

Quick Financial Projection Worksheet

Projected Revenues

Anticipated number of meals served:	250 / week	
Average gross revenue per meal:	$ 37.50	
Total weekly gross revenue:		$ 9,375

Projected Fixed Costs

Restaurant space rental:	$ 1,000 / week	
Loan payments on equipment:	$ 350 / week	
Utilities, insurance, and other costs:	$ 225 / week	
Full-time personnel costs:	$ 2,350 / week	
Total weekly fixed costs:		$ 3,925

Projected Variable Costs

Food / wine wholesale costs:	$ 3,000 / week	
Temporary service staff:	$ 500 / week	
Total weekly variable costs:		$ 3,500

Expected Profits

Total weekly profits:		$ 1,950

FIGURE 5-5: Use this form to calculate revenues and costs and to project profits for your business.

© John Wiley & Sons, Inc.

On the revenue side, the restaurant owners calculate how much they'll make on each meal and how many meals they plan to serve. On the cost side, they enter their fixed costs (for rent, loans, utilities, insurance, and wages) and their variable costs (food, supplies, part-time help, and so on). Their estimates show that they plan to turn a profit of $1,950 a week, or almost $8,000 a month.

Based on their experience in the restaurant business, however, the owners know that their projections won't turn into reality overnight — that's part of the reason they want investors. They project that the restaurant will incur losses during the first six months, break even during months seven and eight, and turn a profit starting in month nine. (To brush up on planning time frames, check out Chapter 1.)

Knowing your burn rate and runway to profitability

Your business model is all about how you plan to make money. To get to that point, you'll need money. Maybe a lot of it. Accurately determining how much money you'll need before you start generating revenue is critical. If you run short of cash before your business takes off, you may be grounded forever. The term *burn rate* refers to how fast you'll go through the money you have set aside to start your business. After you estimate your burn rate, you can determine how long your start-up reserve will last. The amount of time you have to get your business off the ground is — appropriately enough — called your *runway to profitability.*

Your business model must include a timeline that takes the following into account:

>> The up-front costs you expect to incur when setting up your business

>> The source of funds to pay for your up-front costs

>> A schedule showing when you expect revenues to pour in

REMEMBER

The question of timing when revenues will roll in and how they cover the business burn rate isn't only for start-ups or big companies with factories to build and products to design. Timing can impact businesses of any age or size.

EXAMPLE

Take the example of a fledgling bed-and-breakfast (B&B) on Cape Cod, where the tourist season begins on June 1 and ends with Labor Day weekend in September. Except for a few other holiday periods, the B&B will bring in all its revenue during those three summer months. The owners need to generate enough summer revenue to cover its burn rate — its fixed costs for mortgage, utilities, taxes, salaries, and upkeep — all year round. Timing issues apply to many retailers, too, who often make the majority of annual sales during the year-end holiday or other prime selling seasons. For more on burn rates and runways, flip to Chapter 9.

REMEMBER

Especially if you're starting a business with limited cash — like most start-ups — a carefully detailed estimate of your burn rate and runway to profitability should be part of your written business plan. Be conservative and cautious in your estimates. No one complains about having a little money left over after the business is up and running. Everyone is unhappy if you run out of funds before that happens.

Generating and collecting revenue

In the simplest business model, your business makes a product or provides a service, sells it to a customer, and collects revenue directly. You might collect revenue on the spot, or you might sell on credit and collect in 30 days or over a longer time frame, if that's part of the deal. Or, you might lease your offering or provide it on a subscription basis. Or maybe you sell your product along with a service package, which would give your business model two streams of revenue: one from the sale and one from the service fee. In any of these scenarios, however, the sales transaction is between your business and your customer, and it's pretty straightforward and direct.

Other business models employ less direct, more complicated revenue-generation approaches. For example:

>> Instead of selling directly to customers, some businesses sell through wholesalers, distributors, franchises, multilevel marketing schemes, auctions, licensing agreements, or countless other indirect approaches.

>> Some business models involve selling the primary product for practically nothing, generating profit by selling accessories or other offerings the primary product requires. For example, think of the usage contract you sign when you get your cellphone for free, or close to it, or the ink you buy to keep your almost-free printer in use.

TIP

>> Some business models involve giving away the primary product and then converting a minor percentage of free users into buyers of a value-added version under what's called a *freemium* business model. LinkedIn, Pandora, Skype, and SurveyMonkey are among the highly visible examples. See the nearby sidebar for more information, and use Form 5-6 if you're weighing whether a freemium business model is right for your offerings.

>> Other businesses — especially broadcasters and bloggers — charge consumers nothing at all. Instead, they generate content that they basically give away, earning revenue by selling ads or sponsorships to those who want to reach the audiences the stations or sites attract.

Your business might generate revenue from retail transactions, hourly service fees, membership fees, user fees, advertising sales, premium-level product sales, or any combination of these or other revenue-generating approaches. Be sure that your business model clearly defines what you're selling, how you're selling it, when and how you'll collect payments, and your strategy for growth.

FREEMIUM: MAKING MONEY BY GIVING PRODUCT AWAY

Although most businesses invest marketing dollars to build awareness and prompt purchases, a growing number take a no-cost viral approach to building their brands and their sales through a freemium business model. Venture capitalist Fred Wilson, who chose the name, explains the model like this: "Give your service away for free, possibly ad supported but maybe not; acquire a lot of customers very efficiently through word-of-mouth, referral networks, organic search marketing, and so on; then offer premium-priced, value-added services or an enhanced version of your service to your customer base."

To get a freemium model right, you need to develop a clear balance between the free and profit-generating versions of your product.

If you're among those who've upgraded to a premium LinkedIn account, or who pay a fee to listen to Pandora radio without the ads, then you've experienced how the freemium-to-premium conversion works. When you selected the premium-level option, you made a decision that, in return for additional services and value, you were willing to pay for what you could have gotten — in a stripped-down version — for free.

Another example of the freemium model takes the form of e-books that can be downloaded for free. Plenty of business consultants, investment counselors, lawyers, and other professionals offer them. Why? The books are there to demonstrate their expertise, in hopes that you'll retain their services — at a price, of course.

See Form 5-6 for a checklist of considerations to assess if you're considering a freemium approach for your business.

Putting a price on your products

As you define your business model, be prepared to explain your pricing strategy, covering these points:

» How your pricing is structured — to cover all costs involved with purchasing your offering or to inspire additional purchases of features, services, or benefits; to feature a single price option or options for products at basic and premium levels; to be firmly maintained or frequently discounted through quantity discounts, contract rates, rebates, coupons, social media network deals, and other offers

» How you've determined that people will pay the prices you've set

» What discounts, price alterations, or pricing incentives you'll employ, if necessary, to spur trial, repeat, or volume business, and how your revenue forecasts account for those pricing variances

» How your pricing compares with that of your competitors, including a discussion of how your competitors' pricing policies have changed as a result of consumer or financial changes your market has undergone

TIP

Pricing has always been an important factor in business success. Its importance is even greater in a recessionary economy. Use the checklist of considerations in Form 5-7 as you set prices for your offerings.

Planning to control costs

As you develop your business model, consider not just how your business will achieve sales, but also how it will control costs that can erode your profits.

Control costs in the following ways:

>> **Reduce expenses** by eliminating purchases that don't contribute to your business and marketing strength, by finding lower-priced suppliers, by reducing payroll and benefit costs if doing so doesn't risk the morale or vitality of your business, and by conserving and recycling both for cost savings and for environmental contribution.

>> **Reduce your cost of sales** by putting supplier purchases out for competitive bid, by negotiating for favorable prices and terms, by signing contracts for lower-cost bulk purchases, and by refining product designs and production process to shave unnecessary costs.

>> **Eliminate unprofitable clients** by helping them find businesses that can better address their needs, allowing you to focus on those who deliver greater bottom-line results for your business.

>> **Reduce uncollected revenues** with advance-payment and tighter credit policies, interest on past-due accounts, and termination of relationships with customers that cost your business more than they return.

Cost-control contributes to a healthier *profit margin*, which is the percentage of sales revenue that makes it to the bottom line as profit to your business. State your projected profit margin as part of your business model description.

Creating a business model that works

TIP

Before writing your business model description, use the questionnaire in Form 5-8 to describe how your company makes money. After completing it, ask two more questions:

>> Can I spot additional potential sources of revenue that I may be able to develop in the future?

>> Can I come up with alternative payment plans — such as membership or subscription fees — that would entice new customers, keep customers loyal to my company, increase my revenue stream, or develop recurring streams of revenue down the road?

Business Model Questionnaire

1. List all your principle sources of revenue. (Don't forget to include things like product accessories, service agreements, upgrades, revenue from ads and sponsorships, and so on.)
   - •
   - •
   - •
   - •
   - •
   - •

2. List where you expect your fixed costs to come from. (Remember the obvious, such as utilities, a bookkeeping service, city taxes, insurance, and so on.)
   - •
   - •
   - •
   - •
   - •
   - •

3. List the sources of your variable costs.
   - •
   - •
   - •
   - •
   - •
   - •

4. Jot down the key timing issues your business faces. (Make sure to include the start-up interval, seasonal variations in sales, and any cost or price cycles.)
   - •
   - •
   - •
   - •
   - •
   - •

5. Describe your revenue-generation structure, detailing how customers will pay for your products or services (single or multiple payments, weekly or monthly fees, subscriptions, and so on).
   - •
   - •
   - •
   - •
   - •
   - •

© *John Wiley & Sons, Inc.*

FORM 5-8: Answers to these questions can guide development of your business model.

Use your findings to adjust your financial projections, returning to Form 5-5. Your calculations don't have to be fancy; you just want a good indication of the likely success of the cost and revenue projections that will form the basis of your business model.

TIP

Next, use Form 5-9 to assemble all the elements of your business model, including your business description, value proposition, competitive strategy, target customer, marketing approach, revenue generation approach, revenue and cost structure, and timing and success milestones.

REMEMBER

Your business model is the formula for your success over the long term. Include a summary of it in the Executive Summary of your business plan and early in your Company Overview.

Charting Your Future

Business plans serve three purposes: to lay the groundwork for new enterprises as they get up and running, to guide successful businesses to greater success, and to help struggling businesses overcome challenges and get back on the track.

Under all three scenarios, the objective is the same: to acquire customers and to generate revenue and profit. The variables are *how* your business will grow — and how big you want it to get. Use these sections to think through your answers so you can include them in your business plan.

Understanding your options

Companies grow in two basic ways:

>> **By acquiring new customers:** You can grow your clientele by

- Heightening promotion of established products
- Developing and marketing new uses for your established products
- Developing and marketing new products

>> **By generating increased sales volume from established customers:** You can grow your business from within by

- Making changes in your pricing or product line
- Repackaging your products, or bundling products and services
- Generating purchases of greater volume, greater frequency, or premium-level services
- Developing and marketing new products

If you're planning for a new business, your entire emphasis will be on acquiring new customers, while established businesses will likely plan to increase business from established customers while also attracting new customers in order to achieve desired growth.

TIP

If your plan relies on the development of new products or new customers, dedicate sufficient patience, assets, and capabilities to the task. Product and market development take time.

Planning for growth

How do you plan to grow your company? Before you answer that question, review your goals and objectives (see Chapter 3). Chances are good that they lay the groundwork for growing your business — by reaching more customers, expanding your product line or services, or entering new markets.

TIP

Form 5-10 lists resources you may need to develop your growth strategy. Form 5-11 presents questions that guide your thinking as you plan for growth. The results of your SWOT analysis (see Form 5-4) may prompt your answers.

Planning for Growth Questionnaire

1. What are your goals for company growth over the next year? (Use revenues, profits, number of clients, market share, or any other measure that makes the most sense to you.)

   •

   •

2. What are your three- and/or five-year goals for growth?

   •

   •

3. What will it take to get your company where you want it to be? (List three or four key requirements.)

   •

   •

   •

   •

4. Which of your key strengths will be most important in helping you meet your goals for growth?

5. What company weakness could be most significant in limiting your company's growth?

6. What are the major milestones you intend to reach along the way?

   •

   •

   •

7. What external threats could possibly affect your business growth?

© John Wiley & Sons, Inc.

FORM 5-11: This form presents questions that help guide your thinking as you prepare for business growth.

In addition to deciding *how* you want to grow, define *how much* you want to grow. Answers vary widely. One independent contractor may want to grow her business just enough to stay busy and keep the bank account healthy — but not so much that she needs to hire employees. In contrast, another entrepreneur may want to grow big — and fast — so that he can move away from doing the work himself and concentrate on expanding his business.

TIP

Include your growth plans in the Executive Summary of your business plan and also in the Company Strategy section, the Financial Review, and in your Action Plans.

Knowing your Plan A and Plan B

Strategic planning requires a best guess about what the future may hold. Your plan depends on a number of assumptions, which may or may not prove right.

Now is a good time to take a close look at those assumptions and then ask "what if?" What if the cost of raw materials soars? What if the neighborhood doesn't develop as you hoped? What if the favorable regulatory changes you planned for don't happen?

List all the assumptions that underlie your strategic plan. Be as thorough as possible. The tricky thing about assumptions is that people tend to take them for granted.

After you have your list of assumptions in place, ask yourself how you can re-jigger your strategic plan in case any one of them proves wrong. In addition to your Plan A, give some thought to what a Plan B would look like.

Dealing with bad news: Crisis management

Even the best-laid plans sometimes veer off course, usually as the result of unanticipated events or conditions. By gaining a clear understanding of your business environment (Chapter 4), you open your eyes to possible threats on your business horizon. And by conducting a SWOT analysis (refer to the earlier section, "Conducting a SWOT analysis" in this chapter) you gain a clearer understanding of why to bolster business strengths and overcome weaknesses to address external factors that could rock your plans.

The most successful businesses take crisis planning one step further by preparing for three crisis-management steps:

>> **Pre-crisis planning:** Most business crises result from real or rumored incidents in one of the following areas:

- Lapses in social responsibility that result in harm to employees, customers, the community, or the environment

- Violations of corporate standards, regulations, or laws that result in a loss of public trust

- Inappropriate personal behavior by the owner or a high-profile business representative

- Departure of a business owner or high-profile leader

- Product failures or dangers

- Natural or man-made disasters

- Unanticipated business upheaval, such as loss of a large account or reliable revenue stream

TIP

Consider how your business may be vulnerable in each of these areas. Where you see risk, plan preemptive actions, whether by instituting safety precautions, conducting internal audits, announcing succession plans, or other protections.

Also, prepare a crisis-communication checklist that includes media, security, and emergency contact information as well as the person who will serve as your crisis manager and the immediate steps that person will take.

>> **Crisis management:** Should you need to implement a crisis-management plan, waste no time. Figure out what happened, who is affected, how your business can correct or stem the problem, and what you're doing to protect public safety. Be visible, truthful, brief, and clear, communicating through a single spokesperson and consistent message, preferably delivered through the same media channels through which the bad news is spreading.

>> **Post-crisis remedies:** Conduct a careful after-the-fact evaluation. Assess whether crisis signals were missed in order to strengthen the way your business monitors and fortifies against threats. Also, assess the quality and effectiveness of your crisis response, aiming to improve the way you protect public safety, control damage, and communicate crisis updates.

TIP

If your business is vulnerable to crisis situations or has recently had to deal with a crisis, include in the strategy section of your business plan a summary of preemptive actions you've planned, as well as crisis-management strategies you have in place — just in case.

Outlining an Exit Strategy

It may surprise you to hear that you should give space in your business plan to a description of an *exit strategy* — the plan for leaving your business at some point in the future — but you should, especially if you're seeking investors, for two reasons. One, investors will factor your personal exit plan into their funding decisions and two, they'll make their decisions based in part on the investment exit strategy that accompanies your funding request. These sections take a closer look at these two reasons.

Owner exit strategies

It's counterintuitive, but smart business owners have plans for someday leaving their businesses — and leaving them in strong shape when that day comes. Even if you expect to stay with your business for the foreseeable future, an exit plan is important for the simple reason that most owner exits are unanticipated. From health issues to relocations to divorces to partnership disagreements, out-of-nowhere situations can change your intentions. So know your exit plan, just in case.

TIP

Form 5-12 shows some of the most common owner exit strategies. Put check marks beside ones that may be part of your long-term plan. By planning your exit early on, you put yourself in a position to steer your business toward your desired outcome.

For each of the exit options you consider, make a short list of the business capabilities and resources you need to have in place for the strategy to eventually become a reality.

Investor exit strategies

People willing to fund your business want to know how and when they'll receive a return on their investments. The most common investor exit strategies involve payoff through one of the following approaches:

>> **Buyout** of investor shares by owners or key business principles

>> **Acquisition by or merger** with another business

>> **An initial public offering (IPO),** which raises funds by selling shares of stock in your business

>> **Recapitalizing** and paying off early-round investors with funds from venture capitalists or other later-round investors

Be aware that simply stating your investor exit strategy isn't good enough for serious investors. You need to back your strategy with facts about acquisitions, IPOs, or major investments in businesses similar to yours, along with summaries of research you've undertaken that supports your assessment of the worth of your business as an investment risk.

Be ready to include a description of your investor exit strategy when and if you present your business plan to wealthy entrepreneurs who might serve as angel investors, to professional asset managers you hope will provide your business with venture capital, or others who may help fund your business.

Forms

The following forms, which you can find at www.dummies.com/go/business planskit, help you establish and explain your company's strategy in your business plan.

Form 5-1	Business Strengths and Weaknesses Survey	A form that helps you rank success factors and rate your abilities in each key area
Form 5-2	Business Strengths and Weaknesses Grid	A grid that lets you see at a glance how your abilities align with the capabilities needed for success
Form 5-3	Business Opportunities and Threats	A form for listing the potential opportunities and threats facing your business
Form 5-4	Business SWOT Analysis Grid	A grid designed to line up your company strengths and weaknesses against the business opportunities and threats you face
Form 5-5	Quick Financial Projection Worksheet	A worksheet for making quick financial projections as you develop your business model
Form 5-6	Freemium Business Model Considerations Checklist	Issues to address when considering a freemium business model
Form 5-7	Pricing Considerations Checklist	Issues to address when considering how to price your offerings
Form 5-8	Business Model Questionnaire	Questions to help you plan the revenues and costs that contribute to your business model

(continued)

(continued)

Form 5-9	**Elements of Your Business Model Worksheet**	Issues to address as you prepare to describe your business model
Form 5-10	**Resources for Growth Checklist**	Critical resources you may need as your company grows
Form 5-11	**Planning for Growth Questionnaire**	Questions to answer as you plan your company's growth
Form 5-12	**Checklist of Common Owner Exit Strategies**	A list of the most common exit strategies for business owners

IN THIS CHAPTER

Explaining what your business does

Planning your elevator pitch

Describing your business capabilities

Building on what your business does best

Chapter 6

Describing Your Business and Its Capabilities

When a banker or potential investor looks at your business plan, the first thing that person wants to know is what your business does. Your job is to give a good description — without getting lost in the details and without lapsing into industry jargon. And you have to keep it short, too. After all, you're writing a business plan, not the great American novel.

In a statement quick enough to hold attention in today's information-overloaded world, your business description needs to convey the most important aspects of your business, the customers you serve, the products and services you offer, and why and how you'll succeed in your competitive environment.

If you think explaining your business hardly requires this chapter full of advice, think again. Or, better yet, ask a few other entrepreneurs what their businesses do — and watch as they grope for explanations or drone on with their answers. Describing a business in simple, understandable, engaging terms isn't quite as easy as it sounds, and that's why this chapter is so important.

Introducing Your Business

Imagine that you're at your high-school reunion and old classmates ask what you're up to. As you describe your business — or your business concept if you're just getting started — you want to cover the high points, and you also want to build enthusiasm by conveying that it's a really great idea.

EXAMPLE

Here's an example of what the conversation may sound like:

"I've put together a new way for people to find and join groups. The concept started when I began thinking about how people use dating sites. It occurred to me that a lot of people want to meet people and socialize, but not in a dating situation. So I started a site where they can fill out a questionnaire about their location, favorite activities, and daytime availability so that the site can match them to opportunities that match their interests.

"After this site attracts a strong number of followers, I'm planning to extend the idea so that in addition to linking people up with groups, it'll also link them to places where they can buy the gear or services used in their preferred activity, and I'll capture a percentage of those sales."

The venture sounds interesting, and the entrepreneur is obviously enthusiastic. But what if those listening start asking questions, such as, "So will the business make enough money to support itself?" "How will people learn about the site?" "How do you choose which groups to send people to?" The answers to these questions determine whether the idea gains support or lands in a pile labeled "It's a nice idea, but . . . ."

The upcoming sections help you prepare for that all-important question, "What do you do?"

Describing what you're selling

If you've watched entrepreneurs pitch their latest, greatest ideas on programs like *Shark Tank*, then you've seen a full range of great, good, mediocre, and lousy business descriptions. This section helps you create a description on the winning end of the spectrum.

EXAMPLE

Here's a true story: An entrepreneur was presenting her business idea to a group of potential investors. The business idea involved summarizing the latest medical research into easy-to-understand short reports designed to encourage people to lead healthier lifestyles. She talked about the accelerating pace of medical research and new insights by behavioral scientists regarding how people change habits.

She waxed eloquent on the subject of preventive healthcare and showed statistics detailing the aging of the American population. Ten minutes into her presentation, an investor interrupted to ask the simple question, "What is it you're selling, anyway?" The answer: an online health newsletter directed at people older than 50. In her excitement, the entrepreneur forgot to state the obvious.

TIP

When describing your company, get to the point, beginning with a clear description of your product or service. For help, go to www.dummies.com/go/business planskit to view and download Form 6-1, the Product/Service Description Checklist.

TIP

Include a concise description of your products or services in the Company Overview and Company Description sections of your written plan. (See Chapter 3 for help describing your business and Chapter 1 for information on these sections of your plan.) Too much information can confuse people fast, so only include what your audience needs to gain enthusiasm and to make sense of your products or services. (Chapter 1 helps you identify the audience for your plan.) Worth mentioning are features that make your offering appealing and meaningfully different, such as cost, quality, capabilities, usability, and applications. Most importantly, the plan should tell how the features deliver valuable customer benefits.

TIP

Include a product photo or rendering in your business plan, if you think it can help readers get a better idea of what you intend to offer. As the saying goes, a picture is worth a thousand words — and generally takes up considerably less space.

Perfecting your elevator pitch in the digital age

Marketers and investors have traditionally called the response to "What do you do?" your *elevator pitch*. The reason: You should be able to deliver it in the time it takes to ride an elevator through a high-rise building. Today your pitch is more apt to take place at a conference or networking event — or online, where your website and social media pages present your business. One way or another, in 20 to 30 seconds or, online, in a couple dozen words — you need to

>> Introduce yourself and your business in a way that seizes interest and makes people want to know more.

>> Tell what you do in nontechnical words that someone outside your business or industry can easily understand.

>> Describe your product or service and the value and benefits it delivers.

>> Define the target market for your offerings.

>> Set yourself apart by highlighting your competitive advantages, your business model (Chapter 5 has more on this key issue), and the people behind your business, such as prominent investors, board members, associations, or business partners.

>> Generate interest, prompt questions, and begin to develop a relationship.

WARNING

Don't hurry through this task. You need to devote time to perfect your response and then tailor it to the interests of your varied audiences.

Preparing for your in-person elevator pitch

As you begin to develop the introduction you'll present when meeting people face to face, be aware of what you *shouldn't* do or say:

>> Don't begin with a dull, generic introduction, such as "I sell insurance" or "I run a social service agency." Start by inspiring interest and prompting questions rather than evoking stereotypes.

>> Don't dive into a sales pitch. Remember, you're presenting your business here, not the bells and whistles included in each of your products.

When planning your pitch, begin by imagining that you're talking to a group of friends. You're apt to relax, get right to the point, and explain your business — or your new business idea — in the simplest, most persuasive language possible.

Jot down a first draft, or use a voice recorder so you can capture your pitch and transcribe it for later editing. If you find yourself at a loss for words, revisit your mission and vision statements for inspiration. They should capture what your business is all about in a few phrases. (Don't have a mission statement or vision statement? Chapter 3 helps you put them together.)

TIP

View or download Form 6-2, Elevator Pitch–Planning Questionnaire, which guides you toward aspects of your business that are worthy of highlight in your introduction. Then use Form 6-3, Writing Your Elevator Pitch, to assemble your findings into the short description you'll have ready when the chance to introduce your business arises.

TIP

Drawing from the final draft of your elevator pitch, include a short description of your business in the Company Overview and the Company Description sections of your plan (Chapter 1 has more on these sections).

Presenting your elevator pitch online

After you get the wording of your in–person introduction down pat, shrink your message for presentation online, which is where many people are apt to first encounter your business description. Cover the following points:

>> Convey what your business does, its target market, and what makes it distinct and credible.

Elevator Speech-Planning Questionnaire
1. What business are you in?
2. What is your product or service? Give a broad-brush answer without getting hung up on details.
3. Who is your target customer? How large is your market?
4. What benefits do your customers receive, or what problems do you help them solve?
5. What sets your business apart? Think about unique technologies, special expertise, marketing potential, and the strengths of your management team, investors, board members, and industry associations.
6. Who are your competitors and how is your business different and better?

© *John Wiley & Sons, Inc.*

FORM 6-2: Plan a concise, interesting description of your business, incorporating the answers to these questions.

>> Include keywords that those looking for businesses like yours are apt to use in their search terms. The Google Keyword Planner tool offers the example of a business selling men's athletic footwear that might use such key terms as "men's sports shoes," "men's sneakers," and "men's tennis shoes," as well as brand and product names.

>> Convey a sense of your brand promise (there's more on brands in Chapter 7).

>> Keep it short. Twitter limits user bios to 160 characters, and that's a good length to keep in mind for introductions you use across other networks as well. See the nearby sidebar on shrinking attention spans for information on why shorter is better in today's environment.

EXAMPLE

As proof it can be done with 140 characters — or far fewer — here are Twitter introductions from a few of the decade's *unicorns*, those highly publicized start-ups whose valuation soared above the billion-dollar level. Each begins with the @ sign that precedes Twitter usernames:

>> @Airbnb: Airbnb is the world's largest community-driven hospitality company. With unique listings in 190 countries, travelers can belong anywhere.

>> @Spotify: Music for every moment. Play, discover, and share for free. Need support? We're happy to help at @SpotifyCares.

>> @SurveyMonkey: We're the world's leading provider of web-based survey solutions, helping people gather the insights they need to make more informed decisions.

WARNING

Although the format and length of your in-person and online introductions will differ, be careful that both convey the same message about what your business is, does, and stands for. Also, be sure that both are consistent with the facts and experience people will encounter when they take the next step by venturing through your front door, into the pages of your website, or beyond the cover of your business plan.

SEIZING SHRINKING ATTENTION SPANS

Plan to move at lightning speed to catch the eyes, ears, and minds of those you're trying to reach. Lead with your most interesting content, edit out any boring statements, and convince people immediately that what you have to say is worth reading, watching, or hearing — and after that, worth sharing with others. Consider these facts:

- **The average attention span in 2015 was 8.25 seconds,** down from 12 seconds in 2000 and lower than the 9-second attention span of a goldfish.

- **A third of web users abandon slow-loading websites within five seconds,** and most of those who stick around remain less than a minute with half staying only four seconds. Plus, web pages with fewer words are more likely to be read than those with more words.

- **On social media, Twitter-length posts with photos work best across all networks** with 80-character posts winning more engagement than longer messages.

- **When watching video, two of ten viewers click away within ten seconds** and only four remain at the two-minute mark.

- **Face-to-face, you have seven seconds to win interest,** and even if they're interested most people stay engaged for no longer than seven to ten minutes. If you need to make a longer presentation, segment your material into components that each begin with a new interest-grabbing introduction.

Describing Your Business Capabilities

To leverage a good idea into a thriving business, a company needs a set of assets called *business capabilities*. They include

>> Research and Development (R&D)

>> Operations

>> Marketing

>> Distribution and delivery

>> Data collection, management, and usage

>> Customer service

>> Management

>> Organization

>> Financial condition

If this list looks familiar, it's because it presents the same capabilities you assess when rating your company's strengths and weaknesses. (Flip to Chapter 5 for information on how your strengths and weaknesses relate to the opportunities and threats that your business faces.)

This chapter takes a closer look at how your business capabilities affect your company's success. The following sections help you scrutinize your abilities in R&D, operations, distribution and delivery, data, management, and organization.

The reason that we don't cover marketing (including customer service) and financial capabilities in this chapter is because those capabilities are so essential to your success (and so fundamental to your business plan) that each gets a chapter to itself (see Chapters 7 and 9).

TIP

In your business plan, provide an overview of the key capabilities that give your business strength and competitive advantage. If you're in a one-person business and a few of the capabilities truly don't affect your success, you can take a pass on those areas. But don't let yourself off the hook too easily. In one way or another, each of these eight capabilities is likely to be an engine that drives you toward your business goals and objectives.

Research and development

Research and development, known as R&D, refers to your ability to gain knowledge in order to design, develop, and enhance your product, services, technologies, or processes. If your company is a high-tech firm, R&D is No. 1 on the list of capabilities crucial to your long-term success.

WARNING

Even if your company isn't technology- or manufacturing-based, though, don't assume that R&D isn't a necessary capability. Every business — even a one-person consulting business — needs research ability to track the competitive arena, find out about prospective customers, and keep on top of industry and client news.

EXAMPLE

For example, the owners of a business that liquidates households for people who can't do so on their own may think they hardly have need for R&D capability. But, think again. Online auctions and specialized antique sale sites now play a central role in the estate sale arena. Even if the business owners steer completely clear of online sales, almost certainly they'll want to use the sites and other online resources to determine what people are paying for items like the ones they're selling.

For other businesses, R&D is the key to enhancing business skills, enlarging product and service portfolios, and staying on top of customer, industry, and competitive research. In planning ways to improve R&D skills, consider

>> Attending trade shows with research-related sessions

>> Taking industry-specific courses, in person or online

>> Participating in social media networks with people in your field who share findings, ideas, and advice

>> Subscribing to mailings from innovators in your industry

>> Completing certification programs

>> Updating your computer skills

>> Keeping up-to-date through trade journals and sites

>> Joining an industry group

>> Broadening your awareness of industry, market area, consumer, and industry issues and opportunities

Your business plan should include a section that addresses your R&D capabilities, including the following:

>> The importance of R&D to your competitive success

>> A description of your current R&D capacity (including a description of the expertise of staff and contract sources)

>> Your agenda for R&D over the next year

>> Planned R&D expenditures over the next year

>> Your long-term R&D goals

Operations

In the lineup of key business capabilities, the term *operations* describes the processes and resources that you use to produce the highest quality products or services as efficiently as possible.

Business operations typically include four key areas:

>> **Location:** Where you do business — physically and online

>> **Equipment:** The tools you need to get the job done

>> **Labor:** The human side of business operations

>> **Process:** The way you get business done, including your systems for quality control and improvement

The importance of each of these areas depends on the nature of your business. For example, physical location is critical to a retail outlet that lives or dies by walk-in customers, while physical location may not matter a bit to an Internet-based company — unless the business depends on highly skilled talent or the kinds of resources that cluster in places like Silicon Valley or other technology hubs.

TIP

Download, review, and complete Forms 6-4, 6-5, 6-6, and 6-7. These four Operational Planning Surveys can help you evaluate and develop your business capabilities in the four key operational areas — location, equipment, labor, and process.

TIP

If you're planning for a start-up, include a description of your strategy for developing each of the four key operational areas. For established businesses, detail what operational changes are necessary to achieve the new goals and objectives detailed in your business plan and how you intend to implement and fund an expansion of your operation.

Distribution and delivery

How you get your products and services into your customers' hands is what *distribution and delivery* is all about. It's also a fast-changing arena as restaurants sign on to two-hour home delivery services, businesses acquire an increasingly far-flung clientele, virtual work groups necessitate delivery systems to support their remote participation, and retailers move into the realm of customized fulfillment options, same-day and speedier service, drone usage, and crowd-sourced across-town delivery offers.

EXPERIENCING OPERATIONAL GROWING PAINS

Even for a small company, operations can be critical to success. Take the example of a talented San Francisco florist who watched his small business blossom almost beyond his control. At the beginning, he managed all the designs and arrangements himself. He bought new inventory at the flower market early in the morning and finished the bookkeeping late at night.

But as business expanded, the florist could no longer do everything himself, so he scrambled to hire and train employees. In the rush to meet growing demand, he failed to establish a clear set of operational procedures. The result: a business breakdown. Suddenly, his company had no mechanism for quality control. Flower arrangements were delivered to customers before receiving approval, and no single person was put in charge of going to the flower market.

For a brief, rocky period, a number of influential and unhappy clients threatened to find other suppliers. Just in the nick of time, the florist sat down with a consultant and worked out a new way of doing business based on the larger staff size. New operational procedures spelled out each person's duties and responsibilities. They also described the process of filling customer orders from the initial telephone call to final bill. To his surprise, the florist discovered that, thanks to the new procedures, he could devote more time to do what he did best — the creative end of the business — and still meet the growing demand.

Not all businesses are equally concerned with distribution and delivery systems, of course. For example, phone and email access, along with a means for personal transportation, may be the extent of the distribution and delivery needs of a psychologist whose clients come to a single office for counseling, or for a freelance design business or a dog-walking service.

EXAMPLE

For some businesses, however, capabilities in distribution and delivery are important, if not downright critical, to success. Consider these examples:

>> Every time the holiday season rolls around, catalog companies and online retailers face the same nail-biting challenge: how to ensure that customer orders reach their destinations in time for the big day. Some retailers absorb overnight express delivery costs in order to meet promises. A few companies have seen their reputations plummet — and their customers disappear — when they've missed delivery deadlines.

>> One of the biggest challenges for new product marketers is getting valuable shelf space in retail outlets. The same goes for food manufacturers. With

grocery store aisles already overcrowded with thousands of products, achieving store visibility for a new breakfast cereal or snack chip is a tall hurdle to clear.

>> Even businesses in service industries sometimes have to focus on distribution and delivery. Management-training companies, for example, often deliver programs to thousands of managers in dozens of locations — all at the same time. They can't deliver on their promises unless they have trainers and equipment in place when and where they need them.

>> Those who do business primarily online have distribution challenges of their own. They need to reach and serve customers with sites that load quickly, with easy navigation, links that work, live help options for those who need them, and bandwidth sufficient to handle anticipated surges in traffic. What's more, if sensitive information is requested, they need secure web connections and systems that deliver digital communications with protections from abuse or subsequent distribution. And if they provide help or customer service, they need to consider online chat software backed by staffing that ensures acceptable wait times as well as offline contact. Plus, they need good search engine optimization (SEO), to increase the odds that they end up at the top of search results, along with an aggressive program to drive traffic to the site through marketing and online link-building.

WARNING

Failing to plan for the method and cost of distribution or delivery can be a fatal business mistake. Consider the Internet grocery service that staked its reputation on the promise of free delivery on orders of any size. Customers accepted the offer — ordering a single frozen dinner, a bottle of wine, or even a candy bar. Delivery costs ran more than $10 on each order. It didn't take long before the business promise faded away — along with the company.

TIP

Assess the importance of distribution and delivery to your business success by downloading and filling out the Distribution and Delivery Survey in Form 6-8. Be as specific as you can. Flag areas where you need to track down more information and then do the necessary research.

As you complete the form, consider the following:

>> Include all costs involved with product distribution and delivery — including warehouse space, transportation, shelf space allocations, product returns, and other necessary expenses.

>> Consider how you can use distribution and delivery to your competitive advantage, for instance, by offering home delivery, subscription delivery, online service, or other approaches that fit the realities of your product and market area and the desires of your customers.

Distribution and Delivery Survey
1. Outline the steps required in distributing and delivering your product or service:
2. Describe the extent of the geographic area you intend to cover, including any plans to expand:
3. Estimate the costs associated with the distribution and delivery of your product or service:
4. List the relationships and agreements you plan to forge with distribution or delivery companies in your industry:
5. Review any contingency plans you have in place in case your primary distribution or delivery services are interrupted:

© John Wiley & Sons, Inc.

FORM 6-8: Use this form to survey your distribution and delivery systems and to plan for changes that will impact your business success.

>> View distribution as an expansion strategy, looking for new *distribution channels* — new paths that your products follow from your company into your customers' hands — as a way to expand into new markets. Offering your products online, for example, or through new distributor or retailer relationships, allows your business to open new distribution channels.

Use your responses to Form 6-8 to assess the importance of distribution to your business success. If you think it's an essential element, include a description of your distribution system in your written plans.

Management

Long-term business success depends, above all, on the quality of the team providing the leadership, direction, and vision. In fact, in some cases, investors have funded start-up companies primarily on the basis of the people who will run them.

TIP

Assemble background information on yourself and each of your senior team members. Download Form 6-9, Management Team Member Profile, for use as you compile a profile for each key person.

FORM 6-9: Use this form to complete profiles on each senior person in your company.

In your business plan, condense each key person's profile into a brief description, following these tips:

>> **When describing team members,** include everything that's relevant to the potential success of your business. But keep each biographical description to the point and no longer than a half page in length.

>> **If yours is a single-person operation,** you don't have to spend too much time describing yourself in your plan, but do have a résumé highlighting your education, experience, and accomplishments ready for when the information is requested by a banker, supplier, or prospective investor.

>> **If you're running a larger business,** feature biographies of up to five top managers in your business plan, including all the big Cs: CEO (Chief Executive Officer), COO (Chief Operating Officer), CFO (Chief Financial Officer), and CTO or CIO (Chief Technology Officer or Chief Information Officer). Depending on the size of your company, you may also want to include brief descriptions of the members of your Board of Directors, Board of Advisors, or consultants who play a major role in making your business a success.

Conduct a web search for the name of each person featured in your business plan to be sure the results lead to positive, credible, current information. Chances are good that prospective customers, investors, and suppliers will search for your business and its more visible people online as part of their research efforts. You want links to lead to pages that affirm their interest.

Organization

Your company's success hinges on the quality of the people around you, but it also depends on having an organization in place that allows those people to work effectively and efficiently. By defining your organization, you define the relationship of employees to one another — who reports to whom, for example. You also define each employee's access to important company resources.

Organization is a pretty straightforward issue for small businesses, but in large companies, organization is more complicated. And if you don't plan well, it can undermine the efforts of even the best staff.

EXAMPLE

Consider the saga of one of the biggest online health information and management companies. Part of the firm's early strategy was to gobble up smaller online information providers, acquiring their assets and eliminating competition. Trouble was, each of these small companies had its own organizational structure and editorial procedure. Before long, groups within the larger organization were unnecessarily duplicating efforts. No one was sure who was supposed to report to whom, and the company lost editorial control over the site. What's more, content that should've taken only three weeks to produce began to require six and seven weeks. The result: The company bled money. The lesson: Organization matters.

REMEMBER

An organization is a living thing and its form grows and changes with business circumstances. Use the suggestions in this section to come up with an organizational plan that allows everyone to make his or her best contribution. Then, be ready to reevaluate and to adopt a different organization if your business experiences rapid sales or staff growth, adds divisions or product lines, alters its production processes, or struggles to meet goals and objectives.

TIP

Your written plan needs to include a section on your company's organization. Use charts or diagrams to help make a complicated organization a little clearer. For example, an organization chart can quickly illustrate who reports to whom or how the company's divisions relate to one another. Don't get hung up in the details; your goal is to present a coherent presentation of what your company's organization looks like — and why.

The following sections offer examples of organizational structures used by businesses of various types and sizes.

The pack

In this structure, one person holds the top position and everyone else in the business is an equal member of the pack. This organizational style works well in small companies — no more than 20 people — where everyone on staff has the training and the expertise to do almost any job required of him or her.

> *Advantages:* A simple, flexible organizational structure that allows the entire team to work together and to adjust quickly to changing business conditions.

> *Disadvantages:* A business can grow to the point that the top dog can't keep track of and manage the whole pack. Also, people may end up doing jobs they've never done, which can compromise both quality and efficiency. As businesses scale from start-up to larger enterprises, pack structures almost always shift toward organizations that align by functions, which can be expanded to handle business growth.

Form follows function

In this type of organization, you divide people into groups depending on what functions they perform. For example, a company may have an engineering department, a marketing department, a production department, and a finance department. Each department has its own manager, and a general manager or Chief Executive Officer typically takes on the role of coordinating the activities of the various functional groups.

> *Advantages:* You assign people to do the tasks that they do best, and each person knows his or her responsibility. If your business is medium sized and markets only one type of product or service, this structure is probably the one for you.

> *Disadvantages:* Without good communication and oversight, functional hierarchies can break down into separate groups that work well on their own but aren't very good at working with other departments or carrying out the company's larger strategies and goals.

Divide and conquer

Companies that provide more than one product line or that operate in more than one business area often organize around separate divisions. A firm that sells, installs, and services computer networks, for example, may separate those functions into independent divisions. In this organizational model, each of a company's divisions may be responsible for a particular product, service, market, or geographical area, and all the divisions may have to justify themselves as independent profit centers. In some of the largest companies, each division consists of a *strategic business unit* (SBU) — almost a company inside a company. For more details on SBUs, check out the latest edition of *Business Plans For Dummies,* by Paul Tiffany, Steven Peterson, and Colin Barrow (John Wiley & Sons, Inc.).

Advantages: Companies that organize into divisions encourage each separate part of the company to focus on its aspect of the business — selling computers, servicing them, or installing them, for example. Division managers can zero in on their own sets of customers, competitors, and strategic issues.

Disadvantages: Divisions may find themselves competing for the same customers. They may also duplicate overhead costs and lower efficiency.

The matrix

In a matrix organization, people with similar skills are grouped together and assigned as needed to various projects and project managers. For example, an engineer may be assigned to several projects and to more than one manager at a time. Likewise, a web designer may be assigned to develop new content for the company website while also working with the marketing team on special projects designed to bring in new business.

Advantages: This structure fosters flexibility by allowing different parts of a company to share talent, expertise, and experience. It also fosters collaboration between individuals with similar skills. Companies using a matrix structure are often able to respond quickly to changing business conditions.

Disadvantages: Managing employees can be tricky when each person wears several hats. Plus, employees can feel a tense tug of war as they try to respond to the demands of several bosses. This structure can also lead to confusion about business priorities unless a strong general manager sees that the company stays on track.

Data management

To the long-standing list of business capabilities, smart businesses are adding another category: data management. How you collect quality data, capture and maintain business and customer information, extract usable information, monitor key indicators, insure data security, and apply your findings to enhance marketing, production, productivity, growth, and product innovation has become an increasingly important aspect of running a successful business.

Businesses leverage collected data in an ever-lengthening list of ways, including, but by no means limited to, these examples:

» Increase efficiency by making customer information, production status, inventory, and other business information accessible to on-site and remote employees.

» Segment target customers in order to tailor offerings and messages accordingly.

>> Offer customers predictive services; for example, social media sites present "people you may know" and online retailers provide recommendations of "purchases made by others shopping for this item" suggestions.

>> Anticipate customer volume based on trends from past purchase patterns and forecasted anticipated conditions; for example, forecasts for utility usage or restaurant volume and selection based on weather forecasts.

>> Track, enhance, and benefit from customer on-site visits. Some retailers use a hardware device called a *beacon* to activate and send customized messages to downloaded apps on customer mobile devices. Others improve retail and display layouts by monitoring captured video to map customer traffic and to monitor where customers stop compared to purchase volume from that point.

>> Stay on top of reviews and ratings, encouraging customer posts by following purchases with review invitations and consistently monitoring review sites for insights and possible responses.

EXAMPLE

>> Create data-driven products or services that can generate revenue or deliver competitive advantages. As an example of a data-driven revenue generator, LinkedIn bundles its user profile data into a recruiting and staffing tool purchased by headhunters and hiring companies. As an example of a value-added data-driven service, the real estate site Zillow offers a free automated home value estimation tool, Zestimate, that's helped the site attract visitors, achieve top-of-mind awareness, and draw industry-leading visitor counts.

TIP

In your written plan, include a statement about your data management plans, including the objective of data collection, the source and ownership of data, and how you plan to apply collected data to strengthen products, operations, marketing, and business operations.

REMEMBER

As you develop data capabilities for your business, keep in mind that you need to either own or have permission to use the data you're accessing and leveraging. Social media networks, for example, collect enough data to serve as their own data sources, whereas other businesses form data-gathering affiliations, purchase data, or harvest data from publicly available sources.

Updating Capabilities to Meet Challenges and Seize Opportunities

The word *rapid* is inadequate to describe the speed of change your business faces: shifting population demographics, global trade, digital and technological innovation, climate change, new rules and regulations, economic and political uncertainty, transformations in healthcare. The list of possible challenges — or opportunities — goes on and on.

Keeping business capabilities updated amidst the turmoil is more essential than ever and that's why we've added sections throughout this updated edition of *Business Plans Kit For Dummies* to help you deal with planning for change. Flip to Chapter 2 for help spotting and anticipating trends, innovations, and upheavals that can affect the very idea behind your business plan. Then, count on Chapter 15 to guide you through the steps involved to build a business plan for success in today's transformed environment.

For now, though, use this section to focus on how to align your capabilities with the current and looming realities of your business environment.

Putting your capabilities to the test

On a regular basis, not once a year but more frequently, tick through the list of business capabilities — R&D, operations, marketing, distribution and delivery, customer service, management, organization, financial condition, and data management — and ask an important question about each. What's changed, or what may change, to affect your strength in this capability or, on the reverse side, to provide you an opportunity because of your strength in this capability?

REMEMBER

Pay particular attention to *megatrends* — major shifts that have a long-term impact — and how they're likely to rock or boost your business capabilities. Associations that serve your business arena likely forecast and share trends you can consider, as do consulting groups whose reports you can find by searching for "business megatrends" online.

Likely you'll see these trends among those on most forecasts:

>> **Population, demographic, and social shifts** due to changes in birth rates and life spans, human migration and gender, and ethnic and social diversity

>> **Empowered customers** who demand transparency, participation, and interactive communication from the businesses with which they deal

>> **The digital future** including technological advances, connected devices, the rise of mobile device usage, data management, and cybersecurity

>> **The rise of interest in bricks-and-clicks businesses** that feature both online and offline presence and a seamless customer experience between the two

>> **Changes in climate and resource availability** leading to an increased focus on consumption efficiency and sustainability

>> **The global economy** and how it affects everything from product development, marketing and distribution plans, access to resources, and consumer interest in cultural identity

>> **The rise of entrepreneurship** (*The New York Times* even renamed its small business section to acknowledge this shift) affecting competition, labor availability, funding options, community and business resources, and more

REMEMBER

Add to this list other trends that are likely to affect your business. Then, assess whether your business has the capabilities it needs to adapt to changes on your horizon or to capitalize on the changes you foresee. Your answers help guide business improvements or growth plans, which you need to include in the strategy section of your business plan.

Pivoting your strategies

The term *pivot*, introduced by Eric Ries, made its way into the start-up vocabulary in 2011 as a way to describe fundamental strategic changes young businesses sometimes make in order to survive and succeed.

EXAMPLE

Frequently cited examples include Twitter, which pivoted from a podcasting platform to a microblogging behemoth, and Groupon, which started as an online fundraising site called The Point before transforming into the daily deals site we know today.

In each case, an "aha" moment prompted a complete course correction that recharted the path to success.

Watch for these signs to indicate that it may be time to channel your business capabilities into a major redirection or even a total reinvention of your product, market, business model, processes, or operations:

>> When the market you serve diminishes greatly

>> When demand for the products you sell collapses

>> When the way you do business is eclipsed by new innovations

>> When costs require that you rethink how you staff, equip, and organize your business

>> When the market or business arena presents opportunities that you can seize only by dramatically altering the way you do business

REMEMBER

Chapter 15 is all about planning around transformations in your market or business environment. Sometimes, though, you need to make changes that aren't temporary or incremental. Sometimes you need to adjust by making major changes that overhaul your product or alter your location, staffing, operations, and business model in order to adjust to the new situation your business faces. The upcoming sections can help.

Making product and product line changes

To assess whether your product is in need of a minor-to-major overhaul, refer to Form 6-1, this time completing it with change in mind and following these steps:

1. **Summarize your product and its features.**

    This time, frankly assess whether the features of your offering are still competitive in your marketplace and, if not, what new features you could add or what redesigned offering you could present to address transformed customer wants and needs.

2. **Summarize your target customers.**

    Assess whether your current products might appeal to different groups, within your current market area or whether they may gain traction in new market areas or distribution channels.

3. **Summarize the benefits your product provides.**

    Ask whether customers still value those benefits and, if not, how you can revise your offering to create a different value proposition.

4. **Consider whether your company can adapt to its market environment by creating and offering an altogether new product that fits with the capabilities of your business (see Form 6-1).**

    To assess the opportunity of a new product offering, complete Form 6-1 yet again, this time describing the features of your proposed new offering, the market to which it would appeal, and the benefits and value it would provide to customers.

Moving your business

Whether your location is online or in a brick-and-mortar building, sometimes a move is necessary. Offline businesses open online locations. Online businesses open offline locations. (Online sales giant Amazon, for instance, has announced that it will open retail bookstores in malls around the country.) And businesses of all types open additional locations to reach and serve the evolving wants and needs of customers. As you weigh your situation, refer back to Form 6-4,

Operations Planning Survey (Location), this time assessing how changes to your location could benefit your business.

>> Consider where your business *could* be located — physically and online. Can you achieve greater success in a different location or market area? Can you realize higher profit margins if you shift the nature of your location, reducing or eliminating physical inventory in favor of virtual inventory, for example? If your business is online, would it benefit from a street-address location or by affiliating with businesses that provide customers with the ability to shop, receive service, or get quick-turn deliveries? If your business serves customers at a brick-and-mortar location, would it benefit from increased Internet presence either for greater online visibility and contact or for sales, service, or other customer benefits?

>> Outline what would be involved to physically revamp or relocate your business, or to establish an additional location.

>> Outline how you'll expand Internet presence by improving your website, expanding your online social networks, establishing online marketplace affiliations, or establishing new ways customers could access your products online.

Revamping your operations and processes

Some business reinventions involve changes to the very way companies operate. For example, a manufacturer that can't achieve competitive pricing due to high costs might orchestrate a major business redesign by its licensing proprietary designs for manufacture by third parties. A business that can't keep full-time staff productive might revise operations to migrate from an employee-based business to a virtual workplace staffed by freelance contractors. A business that requires large volumes of supplies or services may decide to create business divisions that provide such components internally.

>> Use Form 6-5, Operations Planning Survey (Equipment), to consider whether your business would benefit from a major change in how it's equipped. Would adding equipment allow your business new production options? Would selling equipment and leasing or subcontracting through third-party suppliers provide your business with higher profit margins?

>> Use Form 6-6, Operations Planning Survey (Labor), to assess whether your business might benefit from a redesign of the way it's staffed and organized.

>> Use Form 6-7, Operations Planning Survey (Process), to reconsider how you produce your product, how you handle inventory and delivery of your product, and how you maintain and guarantee product quality.

Altering distribution channels

Especially if your plan aims to dramatically increase sales or to reverse declining sales, use Form 6-8, discussed earlier in this chapter, as you consider how you might improve or overhaul your distribution capability and how you get your product into the marketplace.

>> Outline new ways your product might reach your marketplace. If your business is a brick-and-mortar operation, consider what an online distribution model may look like. If you currently sell through an internal sales force, consider how you could benefit from shifting to or adding wholesalers, distributors, sales representatives, auctions, or other new sales approaches. If you currently sell directly to consumers, assess whether your business might benefit from strategic alliances with intermediaries that might purchase in bulk for resale to consumers.

>> Consider whether the market area you serve is sufficiently large enough to sustain your business or whether you should expand or shift emphasis to distribute your offerings into new markets.

TIP

In your written business plan, define how you intend to alter and strengthen your business capabilities. When describing your strategic adjustments, explain what business or marketplace condition makes the change necessary and how the change will result in positive outcomes that outweigh anticipated disruptions.

Staying Focused on What You Do Best

No business can be all things to all people. In fact, companies that try to please everyone all the time usually find themselves becoming less effective at almost everything they do. Business history chronicles a long list of companies that tried to build on success by expanding in new directions — only to lose the focus that made them sharp and successful in the first place.

TIP

Whether you're starting a business, growing a business, or turning a business around, think about what you do best and how you can build on that strong base. If you're having a hard time zeroing in on a description of what you do best, ask yourself this question: If your company closed down, what products, services, or attributes would customers miss most or have the hardest time replacing? Your answer unveils what makes your company and its offerings unique — and what things your company does best.

After you pinpoint where you excel, ask yourself *how* you do it. Your answer leads you right back to the list of key business capabilities.

Is your success tied tightly to your R&D? Or to the efficiency of your operations? The flawless systems that back your distribution and delivery? The quality of your management? The effectiveness of your organization? Your products or location? The way you collect, use and leverage data? The power of your marketing and customer service (see Chapter 7)? Or the strength of your financial condition (see Chapter 9)?

Make a list of your answers. As you pursue growth opportunities, be careful that your expansion plans do nothing to weaken your key capabilities or lead your business away from the strengths that got you where you are.

In your written plan, give special attention to the business capabilities that contribute most to your success and also to the capabilities that provide the greatest value to your customers. These capabilities represent the heart and soul of your company. They're your strongest assets. Your business plan should include details about how you intend to make the most of each one.

Reevaluate how well you're doing in these key areas on at least an annual basis — and more frequently if you sense opportunities to seize or threats to avert. And also take time to brainstorm ways to build on your strengths and increase the overall value you provide to your customers.

Forms

Go to www.dummies.com/go/businessplankit to view and download these forms that help you come up with descriptions of your business and what your business does.

Form 6-1	Product/Service Description Checklist	A form to help you create your product or service description
Form 6-2	Elevator Pitch Planning Questionnaire	Six questions to guide the development of your elevator pitch
Form 6-3	Writing Your Elevator Pitch	A formula to follow when preparing your business introduction
Form 6-4	Operations Planning Survey (Location)	Key factors when planning the location of your operations
Form 6-5	Operations Planning Survey (Equipment)	Key factors to consider in planning your equipment needs

Form 6-6	**Operations Planning Survey (Labor)**	Key factors to consider in planning your labor needs
Form 6-7	**Operations Planning Survey (Process)**	Key factors to consider in planning the process requirements of your operations
Form 6-8	**Distribution and Delivery Survey**	Questions designed to help you get a handle on your distribution and delivery capabilities
Form 6-9	**Management Team Member Profile**	A form for collecting relevant background information on top management-team members

Chapter 7

Crafting Your Marketing Plan

Business plans. Marketing plans. What's the difference, anyway?

Here's a quick answer: Your business plan sells your company — to investors, lenders, partners, key employees, and associates — whereas your marketing plan tells how you'll offer and sell your products or services. Because selling is fundamental to success, an outline of your marketing plan should be included as a key element in your business plan.

People reading your business plan expect a description of the people you believe are the potential buyers for your offering and whether your market is growing or shrinking. They want to know the extent of your competition and where your business fits in the competitive hierarchy. And they want details about how you'll reach customers and present your product, including your plans for pricing, packaging, distribution, promotion, sales, and customer service.

Marketing is one of the top issues on the minds of most business executives, entrepreneurs, and small-business owners. In fact, most business advisers and investors consider marketing the one area that can make or break a business plan, which is why the following pages are so important.

Marketing at a Glance

You're not alone if you're wondering, "What is marketing, anyway?" For a complete answer, pick up Barbara's book *Small Business Marketing Kit For Dummies* (John Wiley & Sons, Inc.). For a quick overview, this section uses excerpts and forms from that book to provide what you need to know to write the marketing strategy section of your business plan. For yet more start-up marketing help, also turn to *Micro-Entrepreneurship For Dummies* by Paul Mladjenovic (John Wiley & Sons, Inc.).

The big marketing picture

In a sentence, marketing is the process you use to get and keep customers. Figure 7-1 shows a bird's-eye view of the marketing cycle, which includes

>> **Customer, product, and competitive research** that enables you to understand your customers and your market environment

>> **Development of marketing strategies,** including pricing, packaging, and distribution strategies designed to meet the interests of your customers and the realities of your market environment

>> **Promotion,** including advertising, public relations, web presence, social media, customer interactions, and other communications that grab attention, inspire interest, and prompt product purchases

>> **Sales programs** that convert consumer interest into purchases that are backed by outstanding payment and delivery systems

>> **Customer service** that builds satisfaction, prompts repeat purchases, develops loyalty to your company, and inspires positive reviews, recommendations, and word of mouth

The nuts and bolts of a marketing plan

A marketing plan includes the following components (each detailed in following sections of this chapter):

>> Description of your market situation, including your customer profile and assessments of changes affecting your customers, competitors, and business climate

>> Your marketing goals and objectives

>> Your company's positioning and brand statements

>> Your marketing strategies, including plans for your product, distribution, pricing, and promotions, along with plans for retaining customers, gaining repeat business, and building loyalty

>> Your marketing budget

>> Your tactical and action plans

>> Your long-range plans

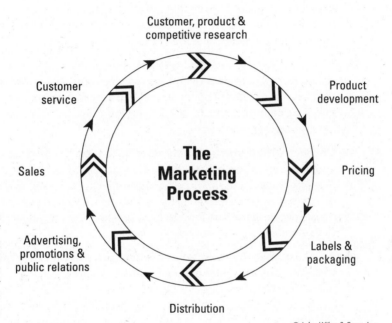

FIGURE 7-1:
An aerial view of the marketing process, from *Small Business Marketing Kit For Dummies* (John Wiley & Sons, Inc.).

© John Wiley & Sons, Inc.

TIP

Detail all these essential topics in your marketing plan. Then include a summarized version that provides the highlights in the strategy section of your business plan (see Chapter 1).

REMEMBER

Your business plan is mainly for external audiences — financial backers, business advisers, and key partners — so edit out details that people outside your business don't need to know and that you may want to hold close to your vest. These include your tactical and action plans and details of how you plan to allocate your marketing budget.

Marketing to a Digitally Connected and Mobile Market

The idea of *marketing* — the process through which you get and keep customers — is as old as commerce itself, but *how* you market to today's screen-connected customers requires radical changes to long-standing tactics and approaches. As you prepare the marketing plan for your business, take today's realities into account:

REMEMBER

» **No matter the size, industry, or location of your business, it needs an online home base.** If the people you're trying to reach aren't looking for your business online, those who influence them are. They expect to find and reach you on their computers and mobile devices.

» **Your website has to load quickly and show well on all screens — from smartphones to tablets to laptops to living room TVs — with buttons that even the fattest fingers can click to access customer-desired information.** If your site doesn't show well on all screens, plan to work on a redesign sooner than later.

» **Online or offline you have only seconds to seize the interest of those you're trying to reach.** In today's instant-gratification society, a third of web users click away from slow-loading sites within five seconds. Two out of ten video viewers leave after ten seconds. And in face-to-face presentations, people decide in the first seven seconds whether they're interested or bored. Grab attention quickly — or not at all.

» **Your customers don't differentiate between whether they're dealing with your business online or face-to-face.** If your business has online and offline locations, they expect a consistent experience no matter how they reach you. For example, they expect your website to provide one-click phone call and location directions, and they expect online purchases to be serviced at your physical place of business.

» **Your online reputation can make or break your business.** More people form opinions based on what they hear from friends or read online than from what they see or hear in business-produced messages. Monitor your online image by typing your business name into a search engine (use incognito or private browsing options so results aren't skewed by your personal browsing history). If results are few, outdated, or less than impressive, get busy building a website and social media pages that people can find. Then, build links to your sites following the steps in the upcoming section on boosting online presence.

» **Marketing needs to pull people to your business.** For decades, marketers pushed messages out, using ads and other one-way communications to interrupt consumers and urge them to take a specific action. Today, pull marketing rules. *Pull marketing* conveys immediately interesting, useful, entertaining, educational information that's capable of drawing — pulling — people to your physical location or website — while prompting high-value consumer-to-consumer sharing of your messages as a welcome bonus.

Analyzing Your Market Situation

Your marketing plan begins with a snapshot presentation of your marketing arena, including its size, dynamics, consumer trends, competition, and the issues that affect your ability to sell your products — for better or worse.

MBA–types call this overview a *situation analysis* because, to sound like Yogi Berra, it analyzes the situation you face as you plan for success. These sections explain how you can better understand your market situation.

Getting a handle on your market

People who read your marketing plan — or the summary of it in your business plan — want to know that your ideas are grounded in reality. They want to know who will buy what you're selling and whether your prospect pool is growing, holding steady, or shrinking. Cover the following points:

>> **Your customer description:** Define your customers in geographic terms (where they live), demographic terms (facts such as age, gender, ethnicity, education level, sexual orientation, marital status, income level, and household size), and psychographic terms (lifestyle characteristics, including attitudes, beliefs, and behaviors that affect customer-purchasing patterns). If you don't have a ready description, turn to Chapter 4 to develop your customer profile.

>> **How customers divide into market segments:** *Market segments* are comprised of groups of customers who share similar characteristics. For example, women may buy from your company differently than men do and buyers from one geographic area may have different product interests than customers from another. Midweek customers may buy differently than weekend customers, and online and in-person shoppers may differ in their interests and purchase tendencies. (Chapter 4 includes market segmentation information to help you analyze who's buying what from your business.)

Here are a few ways that companies divide buyers into market segments:

- Business-to-consumer companies may segment customers by gender, age, income, location, or buying habits.

- Business-to-business companies may segment clients by size or type of company, nature of client relationship (contract business versus one-time purchase, for example), or product interest.

- Companies using multiple distribution channels (retail outlets, direct-mail, and e-commerce, for example) may find that customers arriving via specific channels share distinguishing similarities — in terms of product interest and buying patterns — from customers arriving via other channels.

EXAMPLE

An accounting firm may segment its market into personal and business clients, but beyond those categories the firm may segment by services offered — for example, tax returns, bookkeeping and accounting services, management consulting, estate tax planning, payroll services, and business start-up or sale consulting. The firm also may segment by size of client served — for example, small businesses, mid-size organizations, or major corporations. By knowing its market segments, the firm can refine its products and promote specific offerings that appeal to each group.

>> **The size of your market and its growth trends:** Project and present size and growth information for your overall market and various market segments. For example, if small businesses represent a sizeable segment of your clientele, include facts about the number and growth trends of small businesses in your market area.

WARNING

Don't base projections on a hunch. Instead, refer to census data, cite industry and expert analyses, refer to findings by organizations that serve your market area, or project trends based on a recap of your sales history. By offering data for what you say about market size, you validate the claim upon which you stake your marketing plan and budget.

Assessing your competition

To grow your business you need to gain *market share* (the portion of all sales in your market area that your business captures, commonly known as your slice of the market pie) by drawing customers and purchases away from competitors. In this portion of your marketing plan, you summarize the competition your company faces, including

>> **Direct competitors:** These competitors are businesses that your customers consider when they think about buying products like the ones you sell. As you list direct competitors, describe what you know about the threats each one poses. (Chapter 4 tells you how to use cloak-and-dagger methods in your intelligence mission.)

>> **Indirect or stealth competitors:** These competitors go after your customers in different and unexpected ways. For example, accounting software poses

indirect competition to accounting firms. (See Chapter 4 for help identifying stealth competitors that can blindside your business.)

Competition creates threats and provides opportunities, and how you handle both affects your success:

>> **Competitive threats** include new competitors, improved or expanded offerings from competitors, and new options that let prospects fill the need that your product addresses in a whole new way — such as online buying, do-it-yourself solutions, or new technologies that replace the need for your offering altogether.

>> **Competitive opportunities** include changes that weaken your competitors, the closure of competitors, or new trends that contribute to greater interest for your offering.

WINNING A SLICE OF THE MARKET PIE

Sooner or later, some banker, adviser, or partner will ask you about your *market share* — the portion your business captures of all the sales of products like yours in your market area. You can calculate your market share by units sold, customers served, or dollar volume. Following are examples of each approach:

- **Share of unit sales:** The manager of Open Fairways Golf Course discovers that all the courses in the market area together host 50,000 rounds of golf a year. Of those rounds, Open Fairways hosts 7,000, for a 14 percent market share. (7,000 ÷ 50,000 = 0.14)

- **Share of customers served:** The owners of Immaculate Carpet Cleaning serve homes within 15 miles of the business. That area includes 2,000 homes. However, the Immaculate owners estimate that only half of the area's homes — 1,000 homes — are potential customers for carpet-cleaning services. The company currently cleans carpets in 125 homes a year, giving it a 12.5 percent market share. (125 ÷ 1,000 = 0.125)

- **Share of dollar volume:** The owners of Forever Green Landscaping operate in a market area where homeowners and businesses buy a million dollars' worth of landscaping services annually. Forever Green has sales of $100,000, or 10 percent market share. (100,000 ÷ 1,000,000 = 0.10)

Some companies track market share using several of these calculation approaches. However, many companies have access to only one of the market size statistics, so they base their market-share assessments solely on that calculation approach.

To protect against threats and capitalize on opportunities conduct a strengths, weaknesses, opportunities, and threats (SWOT) analysis. The process will help you identify ways to align your capabilities with the realities of your business environment. (See Chapter 5 for the whole scoop.)

Getting smarter with big data

Big data is the term for collected facts and figures that reveal trends and patterns. It used to apply to those businesses with big operations and big budgets, but today it's for everyone because data is now so readily accessible, and data analysis tools are often free or almost-free.

To leverage available facts into information that help you define and predict your market and customer conditions, take these steps:

1. **Set your sights.**

   With so much data available, the smartest first step is to focus on what you want data to help you accomplish. Do you want more customers? More sales of certain products or services? A larger, more engaged customer community? These kinds of questions can guide the collection of data that can assist your planning.

2. **Collect the data.**

   Obtain information by studying sales records, by researching customers (Chapter 4 guides this effort,) and by tapping into information compiled by business suppliers, government agencies, industry sources, media outlets, and online searches for the kind of information you're working to compile. Also, check out Google Shopping Insights at shopping.thinkwithgoogle.com, a free tool that explores trends and popularity of products across the United States.

TIP

3. **Analyze the data.**

   Make sense of the facts and figures. Use collected multi-year statistics to plot and project growth trends. Use facts from your recent sales history to determine which of your product, customer, and geographic market segments are growing or declining. Use Google Analytics, a free Google tool, to obtain data on your website visitors, including where they come from, what devices they use, which pages they visit, *bounce rates* or how long they stay on your site, and traffic trends that help you analyze which promotions and social media efforts are successfully driving site traffic.

4. **Use the data.**

   Depending on your marketing goals, the data you collect and analyze can guide decisions regarding which customer or market segments are your best growth targets, which products or product features are most apt to see increased customer interest and adoption, and which kinds of messages and offers are likely to pull the most interest. The result? You can prepare marketing and business plans based not on guestimates but on facts, figures, probabilities, and trends.

Forecasting your business environment

The final step in your situation analysis involves looking at outside forces that may affect your business success. Strategists call this environmental assessment a *PESTLE analysis* because it takes into account Political, Economic, Social, Technological, Legal, and Environmental factors that affect business conditions. In evaluating your business climate, consider the following:

>> New taxes, rules, regulations, and laws that may require changes to your staffing, products, pricing, or operations

>> Changes in economic conditions, inflation, or interest rates that may affect your sales and finances

>> Social trends or shifting consumer preferences that may affect your product strategies and your customers' purchasing approaches and buying decisions

>> Emerging technologies that may alter how you or your competitors operate

>> Changes in your business environment, ranging from such factors as weather patterns that affect your business to prolonged conditions that disrupt customer access to customer demands for green and sustainable offerings to regional or industry events or conditions that may impact visibility for and interest in your offerings

TIP

Chapter 15 guides your assessment of changes that affect the conditions your business faces. In your written business plan, include highlights of your situation analysis, touching on the following key points:

>> The market for your product or service, including facts about the number of prospective customers and whether that group is growing or shrinking

>> Market segments that provide the best opportunities for growth and why

>> Competitive threats and opportunities and how you plan to counter or take advantage of each

>> Market trends and business forces that likely will affect your success, along with plans for overcoming threats and capitalizing on opportunities

Setting Marketing Goals and Objectives

Chapter 3 includes information on setting business goals and objectives. Follow these steps as you set marketing goals and objectives:

1. **Review your business goals.**

   Some goals deal with operational, employee, management, and business-development issues. Others deal with marketing issues and those goals, such as "Increase brand awareness" or "Develop new markets for products and services" also become goals of your marketing plan.

   TIP

   When you adopt business goals as goals of your marketing plan you'll want to add clearly defined targets and timelines. For example, you may expand "Develop new markets for products and services" to "Develop new markets to increase sales of Product X by 5 percent over the upcoming one-year period."

2. **Set objectives to define how you'll achieve your marketing goals.**

   Each objective should specify an action and a desired outcome. Table 7-1 shows an example.

TABLE 7-1   An Example of Marketing Goals and Objectives

Goal/Objective	Action	Timeline	Desired Outcome
Goal	To develop new markets	Over the upcoming one-year period	To increase sales of Product X by 5 percent
Objective	Establish a distributor relationship	During the first quarter	To achieve product placement in holiday gift collections
Objective	Place ads in geographically targeted sports publications	In early spring	To develop summer sales to regionally targeted outdoor enthusiasts
Objective	Enhance a web presence and expand social networking	Over the first quarter	To develop customer relationships in nearby and targeted distant market areas

REMEMBER

Include your marketing goals and objectives in the marketing strategy section of your written business plan.

Putting Your Position and Brand into Words

Your *position* is the niche that your business or product — and only your business or product — fills in your customers' minds. To gain a market position, first define how you offer a meaningful and unique solution that isn't duplicated by any competitor. Then, develop marketing communications and customer experiences that will consistently convey the distinct advantages you offer in order to win a preferred position in the minds of your customers and business plan readers.

Your *brand* is the set of beliefs that consumers associate with your name. You build your brand by consistently conveying a meaningful, relevant promise that consumers can relate to and believe in. For two quickly adopted brand examples, consider the positions of Uber, "Everyone's favorite driver," and Airbnb, "A home where you belong."

TIP

Go to www.dummies.com/go/businessplanskit and look at Form 7-1, which provides examples of positioning and brand statements, along with a formula to follow as you write similar statements for your business. Form 7-2 details six brand-management steps to take as you define and develop the brand for your business.

TIP

Include your brand and positioning statements in the marketing section of your business plan.

Boosting Online Presence: The Most Traveled Route to Most Businesses

The Internet is today's starting point for almost anyone searching for information on people, products, and businesses. Today, if people can't find your business online, odds are good they simply won't look further.

Formula for a Positioning Statement

Your business or product name	+ What makes your business unique and different	+ Your market description
Business Plans Kit For Dummies	is the easiest, most self-contained, do-it-yourself resource	for brand-new or expanding businesses of any size
iPod	is the digital music player	for people who want 40,000 songs in their pocket
Zappos	offers the absolute best service and selection in online shopping	to customers who value a business that's powered by service
Now it's your turn…		

Formula for a Brand Statement

A phrase that captures the promise your business makes to its customers.

Bing	A search engine that brings together the best of search and people in your social networks to help you spend less time searching and more time doing.
Twitter	Instantly connecting people everywhere to what's most important to them.
Amazon	Where people can find and discover virtually anything they want to buy.
Now it's your turn …	

© *John Wiley & Sons, Inc.*

FORM 7-1: Use this form as you make product decisions to support your marketing plans.

In the marketing strategy section of your business plan, outline your program for enhancing Internet presence by covering the following points:

>> Provide the address and purpose of your business website.

   If you don't have a business website, describe your alternative online home base. To be credible, you need a site that's findable by a search for your business name, that accurately projects your brand image, and that you can control and keep updated. Social media pages serve as website alternatives, while listings on Chamber of Commerce sites, industry sites, local media sites, and in other directories provide online presence without the necessary brand-building capability.

>> Use keywords throughout your website to increase rankings in web search results.

>> Describe how your business uses social media and online networking to develop and deepen customer relationships, including which networks you use and your goals for each.

>> Include a summary of how you drive traffic to your site through online advertising, incoming links, and self-promotion along with estimated approaches and costs for conversion of site visitors to customers.

>> Describe how you'll use digital communications — e-newsletters, email promotions, messaging, social networking, search engine optimization, and online interactions — to launch and maintain customer contact.

As you plan your online presence and the framework for digital communications with your target audience, be sure your website is ready for today's users who are increasingly searching on mobile devices. To put it to the test, pull your website up on a smartphone. If it doesn't show well, follow these points:

>> **Simplify your site design.** Reduce elements, use larger font sizes, and place information most of your site users seek at the top of the page so it will show on mobile screens.

>> **Make links and buttons fat-finger proof.** In other words, make them large enough that they're easy to see and tap.

>> **Choose a site design or template that shows well on any device.** Both Bing and Google advise against creation of a second site with a dot-m (.m) URL address, largely because the second site complicates findability and search engine optimization. Instead, choose what's called a *responsive design* for your site, which results in a site that shows well on all devices except the oldest cellphones. (Nearly all website-building DIY tools include responsive-design templates.) Another option is to create a site using *adaptive design*, which detects and responds to a user's device — an expensive option used by big companies and outside the budget range of smaller marketers.

TIP

As you plan your digital communications strategy, check out Form 7-3, a checklist from *Small Business Marketing Kit For Dummies* that guides you through the steps involved to establish, build, and monitor the social media program.

Include a blueprint for your digital communication strategy in your marketing plan and then include a summarized statement of that strategy in the marketing section of your business plan.

Zooming In on Your Target Market

Unless your business is large and extremely well funded, it can't try to serve all people, and even then an all-things-for-all-people approach is rarely a winning strategy. That's why most successful marketers focus on market niches, and you should, too.

By deciding which audience you serve best, and which problems or needs you address better than anyone else, you can target a precise market audience with a relevant and believable message and brand promise. Think about it. If you're seeking legal advice for a business start-up, wouldn't you prefer to deal with a legal firm that specializes in small business start-ups? That's what *niche marketing* is all about.

As you determine the market niche your business serves, keep these thoughts in mind:

» Determine whether a group of individuals have specialized interests and needs that your business can address in a compelling and competitive manner.

» Assess whether the market segment you're targeting is large enough to deliver the sales volume targeted by your business plan but small enough to be overlooked by most competitors.

» Be sure that your target audience can easily access your offerings, whether via your physical location, online presence, or distribution channels (either established or anticipated).

» Determine that the niche market you're targeting isn't already well-served by competitors or, if it is, be clear about how your offering is distinctly more appealing.

To pinpoint your market niche, study what current customers rely on from your business. Ask, "If you closed, what problem would your customers have a hard time solving elsewhere?" If you're planning for a start-up, rephrase the question to ask, "What want or need do customers have? What inconvenience or pain do they experience that isn't being addressed by other businesses?" The answer can lead to your market niche and, sometimes, to an innovation that completely upends established approaches in your market arena, called a *disruptive innovation* and featured in a section in Chapter 2.

Describing your target customer

Turn to Chapter 4 as you conduct customer research, develop your customer profile, and detail how and why customers will choose and buy your offerings, including the want or need they address and the benefit and value they deliver. Include this description in your marketing plan.

Planning to lock in loyalty

Businesses of all kinds and sizes establish loyalty-development programs to win long-standing commitments from customers who are constantly tempted by a barrage of price and deal options from competing businesses.

Customer loyalty programs run the gamut from VIP services to points-and-prize programs — and just about everything in between, including frequent guest programs, multiple-purchase programs, special-status programs, join-the-club programs, buyback programs, games that incent and reward actions, and personal and tailored offers and outreach. Although the list of loyalty rewards is long, the loyalty program goal is always the same: to inspire and reward customers with incentives for remaining true to the business and for buying more and buying more often.

Keep these tips in mind when planning a loyalty program for your business:

>> **Develop relationships, not just repeat business.** A program that puts a reward card in a customer's billfold isn't as useful as one that inspires download of an app that allows a business to collect customer information and then to push out limited-time offers, tailored invitations, and loyalty rewards. Check out the sidebar titled "Is there an app in your plan?" in Chapter 15 for advice to follow.

>> **Customize incentives.** Create reward tiers and targeted offers. Inspire low-profit customers with off-hour or off-season offers or incentives that draw them into higher-level purchases. Draw back lapsed customers with offers consistent with past purchases. Reward best customers with personalized surprises and complimentary upgrades.

>> **Collect and leverage customer data.** Customer loyalty begins with great offerings and experiences, and it deepens through customer knowledge and

relationships. In addition to staff knowledge, collect customer information into a single database that consolidates and protects facts about who customers are, how to reach them, past purchases, previous rewards, and other information that can help your business tailor invitations and incentives.

>> **Build your brand.** Develop a loyalty program that's consistent with your brand image and an extension of the interactions customers expect when associating with your business. Then train and enable your team to promote the program as an extension of your brand promise and customer experience.

REMEMBER

Marketing is the process of not just getting, but also keeping customers. In addition to detailing how to win new customers, also detail how to retain, inspire, deepen relationships with, and build loyalty with established customers in your marketing plan. Loyal customers are the ones most likely to buy more, buy more often, require less costly communication, and provide more useful input to your business than all others. Plus, they're most likely to share positive impressions that lead new customers to your offerings.

Designing Marketing Strategies

Creating a marketing success story is a little like baking a cake. You take a little bit of this, a little more of that, and you arrive at one result. If you change the mix, you get a different outcome.

WHAT'S YOUR VALUE PROPOSITION?

As you develop your product strategy, spend time determining how your product decisions deliver clear value to your customers. When making purchase decisions, customers weigh the price against their impressions of the quality, benefits, convenience, reliability, expertise, and support they'll receive from the product or service they're purchasing.

To develop the *value proposition* you're promising customers, describe the results customers can depend on when they buy from your business. By selecting your product, does your customer increase revenue, save time, cut costs, improve efficiency, receive unrivaled quality, enjoy tremendous convenience, have the peace of mind of unparalleled expertise, guarantees, product support, or other compelling values that make customers believe that what they're getting is worth every penny of what they're paying?

Summarize your value proposition in the marketing strategy section of your business plan.

In marketing, the ingredients you juggle are your *product, placement* (also called *distribution*), *pricing,* and *promotions.* Together, these four elements are known as the *marketing mix* or the *four Ps.*

REMEMBER

Every marketing action falls under one of the four Ps of the marketing mix and you need a marketing strategy for each area. Use the following sections to guide your planning, which you can explain in detail in your marketing plan, and summarize in the marketing strategy section of your business plan.

Your product strategy

Your business may be introducing a product or planning changes to the products you already sell. You may be planning a product strategy to communicate different product uses, benefits, or distinctions, or maybe you're working to shift marketing emphasis from one product in your line to another. Perhaps you aim to target established products to new market segments, to rename or relabel products to make them more relevant in the current marketplace, to add accessories or services to boost appeal, or to bundle products into new package options.

TIP

In other parts of your business plan, you present your product development and production plans. In the marketing section, you summarize how you plan to introduce, reintroduce, or revise products to generate sales and achieve marketing goals. Use Form 7-4 as you set your product strategy.

Your distribution strategy

TIP

Chapter 6 helps you assess your company's distribution capabilities. Include the results of your assessment in the company description portion of your business plan. In your marketing plan — and briefly in the marketing strategy section of your business plan — describe how distribution supports your marketing goals and objectives. Use Form 7-5 to plan your strategy.

Your pricing strategy

One of the decisions most crucial to business success involves pricing your products. Your business needs to arrive at prices that cover all costs and deliver a reasonable profit margin while also hitting the sweet spot of what customers are willing to pay for the value they believe they receive from the purchase.

Product Strategy Checklist

1. How will you present your products to develop customers and sales?

2. Which products or product features will you emphasize?

3. Will you introduce new product names, packaging, or labeling to re-inspire market interest?

4. Can you bundle products into packaged offers to increase sales?

5. Will you develop new products or add new design elements or functions to existing products to achieve market interest, meet competitive challenges, or address consumer demands?

6. Will you introduce or increase emphasis on quality assurances or service policies?

7. Other product considerations ...

© John Wiley & Sons, Inc.

FORM 7-4: Use this form as you tailor distribution and delivery systems to fit your marketing objectives.

To get your pricing right, you need to match your prices to the image of your business and the nature of your clientele (you can't charge premium prices if you've established your business as a middle-of-the-road option), while also covering your production and operational costs and delivering the profits necessary for your business survival. Chapter 5 includes a checklist of pricing considerations and advice for putting a price on your products.

TIP

After developing your pricing approach, use Form 7-6 to design the pricing strategy that you'll summarize in the marketing strategy section of your business plan.

Distribution Strategy Checklist
1. Will you introduce new distribution or delivery systems — such as home delivery, subscription delivery, free delivery to volume customers, free shipping or guaranteed returns with online purchases, and so on — to increase sales, serve customers, or gain advantage over competitors?
2. Can you increase sales by adding new distribution channels, such as online sales, distributor relationships, or new retail outlets?
3. Would your business benefit from business partnerships that allow you to achieve off-premise sales outlets in other retail settings?
4. If you use or are adding distributors or representatives, do you have adequate plans for recruiting, training, motivating, and compensating them, and do you have a clear plan for assignment of territories?
5. Other distribution strategy considerations ...

FORM 7-5: Use this form as you develop your company's pricing strategy.

Your promotion strategy

Your *promotion strategy* blueprints how you'll communicate your marketing message to prospective customers.

For information and advice on planning your promotional strategy, see the latest edition of Barbara's book *Small Business Marketing Kit For Dummies, Marketing For Dummies* by Alexander Hiam (both by John Wiley & Sons, Inc.), or check out one of the other countless marketing books on the market.

In your marketing plan, provide a complete outline of your promotion strategy, including a description of your target customer, your market area, your marketing message, the creative approach you'll use to convey your message and advance your brand image, the media channels you'll employ, and the budget you've allocated to get the job done.

In the marketing section of your business plan, include a summary of your promotion strategy with an overview of how it supports the product, pricing, and distribution strategies your business will follow over the business plan period. When appropriate, include samples of marketing materials in the appendix of your business plan. Samples aren't necessary, but if you have professionally produced materials that contribute to a strong image of your business, including them in your plan will contribute to a favorable impression.

TIP

Download Form 7-7 for help with promotional planning.

TIP

CREATING A CUSTOMER-SERVICE ENVIRONMENT

Refer to the aerial view of the marketing process in Figure 7-1 to see that marketing doesn't end when you make the sale. After-the-sale service is the key to achieving customer satisfaction, earning repeat business, achieving good word of mouth (and avoiding devastating customer rebukes that can go viral instantaneously online), and building a valuable, loyal clientele. Use Form 7-8 to evaluate your customer service and to create a customer-service strategy that includes service standards, service objectives, and plans for continuously monitoring and enhancing the service you provide customers.

Pricing Strategy Checklist

1. What is your pricing-level philosophy?

Are your prices the high-end, middle-of-the-pack, or low-end choice?

If you have high-end prices, do you offer extra value? If your prices are lower, what affects your lower price and can your pricing sustain profitability?

How do you plan to maintain or adjust your pricing level over the business plan period?

2. What is your pricing structure?

Do you offer all-inclusive pricing or pricing for a base-level product plus add-on prices for service, guarantees, delivery, and so on? A single price level or multiple price levels from which to choose? Pricing by the project or product delivered or by the time and costs involved? A free base-level product with premium-level options available for a price? Pricing based on frequent discounts through promotional offers, quantity discounts, or other deals or incentives?

How do you plan to adjust your pricing structure over the business plan period?

3. What pricing and payment options do you offer?

Do you offer introductory pricing to gain trial and acceptance, increasing prices later? Do you allow bargaining? Do you offer financing? Do you offer a range of payment options? Do you offer contract, subscription, or bulk-order discounts?

How will you adjust your pricing and payment options over the business plan period?

4. Pricing considerations ...

Do your prices cover all costs plus a profit margin?

Do your prices cover costs such as shrinkage, returns, bad debt, and allowances for employee errors?

Do you know how each pricing and payment option impacts your financial condition?

Do you — or can you — join a buying group, buy through an association, or establish bulk-buying agreements to reduce the costs of your product?

How do you plan to adjust pricing over the business plan period?

© *John Wiley & Sons, Inc.*

FORM 7-6: This form helps you with pricing.

Forms

Go to www.dummies.com/go/businessplanskit to view and download these forms that help you develop your marketing plan.

Form 7-1	Formula for a Positioning Statement	Formulas and real-world examples to help you write your marketing statements
Form 7-2	Six Brand-Management Steps	A worksheet to guide the steps necessary for building a brand for your business
Form 7-3	Social Media Program Planning Checklist	A form from *Small Business Marketing Kit For Dummies,* listing steps to take as you plan, implement, and monitor your social media program
Form 7-4	Product Strategy Checklist	Questions to answer as you develop a strategy for marketing your products
Form 7-5	Distribution Strategy Checklist	Issues to consider as you tailor your distribution and delivery systems to fit your marketing objectives
Form 7-6	Pricing Strategy Checklist	Questions to weigh as you develop a pricing strategy that takes into account the nature of your clientele and the production and operational costs your sales revenue needs to cover
Form 7-7	Promotion Strategy Worksheet	Issues to address as you select promotion approaches and determine the most effective ways to communicate with prospects
Form 7-8	Customer Service Checklist	Questions designed to prompt plans for improving your customer service

Chapter 8

Finding Your Funding

A great idea sparks most business start-ups, but money is the fuel that turns that idea into reality and gets a start-up off the ground. Most entrepreneurs and even many established businesses need to raise the funds to carry them from business launch to sales lift-off.

Even if you're launching a one-person freelance business, more than likely you need cash to underwrite your early days of operation. If you're starting a bigger company, and especially if you're founding a high-tech or manufacturing enterprise, chances are good that you need *lots* of cash. If your business is humming along but you're planning for growth or major change, you probably also need funds to put that plan into action and to operate until revenue begins rolling in.

This chapter explores how to forecast the amount of money you need in order to provide your business with funding until the momentous day when revenues exceed costs and cash flows freely. It explains the funding sources most entrepreneurs turn to and what it takes to unlock the money you need. It also flags cautions to keep in mind as you seek funding to turn your business idea into a business success.

Forecasting Your Funding Requirements

Most businesses, especially when they're starting up or planning for expansion, face periods when they need to rely on outside resources to stay afloat. Whether the funds come from the owner's pocket, accumulated business profits, or outside funding sources, they provide the lifeline that keeps the business going when expenses exceed revenue for a prolonged period. Use this section to forecast how much money you need — and for how long.

WARNING

Even if you're launching a one-person business located for the time being at the kitchen table, you still need to project the time it takes to sign the first client and cash the first check — and then the next one. While you're waiting for revenue to take off, you'll be burning through cash reserves to fund business expenses.

To estimate the funding requirement your business faces, take these steps:

1. Create a realistic forecast of your financial situation.

For help with this key step, turn to Chapter 9. Follow the steps for preparing a *pro forma* or estimated statement of income, expenses, and profit, along with an estimated balance sheet and cash flow statement.

2. Estimate your funding need.

Use your financial forecasts, and especially your cash flow projection, to determine how long you anticipate expenses to exceed revenue and by how much. Doing so helps you get a handle on when you expect expenses to be incurred, when you expect revenues to roll in, and the amount of funding you need in order to cover the gap.

3. Create a funding time frame.

After you establish how much funding you need, create a schedule for how long you need the funding to last before your business needs to become self-sufficient. This schedule, called your *time frame*, should include dates by which you plan to meet revenue-generating *milestones* — for example, first customer, first major contract, first $10,000 in sales, and so on — that you can monitor as indicators that your business is on track to achieve profitability before funding runs out.

REMEMBER

As you forecast how long your funding needs to last, be aware of these terms:

>> **Runway:** The amount of time funding needs to last before your business becomes profitable and self-sufficient or until additional funding will be required

>> **Burn rate:** The speed with which you expect to spend the funding you've raised — in practical terms, the amount of cash required each month to cover the costs of staying in business

Turn to Chapter 2 for more information on calculating the funding runway required by your business plan.

Searching for Money in All the Right Places

When your business needs more cash than it's generating, you can turn to a long and growing list of business funding resources. Some are easy to tap. Others require high levels of patience and diligence. Some don't have a lot of strings attached. Others do, in the form of fees, interest, or shares of ownership in your business, for example. The following sections lead you through funding options and considerations to weigh.

Funding your business with close-to-home resources

Terms like *venture capital* and *commercial loans* have long dominated talk about business start-up and expansion funding, but business growth is more likely to be funded by sources far closer to home or headquarters. Your savings, your credit card, your friends and family, and your own business cash reserves, accumulated during profitable times, are the go-to resources most likely to tide your businesses over both during its early days and again during high-expense, low-income growth or turnaround periods.

Funding your business needs with your own money or resources from friends or family makes sense for practical and strategic reasons.

» **The practical:** Your business will have a hard time attracting outside funding if you don't have assets that can serve as loan collateral or if you can't yet demonstrate growing revenues and a strong financial position, an impressive operation and management team, a growing customer list, or a business idea so promising that investors are rushing to get behind it.

» **The strategic:** Even if you have business attributes that are likely to impress investors or lenders, you may choose not to turn to outside funding because of the concessions that come with it, which include the following:

- Time and money spent to approach and court investors or lenders, which is time and money diverted from your business

- Reduced personal control of your business, either because investors will want to have input or because they'll want to own an equity position in your business in return for their investment — or both

- Reduced personal accountability for the success of your business, both because outsiders are affecting business decisions and because the funding cushion may reduce the pressure you feel to sink-or-swim

By providing your own early-stage funding, you'll own all your business after it becomes profitable, at which time you'll be in a better position to negotiate funding commitments to your business advantage.

Realize, though, that if you decide to steer clear of lenders and investors, your funding will likely come from the person you see in the mirror — or from people the person in the mirror can reach out to for help.

Your own pocket

The most obvious sources for cash for your business are your own savings, your credit cards, or personal debt that you incur. A third of all start-ups are self-funded or *bootstrapped*, the longstanding term for ventures that succeed using their own rather than outside resources. Here are the pros and cons:

>> **Pluses:** Bootstrapping lets you remain the boss and sole owner of your business. Plus, it forces you to be disciplined about quickly getting your venture off the ground and into profitability, because you'll be growing your business primarily with money it brings in through sales.

>> **Minuses:** Bootstrapped businesses often trim all but essential costs and remain closely focused on profit-generating activities. The result is they sometimes miss opportunities seized by well-funded businesses that have the financial flexibility to pursue innovations, new directions, or pivots into all-new business models. Owners of bootstrapped businesses also run the risk of tunnel vision because they don't have outside investors to bring different points of view that can contribute to stronger business plans and decisions.

As you weigh the go-it-alone or seek-funding decision, realize that either way you're going to reach into your own pocket, savings, or credit sources, because putting some skin in the game is a prerequisite of most lenders or investors.

>> **If you link arms with investors,** you'll still tap your own resources, because investors almost certainly expect you to personally invest. That means you'll share the risk — but also the rewards — with others.

>> **If you seek loans,** financial institutions require you to pledge personal assets as collateral to secure the debt.

>> **If you go the venture capital route,** most investors insist that you ante up some of your own cash, largely as proof of your commitment, before they'll add their own.

The primary benefit of self-funding is that you maintain 100 percent ownership and 100 percent control. The caveat is that you also take on all the risk: If the company goes under, your money goes with it.

Friends and family

Turning to friends or family members is a time-honored tradition in starting a small business. Some people borrow money in return for a simple IOU to be paid back in full when the company starts making a profit. Others set up a more formal loan along with an agreement for paying back money with interest on a specific schedule.

WARNING

Whatever arrangement you reach, make sure that everyone involved understands the terms and knows what to expect and when to expect it. Don't assume that a handshake agreement is enough. Put the terms in writing and ask all parties to sign. Disagreements over money can spoil even the closest relationships. Circumstances like divorce or death can bring others into the agreement and raise lots of questions, unless you have everything in writing.

Turning customers and prospective customers into investors

Customers also can become investors who can help your company get off the ground. For example:

» Community-supported agriculture (CSA) programs pair local farmers with consumers who pay a set fee in advance in return for a weekly load of produce during the summer growing season.

» Condominium projects sell units to prospective owners before the builder ever breaks ground.

» Local businesses reach out to community members, called *locavestors*, who invest in new neighborhood businesses both to earn a return on their investments and to help build stronger local communities.

TIP

When considering customers as potential funding sources, think of people who use and benefit from your company's offerings. They may be willing to provide funding through prepurchases or investments, especially if you provide a clear reason and reasonable incentive or rate of return on their money. Sharing your business idea with prospective customer-investors early in the planning process also offers a useful reality check to test whether they'll actually pay for your proposed products and services.

Navigating the routes to bank funding

A Harvard Business School report, *The State of Small Business Lending*, confirms what most small businesses in need of funding already surmised. Since the 2008 financial crisis, traditional lending — usually through small and community banks — has declined dramatically. The reasons are many, including:

>> Banks loan to businesses with a good credit history, which most small businesses in need of funding haven't yet established and, even if they have, small business creditworthiness is often more difficult for banks to assess.

>> Banks require valuable assets, called *collateral,* to secure loans, and many early-stage businesses don't yet have the cash accounts, real estate, vehicles, equipment, or inventory to pledge as loan security.

>> Most owners seeking small business loans, especially if they don't have collateral to pledge, are asked to sign a *personal guarantee* saying that they are personally responsible for repayment. If the bank requests a personal guarantee instead of loan collateral, many small business owners don't have sufficient assets to pledge.

>> Small business loans typically come through community banks, which have declined in number due to bank failures and mergers.

>> Small business loans are less profitable to banks because banks incur similar costs whether loans are large or small.

Banks, especially community banks and local branches of smaller banks, are still willing to consider loan requests from local businesses, though only a small percentage of applications get funded. The factors that influence a banker's decision include your business financial track record, your personal credit history, your education, your expertise and business experience, and the likelihood that your business start-up or expansion will succeed.

The upcoming sections describe the kinds of bank loans most small business owners consider as they seek funding for their business plans.

Commercial loans

The simplest bank-loan arrangement is a standard commercial loan. The bank loans the money, and you pay it back, usually in monthly installments and with interest. But you can find all sorts of loan variations, from real estate loans on commercial property to loans secured by your inventory or accounts receivable.

The big advantages of bank loans include the following:

>> You gain business funding while maintaining all the equity in your company, which is rarely the case when receiving investor funding.

>> Bank loans usually come with lower interest and longer repayment terms than many other sources of capital.

Bank loans also come with a few drawbacks, beginning with the fact that payments are due on schedule even if your business runs into hard times. If a payment is late or missed, the loan becomes *delinquent.* If a loan remains delinquent for a prolonged period, it's considered *in default,* which can trigger seizure of assets pledged as loan security, a drop in your credit score, and higher interest rates in the future.

Before approaching a banker, be prepared to make your case by presenting your written business plan along with a loan request that defines how much you want to borrow, how you plan to use the funds, and when you'll repay the money. Most banks won't lend unless a business can pledge collateral to secure the loan. In many cases, especially for businesses that haven't acquired equipment, inventory, accounts receivable, or other assets, the loan security comes in the form of the owner's personal guarantee, often backed by a second-mortgage on the owner's home.

Commercial lines of credit

If you need access to money that you don't intend to use all at once, consider applying for a *commercial line of credit,* which is an agreement from a financial institution to extend a specified amount of credit that your company can draw upon, as necessary, to finance inventory purchases or to provide working capital or funds for other cash needs.

With a commercial line of credit, you pay interest only on the funds you actually borrow and only over the period between when you draw on the funds and when you pay them back. Banks may require that you secure a line of credit with business accounts receivable, inventory, machinery and equipment, or real estate.

Equipment leasing

Another way to borrow money from banks is an *equipment lease,* which you can use to buy anything from computers to copiers to manufacturing equipment, tractors, and trucks. Financial arrangements include lease-to-buy options, equipment upgrade options, and master leases, which cover a variety of equipment under one agreement.

The loan length for these options is usually tied to the lease term.

SBA loans

Bravo to the Small Business Administration (SBA), the government agency with a variety of loan programs for small businesses that may otherwise have a tough time securing financing from commercial banks. Keep in mind: The SBA is more likely to fund business expansions than acquisitions or start-ups. And the money isn't free. What's commonly called an SBA loan is actually a bank loan guaranteed in part (usually in large part) by the SBA, which essentially plays the role of a co-signer. Expect to pay fees and interest and be ready for paperwork, oversight, and the responsibility of personally guaranteeing loan repayment. But because the SBA provides the backup guarantee, loans that banks may otherwise turn down get extra attention.

Considering alternative lending sources

With traditional loans harder for small businesses to get than ever before, new alternatives for funding, available online, are making headlines and filling the void.

WARNING

Many of the new online lending options provide faster and easier application processes and far more immediate lending decisions than those of traditional lenders. The downside is that most alternative sources serve only established businesses with annual revenues that meet stipulated minimum standards. When they approve loans, funding is usually for shorter terms, and it almost always comes with higher — often considerably higher — fees and interest rates than those of traditional lenders.

Alternative lending sites

Alternative online lenders, including Kabbage.com, OnDeck.com, and others, raise a pool of funding from investors that they then lend to businesses with funding gaps not likely to be addressed by commercial bank loans. They take greater risks, which, no surprise, are accompanied by higher fees.

The lending process begins with an online application during which you upload your business banking and transaction records. Automated programs then analyze your financial history against risk-scoring models that assess creditworthiness within minutes. The result is a quick-turn lending decision, followed by funding and payback through processes unique to each site.

The sites aren't for new businesses or for those seeking long-term funding. For example, Kabbage.com accepts applications from those who have been in business at least a year with annual revenues of at least $50,000. Loan amounts range from $2,000 to $100,000 and work like a six-month line of credit that can be tapped as needed, with interest and fees accruing as funds are used.

WARNING

Fees, rates, and penalties can add up fast, so take time to study all the terms — and then have an adviser look them over as well.

Peer-to-peer loan sites

Sites such as Lending Club (www.lendingclub/com) and Funding Circle (www.fundingcircle.com/uk), as two examples, are called *peer-to-peer* or P2P lenders.

They connect those seeking business funding with those willing to lend it, some-times pairing loan applicants with several lenders who each provide a portion of the requested loan amount. Loans come with interest rates that are often higher (significantly higher for higher-risk loans) than those offered by traditional banks. Expect to pay loan origination fees and penalties for late or missed payments.

WARNING

Consider P2P sites only if your business is located in a state that's open to P2P lending and only if your company has been established for several years. You must have revenues that meet stipulated minimum requirements, you must back your application with a strong personal credit rating, and you must be prepared for the steep fees you'll pay for the money you get.

Microfinancing

Also called *microcredit*, microfinancing brings financial services to small business owners who lack access to financial services or lending opportunities. The website www.microfinanceinfo.com defines microfinance as "banking the unbankables," explaining that "banks are for people with money, not for people without money."

REMEMBER

Microfinancing unlocks entrepreneurial opportunity in developing and developed markets alike:

>> **Microfinance aids entrepreneurs in the developing world** with small loans of the size and type that earned Muhummad Yunus, founder of Grameen Bank in Bangladesh, the Nobel Peace Prize in 2006.

Loans for amounts as low as $25 help create small business opportunity in poor communities around the world. Nonprofit microfinance sites like Kiva (www.kiva.org), Grameen Foundation (www.grameenfoundation.org), and Global Giving (www.globalgiving.org), among others, raise funds for distri-bution as loans to those who are working to create better lives for themselves and their families.

>> **Microfinance helps small-scale entrepreneurs in developed market areas** by lending amounts smaller than the loan requests considered by most major financial institutions. Most small business bank loans are for amounts around $140,000. Most SBA-guaranteed loans are even higher. Yet the funding needs of many small-scale entrepreneurs are usually for loan amounts of $50,000 or less.

The Small Business Administration (SBA) Microloan program addresses this smaller-scale need with small short-term loans, averaging $13,000, available through intermediary lenders. For information, check out www.sba.gov/content/microloan-program.

Also look into the offerings of the nonprofit microfinance provider AccionUSA at us.accion.org/.

Merchant cash advances

Merchant cash advances require no collateral. They don't even require a strong business history or high credit rating. If you're thinking, *there has to be a catch*, here it is: Merchant cash advances are expensive.

A merchant cash advance allows a business that has high credit card sales volume to receive a lump sum of funding, based on monthly sales volume. In return for the up-front funding, the business agrees to allow the funding business to keep a portion of all future credit card sales, often deducted daily, for as long as it takes to pay off the cash advance and the fees that come with it. Be aware because those fees often mount up to 30 percent or more of the amount originally advanced.

WARNING

Businesses that conduct a large amount of sales volume through credit card transactions — and that have no access to lower-price funding — need to weigh a few cautions before committing to accept a cash advance.

FACT CHECK: WHERE BUSINESS FUNDING COMES FROM

Especially if your business is in the tech arena, you can easily think everyone who is anyone has caught the eye and captured the partnership of a venture firm or angel investor. Think again. Following are findings, based on a Kauffman Foundation survey, of where businesses on the *Inc. Magazine* roster of fastest-growing US companies got their funding.

- Personal savings: 67.2 percent

- Bank loans: 51.8 percent

- Credit card: 34.0 percent

- Family: 20.9 percent

- Business acquaintances: 11.9 percent

- Angel investors: 7.7 percent

- Close friends: 7.5 percent

- Venture capitalists: 6.5 percent

- Government grants: 3.8 percent

It's worth noting that 13.6 percent of the fastest-growing businesses reported that they had never used financing, while the vast majority relied on their own savings or funds from friends and family to launch their businesses.

>> The cost of funding through merchant cash advances is higher than nearly any lending option.

>> Changing credit card providers during a cash advance agreement is difficult.

>> The agreed-upon deduction from credit card receipts reduces the revenue you receive from each sale and the cash flow you usually count on.

Merchant cash advances have been around for a decade or so, but more recently players like PayPal (www.paypal.com) and Square (https://squareup.com/capital) have gotten involved and cash advances have become a more frequently used route to quick and often last-resort funding.

Reaching into deep pockets

It sounds like a match made in heaven — entrepreneur with great business idea but no money finds like-minded entrepreneur with money in search of a great idea. In fact, such partnerships can live happily ever after. Realize, though, that businesses that form successful investor partnerships represent a microscopically small percentage of start-ups and that nearly all share a lineup of similar traits.

>> They have a business idea that fills a unique marketplace void, that's proven to be capable of attracting paying customers, that's able to *scale up* or grow profitably into a large enterprise, and that isn't likely to be easily replicated or disrupted.

>> They establish an up-front agreement that defines how much control the investment partner or partners will exercise over the business strategy, planning, and day-to-day operations.

>> Above all, the parties all get along. It may sound obvious, but a good working relationship with an investment partner can help smooth the inevitable bumps on the road to success.

When it comes to forming investor partnerships, the odds are low, but the rewards are high. The next sections explain the options.

Venture capital

Venture capitalists are individuals or, more often, professional asset managers (in other words, investor groups) who seek a high rate of return for capital invested in businesses, whether at start-up, called *seed capital,* or during growth phases, called *early-stage* and *expansion-stage financing.* Venture capitalists scrutinize hundreds of plans, pursuing only those they believe will reward funds invested with fast-growing, significant returns and a successful *investor exit* or cash-out by a designated date.

When venture capitalists are impressed by a business concept and confident that the management team has what it takes to make the business succeed, they fork over sizeable sums. The catch is that they want something in return, and usually that something is a big role in controlling your business, a major chunk of the ownership, and a clear way to recoup and realize a substantial return on their investment.

Venture capital tends to flow when the economy is booming and slow to a trickle when it hits hard times. Check out Gust (www.gust.com) for free online tools and information from an investor network endorsed by the world's leading business angel and venture capital associations.

Angel investors

Angels are successful and wealthy entrepreneurs who buy into up-and-coming companies, offering not only money but also expertise and guidance. Angels make funding decisions more rapidly than venture capitalists, largely because they operate independently rather than on behalf of a group of investors. Additionally, angels take greater risks than venture capitalists, funding businesses at earlier stages of their life cycles and entertaining smaller financing requests. However, like venture capitalists, angels usually want a piece of the equity pie.

Don't approach angels if your business isn't up and running and if it isn't likely to grow at a double-digit rate and deliver a high return on the funds you seek. Also, steer clear of angel funding if you don't want investor involvement and the scrutiny that comes with it.

Before approaching angel investors, be ready to present your business plan, your business model, and proof that it works to generate revenue, has established an impressive early track record, and that five-year financial projections indicate your business will grow quickly and will deliver profits to both you and the angel by a specified investor-exit date.

Your most likely source for angel investment is either through a high net-worth individual you know or an accredited investor you reach through networks such as Gust.com (previously called AngelSoft) and www.angellist.com.

Getting wise about crowdfunding approaches

Crowdfunding raises small amounts of money from a great number of people, usually through an Internet campaign, to fund anything from disaster relief to music or film productions to, most recently, business start-ups.

For entrepreneurs, crowdfunding takes two forms: Reward-based campaigns and equity-based campaigns.

Reward-based crowdfunding

Reward-based campaigns are the ones that have been around the longest. For years, they've been providing a financial lift-off for businesses that can't qualify for bank loans and whose owners can't call on deep-pocketed family and friends to fill the start-up coffers until product sales can cover business costs. Instead, popular crowdfunding platforms like Kickstarter (`www.kickstarter.com`) and Indigogo (`www.indiegogo.com`) enable businesses to make a broad-reaching appeal for funds, rewarding those who pledge money with perks, rewards, products, or services.

The sites require you to make a concise and engaging funding request accompanied by an offer of interest to those being solicited (a record or concert tickets from an entertainer, for example). Plus, you have to follow the model of the funding platform you choose to use. Some platforms are *all-or-nothing*, meaning no contributions are accepted unless a minimum pledge level is reached.

EXAMPLE

All platforms collect a small percentage of funds received as their hosting and processing fee, and nearly every successful effort begins with strong momentum from an impressive groundswell of first-day contributions, usually from friends, family, customers, and Facebook followers. For example, the Nikola Tesla museum project raised more than a million dollars in the first 9 days before going on to meet its full 45-day campaign goal.

Among the most successful reward-based crowdfunded campaigns are a number of names you likely know:

>> The space simulation game Star Citizen broke the world record for crowdfunded games by raising $4.2 million. Contributors were rewarded with game currency.

>> The virtual reality headset by Oculus Rift exceeded a $250,000 crowdfunding goal by raising a whopping $2.4 million before being purchased by Facebook for $2 billion. (Contributors are still posting that they wish they'd received stock instead of the thank-you notes, T-shirts, and headsets they received as contribution rewards.)

>> *Reading Rainbow,* a TV show which encourages kids to read, raised more than $5 million in 35 days. Contributors received gifts ranging from bumper stickers to a private dinner with *Reading Rainbow* host LeVar Burton.

Exciting as these examples are, realize they're indicative of what's possible but not of what most crowdfunded campaigns can expect. More typical is the success story of a documentary about medical aid in Haiti, which surpassed a $1,500 crowdfunding goal by raising $3,500 from friends and friends of friends, who form the profile of most small-scale crowdfunding contributors.

Before you start making your list of rewards and planning your crowdfunding appeal and video, here are some statistics from the 2015 Crowdfunding Industry Report to help you base your funding expectations in reality:

>> Kickstarter reports that fewer than 40 percent of campaigns reach their funding goal, and for tech-based campaigns the success rate is even lower.

>> The campaigns with huge goals make headlines, but campaigns with a goal closer to $10,000 have the highest success rate.

>> The average successful campaign receives approximately $7,000.

>> The average failed project brings in less than $1,000.

Crowdfunding for equity investments

In 2016, under rules approved by the US Securities and Exchange Commission (SEC), private start-ups and small businesses can offer a share of their financial returns or profits to US citizens (called *non-accredited investors* in government jargon) who invest through crowdfunding campaigns.

In other words, instead of receiving rewards of logo-emblazoned items or early-release products, equity crowdfunding participants will receive shares of private businesses.

The rules for so-called equity crowdfunding fall under the US Jumpstart Our Business Startups (JOBS) Act. The act allows entrepreneurs to raise up to $1 million over a 12-month period from individuals, who can invest up to $2,000 or 5 percent of annual income or net worth, whichever is greater, or up to 10 percent, if annual income and net worth are equal to more than $100,000. No investor can invest more than $100,000 in one year.

As with traditional crowdfunding campaigns, businesses need to reach their full funding goal before accepting any of the investment commitments. Plus, businesses need to meet disclosure and financial reporting requirements that vary depending on equity-raising goals.

WARNING

Equity crowdfunding is still in its shake-out stage. Which sites will become the Kickstarters and Indiegogos of equity crowdfunding is still to be determined. Search for "equity crowdfunding portals" to find out about emerging players. Turn to sites like www.crowdfunder.com for checklists to use when planning an equity crowdfunding campaign. Above all, get advice from your business attorney before venturing into this new funding opportunity.

Chapter 9

Tallying Your Financial Situation

S ome people love adding and subtracting columns of numbers. And then there is everyone else. Fortunately, most businesses owners don't have to do it themselves. They can turn to accountants. Small businesses and sole proprietors can turn to bookkeeping and financial forecasting computer programs.

This chapter helps you understand your business finances and the way the numbers are typically presented. This chapter also makes you better at keeping an eye on your money and assessing your financial situation with an eye to forecasting your company's financial future. As plenty of businesses have found out the hard way, not knowing your financial situation can be disastrous. So bring out the calculators and get ready to talk finance.

Decoding Financial Terminology

People hyperventilate when they hear the term *financial statements,* as if someone just told them that the rest of the conversation would take place in an arcane foreign language with no translation assistance.

Well, here's good news. You can master the language of business finance by understanding three key terms:

>> **Income statement:** This report, also called *earnings reports* or *profit-and-loss statement,* summarizes how much money your business earned and spent up until the minute the report was run. It reports your revenues over a given period of time and then subtracts all the costs of doing business over that same period to arrive at your *net profit.*

>> **Balance sheet:** This report captures a financial snapshot of your business at a particular moment in time, usually the very end of a month or year. The top half of the balance sheet tallies up your *assets* (the things your business owns that have monetary value). The bottom half combines your *liabilities* (the money your business owes) with your *equity* (the portion of your assets that you own as opposed to what you've borrowed and owe). The top and bottom portions of this report must balance each other out — in other words assets must equal the total of liabilities and owner equity — hence the name.

>> **Cash-flow statement:** This financial report tracks money that flows in and out of your business over a given period of time (weekly, monthly, quarterly, yearly, or over a period of years). The top half of your cash-flow statement details funds coming in and going out of your business over the statement period; the bottom half shows the resulting changes in your cash position. The top and bottom halves must match up in order to reconcile the net effect of the inflow and outflow of money with the difference in cash holdings over the report period.

Putting Together an Income Statement

Your company's income statement calculates your *net profit,* or bottom line, using this basic formula:

Net profit = Revenue – Costs

The result of this calculation gives a measurement of how your business performed financially over a certain time period. The IRS, of course, is interested in your income statement for the taxable year. Seasonal businesses — such as winter ski resorts or summer river–rafting operations for example — view statements quarterly, and many other businesses run reports monthly to keep tabs on their bottom line. The following sections introduce income statements and how to use them.

Knowing the sections of an income statement

Having a firm understanding of the numbers an income statement contains can help you see how your business is performing.

EXAMPLE

Take a look at how a gift shop called Broad Street Emporium uses income statements to manage business finances. Figure 9-1 shows the company's annual revenues, costs, and profits for the most recent year as well as for the previous year. By comparing statements for two years in a row, the owners can see how their financial performance has changed over time.

Broad Street Emporium Income Statement				
INCOME STATEMENT AS OF DECEMBER 31				
			Last Year	**Previous Year**
1	Revenue on in-store sales		624,000	595,000
	Revenue on catalog sales	+	105,000	+ 95,000
	Gross Revenue	$	**729,000**	$ **690,000**
2	Cost of goods sold	–	448,000	– 445,000
	Gross Profit	$	**281,000**	$ **245,000**
3	Sales, general, and administration	–	126,000	– 108,000
	Depreciation expense	–	20,000	– 20,000
	Operating Profit	$	**135,000**	$ **117,000**
4	Dividend and interest income	+	3,000	+ 3,000
	Interest expense	–	24,000	– 25,000
	Profit Before Taxes	$	**114,000**	$ **95,000**
5	Taxes	–	22,000	– 19,000
	Net Profit	$	**92,000**	$ **76,000**

© John Wiley & Sons, Inc.

FIGURE 9-1: An income statement summarizes your revenue and costs and shows your net profit.

The Broad Street Emporium income statement includes five sections. Each one provides important information about the company's financial condition.

Section 1: Gross revenue

In business finance, *gross revenue* refers to the total of all sales income collected by your business without subtracting any costs.

TIP

Depending on your business, your revenue may come from sales of a single product or product line or from a number of different products and services. If you have more than one revenue stream, itemize revenues from each source so that you can see at a glance where your revenue is really coming from and then add the categories to arrive at your gross revenue.

In the case of Broad Street Emporium, gross revenue comes from two major sources: money taken in via in-store retail sales and money collected through the store's catalog sales.

Section 2: Gross profit

In general, *profit* is the money that you get to keep after all the bills are paid. *Gross profit*, also called *gross income*, is the first stage of profit. It equals gross revenue minus the *costs of goods sold*, which covers the costs directly associated with producing, assembling, or purchasing what you have to sell.

To Broad Street Emporium, costs of goods sold include the wholesale costs of the merchandise displayed on the gift shop's shelves and in its catalog. To a service business, costs of goods sold include costs directly related to supplying or delivering the service. To a manufacturer, costs of goods sold include costs for raw materials and the labor, utilities, and facilities needed to put the product together.

TIP

You'll have to make judgment calls regarding which expenses count as costs of goods. After you decide, keep your definition consistent over time so that as you monitor gross profit, you're able to compare apples with apples.

Section 3: Operating profit

After you have subtracted your costs of goods from your gross revenue to arrive at your gross profit, the next step is to calculate your *operating profit* (also referred to as the *operating income* or *EBIT*, which stands for earnings before income and taxes).

TIP

To figure your operating profit, follow these steps:

1. **Subtract your *operating expenses* from your gross profit.**

   Operating expenses, also known as *general and administrative expenses* or *SG&A (sales, general, and administration expenses)*, include the costs involved in operating your business, including salaries, research and development costs, marketing expenses, travel and entertainment, utility bills, rent, office supplies, and other overhead expenses.

2. **Account for something called *depreciation expenses*.**

   When you purchase big-ticket items for your business — maybe a car to call on clients, a computer system, or even a building for offices, warehouse space, or other facilities — what you're really doing is exchanging one asset (cash in the bank) for another asset (the car, computer, or building). The business assets you acquire all have useful life spans, so one way to spread out the costs of these assets over the number of years they're actually in service is to calculate and deduct *depreciation expenses* each year.

3. **Subtract your operating and depreciation expenses from your gross profit.**

Operating profit = Gross profit – Operating expenses and Depreciation expenses

EXAMPLE

On the Broad Street Emporium income statement, operating expenses reflect staff salaries, advertising costs, and production and delivery of the store's catalog three times a year. In addition, the company takes depreciation expenses for its store-front building, computer system, and delivery van.

WARNING

When calculating your operating profit, watch your overhead expenses like a hawk. They're not tied directly to your products and services, so they don't contribute directly to your revenue. But if they get out of line, they can quickly eat away at your gross profits.

Section 4: Profit before taxes

Profit before taxes takes into account any income that your business made on investments of any sort and subtracts any interest expenses you paid over the statement period.

Profit before taxes = Operating profit + Investment income – Interest expenses

REMEMBER

You keep investment income and interest expenses apart from your operating profit because they result from money management and aren't really part of your business operations. For one thing, the amount of interest you pay depends on how you've structured your business financially, not on the business itself. For another thing, interest absolutely, positively has to be paid on a strict and unforgiving schedule.

Section 5: Net profit

Net profit (also called *net earnings, net income,* or *bottom line*) is what's left after you subtract your final expenses from your total business income. As you read that sentence, you're probably thinking, "Final expenses? We've already deducted every cost under the sun. What's left to subtract?" In a word, taxes.

Depending on how you structured your business, you may or may not pay taxes directly on its profits. If you're a sole proprietor or if your business is a partnership, for example, your profits are funneled straight to the owners for tax purposes.

But if your business pays taxes, you need to subtract those taxes before you state your final profit. Check out Chapter 3 for details on different ways to structure your business.

EXAMPLE

Figure 9-1 shows that after Broad Street Emporium paid its taxes for the year, the business was left with a net profit of $92,000. That's good news because it amounts to a 21 percent increase over the previous year.

Now it's your turn: Creating your income statement

TIP

To develop an income statement for your business, use the template provided on Form 9-1 at www.dummies.com/go/businessplanskit (which looks just like Figure 9-1 except all the entries are blank). If your business isn't up and running yet, use the template to project what you expect in terms of revenues and expenses. Doing so serves as a good basis when you prepare your new business budget.

More and more companies use accounting or financial software, such as Quickbooks, which makes the task much easier and can even link directly to your bank accounts. If you use accounting software, you can skip Form 9-1. But we encourage you to print your most recent income statement and carefully look it over. Make sure you understand each entry and that your overall financial picture makes sense to you.

REMEMBER

Your income statement is an essential part of your written business plan. If your venture is up and running, include statements for the last year or two for comparison purposes. Also include income statement projections — whether yours is an existing business or a start-up. Show your income plans for a year or two, or even up to five years into the future. Refer to the "Forecasting and Budgeting" section near the end of this chapter for more information.

Creating Your Balance Sheet

Your balance sheet gives you a snapshot of what your business is worth at a particular moment in time. To make the calculation, tally up the monetary value of everything your business owns and then subtract the money you owe to others. What you own are your assets and what you owe are your liabilities. The difference between the two is what your business is worth, usually referred to as the *equity* in your business. The following sections take a closer look at a balance sheet and how you can use one.

Identifying the sections on a balance sheet

You can represent your balance sheet in a really straightforward equation:

Equity = Assets – Liabilities

In a bizarre attempt to ensure job security, however, accountants rewrote the equation as follows:

Assets = Liabilities + Equity

This equation is the very same as the other — it's just harder to grasp. Go figure. Anyway, the layout of your company's balance sheet follows this second equation. The top half of the balance sheet lists your business assets, divided into a number of basic categories. The bottom half lists your liabilities by category and then tacks on your equity in the business.

REMEMBER

The total value of assets must be equal to the value of liabilities plus equity. In other words, the top half has to balance out the bottom half. *How* they balance each other tells you a lot about your company's financial health.

TIP

At the very least, put together a balance sheet on the last day of each year. Include the numbers for the end of the previous year as well so you can compare how your assets, liabilities, and equity have changed over the year.

EXAMPLE

Figure 9-2 shows the balance sheet for the Broad Street Emporium gift shop as of December 31 of the most recent year. It also shows numbers for the end of the previous year for comparison purposes. Read on for explanations of each section.

Section 1: Current assets

Current assets represent all the items your business owns that are liquid enough to be converted into cash within a year. Anything with monetary value that your business owns is an asset. Your balance sheet shows not only how much your assets are worth but also how long it would take you to convert them into cold, hard cash. The length of time needed to dispose of an asset is often described in terms of *liquidity.* The more *liquid* an asset, the faster you can sell it off.

Current assets include

>> **Cash:** You can't get more liquid than cash. Cash can be anything from the bills and change in the cash register or the petty cash drawer to the money you have in checking or savings accounts at the bank.

Broad Street Emporium
Balance Sheet

BALANCE SHEET ON DECEMBER 31

Assets		Last Year	Previous Year
1	**Current Assets**		
	Cash	45,000	36,000
	Investment portfolio	+ 20,000	+ 17,000
	Accounts receivable	+ 15,000	+ 18,000
	Inventories	+ 110,000	+ 97,000
	Prepaid expenses	+ 1,000	+ 1,000
	Total Current Assets	$ 191,000	$ 169,000
2	**Fixed Assets**		
	Land	100,000	100,000
	Buildings	+ 295,000	+ 295,000
	Equipment	+ 15,000	+ 10,000
	Accumulated depreciation	− 65,000	− 45,000
	Total Fixed Assets	$ 345,000	$ 360,000
3	**Intangibles (goodwill, patents)**	$ 10,000	$ 10,000
4	**TOTAL ASSETS**	$ 546,000	$ 539,000
Liabilities and Owners' Equity		**Last Year**	**Previous Year**
5	**Current Liabilities**		
	Accounts payable	4,000	6,000
	Accrued expenses payable	+ 12,000	+ 11,000
	Total Current Liabilities	$ 16,000	$ 17,000
6	**Long-term Liabilities**		
	Building mortgage	210,000	214,000
	Total Long-term Liabilities	$ 210,000	$ 214,000
7	**Owners' Equity**		
	Invested capital	200,000	195,000
	Accumulated retained earnings	+ 120,000	+ 113,000
	Total Owners' Equity	$ 320,000	$ 308,000
8	**TOTAL LIABILITIES and EQUITY**	$ 546,000	$ 539,000

FIGURE 9-2:
Your balance sheet shows your company's worth.

- >> **Investment portfolio:** Cash is nice, but it's even nicer to see your money put to work. Investments may include money market accounts, government bonds, or other reasonably safe securities.

- >> **Accounts receivable:** This asset consists of money customers owe you for products or services you've already delivered. If you provide products on credit, you may give customers 30, 60, or 90 days to pay.

  WARNING

  Watch your accounts receivable carefully. One deadbeat customer can throw your numbers for a loop.

- >> **Inventories:** This item reflects the equivalent cash value of products or supplies you have on hand. Coming up with a realistic estimate for the value of your inventories is often tricky. When in doubt, stay on the conservative side. Your balance sheet should reflect what you can reasonably expect to receive if you have to liquidate these assets.

- >> **Prepaid expenses:** Your business may have paid for services you haven't yet received — professional service retainers or insurance premiums, for example. List these payments as part of your current assets.

Current assets, especially the most liquid ones, are extremely important to your business. They represent reserves available to fund day-to-day operations or to draw on in case of a financial crunch. Figure 9-2 shows that Broad Street Emporium had a total of $191,000 in current assets as of the end of the most recent year, including $65,000 in cash or securities.

Section 2: Fixed assets

Fixed assets are usually big, expensive, and meant to last a long time, so they're not very liquid. Fixed assets include

- >> **Land:** If your company owns land — the ground under your office building, for example — you list it separately from your office building on the balance sheet. Unlike other fixed assets, land doesn't depreciate on your balance sheet because it's considered an asset that doesn't wear out over time. For that reason, you leave the same land value on the books year after year. Land can appreciate in value, of course. But you still keep the value the same on the books until you sell the land.

- >> **Buildings:** As far as your balance sheet is concerned, the value of buildings is equal to the original price you paid for them plus the amounts you've spent on improvements over the years. Again, any appreciation in value that may have occurred is only recorded if you sell the building.

- >> **Equipment:** Equipment includes anything and everything you acquire for your business that's meant to last more than a year. Machinery, cars, office equipment, computers, telephones, and furniture all fall into this category.

When you enter the value of each asset on your balance sheet, use the actual price you paid for it. If you didn't pay cash, assign a reasonable value to include on your balance sheet.

>> **Accumulated depreciation:** Each big-ticket item that you acquire for your business has a useful life span. *Depreciation* measures the decline in useful value of each fixed asset over time. Don't worry, you don't have to come up with the numbers; the IRS provides standard depreciation schedules, depending on the kind of assets you own. *Accumulated depreciation* sums up the value loss of all your assets over your years of ownership and reduces the total value of your fixed assets accordingly.

REMEMBER

On your balance sheet, the value of a fixed asset is based on the original price paid minus any accumulated depreciation according to the IRS's general depreciation schedule. The resulting number may have very little to do with the price you would receive if you sold the asset or the price you would pay if you replaced it.

EXAMPLE

Broad Street Emporium shows fixed assets valued at $345,000 after accumulated depreciation is taken into account, including $5,000 spent on new equipment during the most recent year. Also during the recent year, the book value of all assets was reduced by $20,000 because of depreciation. That same $20,000, by the way, shows up as a depreciation expense on the income statement illustrated in Figure 9-1.

Section 3: Intangibles

Intangibles are assets that, by definition, are hard to get your arms around, but these intangibles can turn out to be extremely important to your business. Intangible assets include things like an exclusive contract to supply services, a franchise ownership, or a hard-to-get license or permit to do business. An intangible asset can also be a patent that protects an invention, software technology, or a production process. Intangible assets are clearly valuable to the company that owns them, but the question is, what are they really worth?

Intangibles usually aren't reflected as assets, although some companies allocate a symbolic $1 on the balance sheet to indicate that intangible assets are there and are valuable but aren't measurable. The exception is a purchased patent that may be amortized over the life of the patent.

REMEMBER

As a business owner, one key intangible asset you have is goodwill. *Goodwill* represents the positive value of a company's name, including its customer relations, its workforce, its reputation, and other factors that contribute to the company's ability to succeed in its marketplace. When a buyer purchases a company at a price above its fair market value, the buyer is probably paying extra to acquire the company's goodwill. Goodwill is only realized when a business is sold, and so it's not carried on a balance sheet unless it was acquired as part of a business purchase.

EXAMPLE

For example, Broad Street Emporium bought an existing gift shop a number of years ago and paid $10,000 more than the net value of the shop's assets at the time. The Broad Street Emporium's balance sheet lists that goodwill purchase as an intangible asset.

Section 4: Total assets

Total assets reflect the value of all the current assets, fixed assets, and intangibles that your company owns. Your assets include equipment, inventory, real property, and anything that is assigned a monetary value on your balance sheet. Your current assets are an indication of your company's liquidity or its ability to pay its current obligations. Your total assets minus total liabilities provide an indication of your company's solvency.

EXAMPLE

Figure 9-2 shows that Broad Street Emporium increased its total assets by $7,000 to $546,000 last year — the result of increases in current assets and fixed assets, as you see in the upcoming cash-flow statement section.

Section 5: Current liabilities

Liabilities are amounts of money you owe to creditors in the form of bills that are due, bank loans you've taken out, and bonds or warrants that you may have issued to raise money. The basic idea behind these so-called financial instruments is always the same: You receive money or something else of value in exchange for the promise to pay back the debt over a certain period of time (usually with interest). Sometimes an asset that you own secures the debts. (If you don't pay back what you owe as promised, the creditor can take the asset away from you.) Other times the debts are unsecured.

REMEMBER

Current liabilities represent short-term debts that you have to repay within one year. These liabilities are closely tied to the current assets listed on the top half of your balance sheet because you have to pay them off with those assets. In most cases, current liabilities fall into two groups:

>> **Accounts payable:** These liabilities come in the form of bills that haven't yet been paid for such things as utilities, telephone service, office supplies, professional services, raw materials, wholesale goods, or other invoices from providers or suppliers.

>> **Accrued expenses payable:** In addition to outside accounts payable, your business continuously accrues liabilities related to salaries or wages (if you have employees), insurance premiums, interest on bank loans, and taxes you owe. Any obligations that are unpaid at the time you run your balance sheet get grouped together in this category.

To figure out the money available on a day-to-day basis to keep your business up and running — known as your *working capital* — subtract your current liabilities from your current assets.

Working capital = Current assets – Current liabilities

The Broad Street Emporium owners have $175,000 in working capital — a strong position that provides them with the financial flexibility to carry on their business activities and fund operations during fluctuations of revenue and expenditures.

Section 6: Long-term liabilities

Long-term liabilities are major financial obligations that you take on to get your company up and running or to expand your business operations. You may get a 10-year bank loan, for example, or issue bonds to a group of investors to be repaid in 15 years. These liabilities are often at the very heart of your company's financial structure.

Broad Street Emporium has one long-term liability: A $210,000 building mortgage that the company will pay off in 26 years.

Section 7: Owner's equity

Equity is the part of a business that the owner or owners actually own. Think of equity this way: Lots of people who say they own their homes really own just a piece of their homes. Banks or mortgage companies own the rest. The same is true for business owners and their businesses.

What's more, the equity in your business might be distributed among a number of owners with various strings attached, defining when equity can be sold or how it can be used. You may be the only owner of your company, or your company may be a publicly traded corporation owned by tens of thousands of investors. Under any ownership structure, though, when you strip away all the complexity, owner equity comes from two basic sources of equity: money coming from outside investors and money generated from profits that are kept inside the company. These two forms of equity are called

>> **Invested capital:** Money invested in your business comes from various sources, including cash you put up as a principal owner of the business or cash you raise by selling small pieces of your company in the form of stock to outside investors. Outside equity may be privately held, or, when your business is big enough, you may decide to go for an initial public offering (IPO) — making shares of your company available for sale on a public stock exchange. No matter how you exchange equity for cash, it's all lumped together as invested capital.

>> **Accumulated retained earnings:** When your business turns a profit (meaning when revenues exceed all costs and expenses), you face the happy decision of what to do with the windfall. You may decide to give some of it back to the owners and investors in the form of *dividends*. Or you may plow some of the profits back into the business so that you can grow bigger and, as a result, create more equity for everyone who has a stake in your company. *Accumulated retained earnings* represent all the profits you've poured back into your business.

Total owner's equity is the sum of invested capital and accumulated retained earnings, which together equal the value of the part of the business that the owners actually own.

Total owner's equity = Invested capital + Accumulated retained earnings

The owners of Broad Street Emporium have a total equity of $320,000: $200,000 from owner investments and $120,000 from profits they've poured back into the company over the years.

Section 8: Total liabilities and equity

Total liabilities and equity sums up the value of a company's assets. It combines the current and long-term liabilities that your company is responsible for with the amount of owner's equity in the business. Basically, this means that your business assets are worth the sum of what you own plus what you owe.

Current Liabilities + Long-term Liabilities + Owner's Equity = Total Assets

As you can see, at the close of last year, the top and bottom halves of the Broad Street Emporium balance sheet were in balance at $546,000. In other words, the sum of the company's total liabilities and total owner's equity correctly equaled the total of the company's assets.

Building your own balance sheet

You guessed it: You need to make a balance sheet of your own. If you're using accounting software, you can complete the task with the push of a button. However, your computer-generated balance sheet is only as good as the numbers you entered in the first place, so take the time to scrutinize them carefully.

If you're starting from scratch or just want to get a hands-on feel for what a balance sheet really means, get out a pencil and create your balance sheet the old-fashioned way — on a piece of paper, using the template provided on Form 9-2 (which looks just like Figure 9-2 but with blank spaces to enter figures showing your own assets, liabilities, and owner's equity).

Include your company's balance sheet in the financial review section of your written business plan to provide a snapshot of what you own, what you owe, and what your company is worth. If you're already in business, include year-end numbers for the most recent two years for easy comparison.

Constructing a Cash-Flow Statement

A *cash-flow statement* tells you how money flowed in and out of your business over a certain time period and how assets of your business changed as a result. Cash-flow statements offer a great way to forecast and plan before plugging numbers into your income statement or balance sheet. Your balance sheet and income statements report revenues as they are earned and expenses as they are incurred, which is called *accrual basis accounting.* The cash-flow statement converts the accrual basis of accounting to a cash basis. Instead of looking at what you've earned and what you owe, it looks at what you've collected and spent, and it lets you see at a glance whether more cash is going out than coming in, or vice versa.

Review your cash flow at least monthly, using a report that presents side-by-side numbers for two periods so you can track changes in your cash position. We guide you through the numbers you need to track, using Broad Street Emporium as an example.

First, to see how a cash-flow statement measures financial activity and tracks the effects of changes in your cash position, look at Figure 9-3, which shows the cash-flow statement for the Broad Street Emporium gift store as of December 31 of the most recent year alongside cash-flow entries for the previous year for comparison purposes.

On the bottom line, you can see that after all the revenue was collected and all the bills were paid, $12,000 was left over, leaving the company in what is known as a *positive cash position.* The following sections explain how cash flowed before arriving at the final year-end position.

Section 1: Total funds in

The cash-flow statement tracks every single dollar as it comes into your company — and not a second before. You can't show the revenue on sales, for example, until you actually have the payment in hand. Following are the income sources that the cash-flow statement tracks:

>> **Receipts on sales:** The money you take in from the sales of your products or services show up in this section, but only after they're deposited in the bank.

Billing a customer may be enough to generate a revenue entry on your income statement, but you can't include the amount on your cash-flow statement until you have a deposit slip to show for it.

>> **Dividend and interest income:** Any interest you make on your business bank accounts or any earnings from your investment portfolio appear in this section — *if* the payments come in during the statement period.

>> **Invested capital:** If your company receives funding from investors, on the date the money reaches your business, it's entered here on your cash-flow statement.

EXAMPLE

The Broad Street Emporium cash-flow statement (see Figure 9-3) shows that the gift store took in $740,000 cash last year. That number syncs with entries on the company's income statement (refer to Figure 9-1) and balance sheet (refer to Figure 9-2). Okay, to be honest, you have to do a little work before you can see how it syncs, but in a minute it'll all make sense.

Here's how it works: The income statement shows gross income of $729,000 and income from dividends and interest of $3,000. Plus, the balance sheet shows that the company also received $5,000 of investment capital from its owners. (This money is reflected in the entry for invested capital, which went from $195,000 the previous year to $200,000 last year.) Additionally, the company collected $3,000 in outstanding accounts receivable last year (shown on the balance sheet as a reduction in accounts receivable from $18,000 to $15,000). Together, these funds total $740,000, exactly as indicated by the cash-flow statement. Ta-da!

Section 2: Total funds out

This section of the cash-flow statement shows where the money went. You may notice a number of entries that don't appear as expenses on your income statement — such as buildings and equipment, long-term debt reduction, and distributions to owners. The reason is because these cash outlays don't result directly from the cost of doing business, and therefore they aren't listed on the income statement, though they're tracked on the cash-flow statement.

EXAMPLE

Figure 9-3 shows that Broad Street Emporium used $728,000 cash last year. Refer to that figure as you walk through these items:

>> **Cost of goods acquired:** This line item includes all the products and materials that you paid for during the cash-flow statement period. It doesn't matter whether you sold the goods you acquired or whether they went into your inventory; if you paid to acquire them during this statement period, they show up here.

Broad Street Emporium
Cash Flow Statement

CASH FLOW AS OF DECEMBER 31

Inflow and Outflow		Last Year	Previous Year
1	**Funds Provided By:**		
	Receipts on in-store sales	626,000	596,000
	Receipts on catalog sales	+ 106,000	+ 96,000
	Dividend and interest income	+ 3,000	+ 3,000
	Invested capital	+ 5,000	+ 10,000
	Total Funds In	$ 740,000	$ 705,000
2	**Funds Used For:**		
	Cost of goods acquired	461,000	442,000
	Sales, general, and administration	+ 127,000	+ 109,000
	Interest expense	+ 24,000	+ 25,000
	Taxes	+ 22,000	+ 19,000
	Buildings and equipment	+ 5,000	+ 1,000
	Long-term debt reduction	+ 4,000	+ 3,000
	Distributions to owners	+ 85,000	+ 65,000
	Total Funds Out	$ 728,000	$ 664,000
3	**NET CHANGE IN CASH POSITION**	$ +12,000	$ +41,000
Changes by Account		**Last Year**	**Previous Year**
4	**Changes in Liquid Assets:**		
	Cash	+ 9,000	+ 28,000
	Investment portfolio	+ 3,000	+ 13,000
	Total Changes	$ 12,000	$ 41,000
5	**NET CHANGE IN CASH POSITION**	$ +12,000	$ +41,000

FIGURE 9-3: Creating a cash-flow statement helps you monitor the cash that flows into and out of your business.

© *John Wiley & Sons, Inc.*

$461,000 was expended for cost of goods acquired — a figure that matches up with the $448,000 entry for cost of goods sold shown on the company's income statement plus a balance sheet increase in company inventories of $13,000.

>> **Sales, general, and administration:** This entry covers payments you made for so-called *overhead expenses,* including everything from paper clips to payroll. When the money actually leaves your hands, you enter those expenses here. Sales, general, and administration expenses took up $127,000, including $126,000 shown on the income statement and a pay down of $1,000 in current liabilities, shown on the balance sheet.

- >> **Interest expense:** This entry reflects interest you paid out during the cash-flow statement period, whether for short-term or long-term loans that your company has taken to finance anything from inventory purchases to buildings and equipment. The company paid out $24,000 in interest expense.

- >> **Taxes:** This line item reflects tax payments you made during the cash-flow statement period. The company paid $22,000 in taxes.

- >> **Buildings and equipment:** Big-ticket items that your business purchased show up as assets on your balance sheet and in the form of depreciation (check out the section "Creating Your Balance Sheet," earlier in this chapter) on your income statement. At the time that you actually make the purchase, the amount of your purchase payment shows up here on your cash-flow statement. The gift shop owners also spent $5,000 on equipment.

- >> **Long-term debt reduction:** This entry includes the cash you paid to reduce any of your business debts. They spent $4,000 on long-term debt reduction, which you'll see reflected as an increase in equipment assets and a decrease in long-term liabilities on the balance sheet.

- >> **Distributions to owners:** If your company makes a profit and your balance sheet is strong, you're probably in a position to give some of the financial rewards back to the owners of the business. If you do, enter distributions or dividend payments in this area of the cash-flow statement. The company distributed $85,000 back to the owners of the gift shop over the year, bringing the total funds out to $728,000.

Section 3: Net change in cash position

Your *net change in cash position* is the difference between the total amount of money your business brought in and the total amount that it expended over the reporting period. To find out the net change in your cash position over a certain period, subtract all the funds that left the company from all the funds that came in to the company.

Net change = Funds that came into the company – Funds that left the company

EXAMPLE

Broad Street Emporium increased its cash position by $12,000 during the most recent year, which means it brought in $12,000 more than it paid out.

Section 4: Changes in liquid assets

The bottom half of the cash-flow statement monitors where the money goes while it's inside your company:

>> **Cash:** This entry tracks the total change in your cash reserves over the course of the statement period.

>> **Investment portfolio:** This entry tracks changes in the value of your investment portfolio over the period.

Notice that the cash-flow statement only tracks the flow of cash. It doesn't reflect changes in the value of other company assets unless those changes delivered cash that was expended or invested.

EXAMPLE

Figure 9-3 shows that, last year, Broad Street Emporium increased its cash by $9,000 and its investment portfolio by $3,000 over the previous year. These increases match up with the corresponding changes to the cash and investment portfolio entries under current assets on the company's balance sheet (refer to Figure 9-2).

Section 5: Net change in cash position

Because the top and the bottom halves of the cash-flow statement must balance, the total changes in liquid assets reflected in Section 5 should be identical to the net change in cash position shown in Section 3. In other words, you can determine a net change in cash position by subtracting money going out from money coming in or by monitoring changes to the accounts where the money is coming and going from.

Creating your own cash-flow statement

As you assemble your cash-flow statement, you'll probably notice that many of the entries are based on numbers from your income statement and your balance sheet. That's because your company's cash flow is tied closely to your revenues and costs, as well as to the assets you own and the debts you've taken on.

If you use accounting software to manage your finances, you can probably run a cash-flow statement by opening the menu and pressing a few keys.

TIP

But you may discover even more by using Form 9-3 (which looks just like Figure 9-3 only totally blank and ready for your numbers) to assemble a cash-flow statement from scratch. Form 9-3 allows you to review the previous two years. If you've been in business longer you can expand the form to look back even further in time simply by creating additional columns for more years.

COUNTING EVERY PENNY

Knowing where every penny goes can be the difference between success and failure in any business — especially during challenging economic times. Take the example of a small chain of restaurants in northern California, which had expanded when the economy was going gangbusters. When the recession hit, sales began to slip. Fortunately, the restaurant owners were tracking sales month by month, outlet by outlet. Furthermore, their financial tracking allowed them to see what customers were spending their money on. By the end of 2010, sales were down 15 percent from the year before. By the end of 2011, they had slid another 10 percent. Most analysts predicted that discretionary spending — the kind the restaurant chain had depended on most — wasn't going to recover any time soon.

The company moved quickly and proactively, guided by what their numbers told them. They decided to close the restaurant that had taken the biggest hit. They revamped the menu for the others, replacing some of the more expensive dishes with "comfort food" alternatives priced several dollars less. Noticing that wine sales were off, they also added several choices under $20. In one location, they experimented with adding a catering business on the side. When that proved a success, they phased it in for the other locations.

"A lot of restaurants, when the downturn hit, were guided by wishful thinking. They went month to month, hoping the economy would recover. And a lot of them went out of business," the owner told us. "We had the numbers in front of us. We knew exactly what our operations cost to run and exactly how much we were taking in. As soon as profits began to fall, we started planning to adapt and survive. And that made all the difference."

TIP

Include a cash-flow statement in your written plan. If your business is up and running, include year-end numbers from the past few years for comparison. If you're just getting started, use a cash-flow projection to show exactly how you'll manage the start-up period.

Forecasting and Budgeting

Your financial statements capture how your company did over a certain period (that's what your income statement is about), where your finances stand (that's your balance sheet), and what happens along the way (your cash flow). *Forecasting* tells you where your business is headed.

Financial forecasts are built around the same three financial statements covered in the preceding sections of this chapter. That means no new reports to master. But this time, you base your entries on what you see in your financial future. Then, using your projections, you develop a master budget summarizing your plans for sales, cost of goods sold, operating expenses, capital expenditures, and cash-flow projections that guide your allocation of anticipated resources toward investments and expenditures that are most likely to help your business succeed. Read on to see how to make informed predictions about your financial future and how to use a financial forecast to guide your business plan. The following sections also explain how to create a master budget and why having one in place is essential for maintaining a healthy bottom line.

Your financial forecast

Your *financial forecast* includes your best guesses about the future based on a set of assumptions about what you expect to happen down the road. A carefully thought-out financial forecast can help guide many of the decisions you make, from hiring new employees to managing your inventory. It can also help you know how much money you need on hand, called your *cash reserve.* A cash reserve contains money you can draw on at any time to meet operating expenses in case of a shortfall in revenues.

When business is going well, it's always wise to build up your cash reserves. When you start a new business, many experts advise that you have a reserve equal to at least six months of your projected expenses. The more conservative you are in your projections — and the more cash you can set aside — the stronger your position in the event of a downturn.

How much is enough? Your financial forecast can help guide you to the best answer. Here are descriptions of the three basic parts of a financial forecast and tips on how to make the most informed estimates.

Pro forma income statement

Pro forma is one of those Latin phrases that sounds more complicated than it is. In this case, *pro forma* refers to anything you're going to estimate in advance. So your pro forma income statement estimates your revenue, expenses, and profit: one, three, or even five years in the future. You may even want to subdivide the first few years into quarterly projections to allow you to monitor progress in short-term increments during the early days of your company's life. To estimate your financial future, start with these steps:

>> If you've been in business for a while, get together past income statements to serve as a starting point in making future projections.

>> If you're just starting your business, you won't have a financial history to fall back on. Instead, search out people in similar businesses, go to trade shows, do online research, and find consultants who can give you guidance. It's work, but if your financial projections end up close to the mark, the results will definitely be worth it in the end.

TIP

To assemble your estimates, think about using the business income statement template in Form 9-1, following the income statement construction steps earlier in this chapter. When you're finished, your pro forma income statement should look quite similar in format to its real counterpart. That makes comparing your projections for future performance with what really happens easy.

Carefully consider every business assumption that goes into your financial forecast. Make sure you know what each one is based on. For example:

>> If you're assuming that the economy will grow at a given rate, state the growth rate on which your plan is based.

>> If you believe that you can raise the cash you need from at least three different funding sources, be specific.

>> If you're almost certain that a new technology is going to completely change the way your industry does business, explain your reasoning.

>> If you think competition will increase in a certain segment of your market, say so.

REMEMBER

At the end of each quarter or year, take time to go back to your pro forma income statements to compare actual financial performance with projected performance. Make notes indicating where you were right and wrong. After all, practice makes perfect.

Estimated balance sheet

The difference between an estimated balance sheet and the real thing is that the estimate projects what you will own, what you will owe, and what your company will be worth year by year — looking ahead four or five years. Projecting those numbers sounds tough, and it is. But do it anyway. Even if your projections prove to be less than perfect, they provide you with a financial road map to the future.

Start by listing the assets you think you'll need to support the growth you're looking forward to. Then think about how you'll pay for those assets, and that means making major decisions about how much debt you're willing to take on, what company earnings you'll be able to plow back into the business, and how much equity you need to invest in the future.

TIP

The business balance sheet template in Form 9-2 provides a useful format that works just as well projecting the future as it does your current condition.

Projected cash flow

Want five good reasons to project your cash flow? Well, here they are. When you have a good sense of how cash will flow in and out of your business, you can

>> Anticipate inventory purchases to meet seasonal business cycles.

>> Take advantage of discount- and bulk-purchasing offers.

>> Plan equipment and building purchases to meet your growth needs.

>> Arrange financing if you're going to need it — whether that means recruiting investors, assuming long-term debt, making a personal loan, or establishing a short-term line of credit with your bank.

>> Stay in control of your finances by anticipating cash needs before they arise and meeting obligations in an organized, timely way.

TIP

When you estimate your future cash needs and sources, use the business cash-flow statement template in Form 9-3. That way, later you'll be able to compare your projections with your actual cash-flow statements. Form 9-3 allows you to look ahead over the next two years. If appropriate, you can expand the form to look even farther ahead. Many large companies do five-year cash flow projections.

REMEMBER

Without a financial forecast, your business plan is incomplete. In the financial review section of your plan include your pro forma income statement, estimated balance sheet, and projected cash-flow statement along with the business assumptions behind your projections. Then review and revise your forecasts on a regular basis. Your financial forecast just happens to be one of the most important — and fragile — parts of your business plan. Be able and willing to change it when the business circumstances around you change.

The master budget

The master budget you create for your company allows you to do two extremely important things:

>> **Live within your means.** Your master budget summarizes your company's anticipated sales, cost of goods sold, operating expenses, capital expenditures, and cash flow. By constructing your company's budget to align with your projected cash flow, you establish spending guidelines based on the most realistic financial picture you have. The budget, of course, fills in all the details.

>> **Use your money wisely.** The master budget allows you to keep spending in line with your business plan. That way, you allocate funds in the most effective way possible to achieve company long-term goals.

To prepare a budget, start with copies of your projected cash-flow statements for the next year or two, paying particular attention to the section that lists where you expect to use cash (refer to Figure 9-3). Then take each of the broad categories (cost of goods acquired; sales, general, and administration expenses; buildings and equipment; and distributions to owners) and create detailed plans for each entry, defining, for example, exactly how much money your business should spend on a service or a piece of equipment.

TIP

If your business is large enough, you may want to get a few of your colleagues involved in the budgeting process. Creating a master budget is a big job. By working with the key people around you, you spread the effort while also upping the odds that your management team will buy into the master budget that you come up with.

REMEMBER

Your master budget is a key part of your business-planning efforts, but you may or may not want to include it in your written business plan. For most of your audience, your pro forma income statement, estimated balance sheet, and projected cash-flow statement will provide enough information about your future finances.

Dealing With Regulations and Taxes

Because preparing for the inevitable is a crucial part of business planning, your new venture must address all tax liabilities and regulatory requirements. That's not always as straightforward as it sounds. Business taxes vary widely from country to country, of course. In the United States, the federal government, your state government, and in some cases your local government, such as your county or city government, may levy business taxes. Your business's tax liabilities depend in part on the business structure you choose. Chapter 3 goes into more detail about various business structures.

REMEMBER

For small businesses and sole proprietors, for example, the federal government levies four basic kinds of business taxes:

>> **Income tax:** Money owed to the feds based on an individual's income after deductions

>> **Self-employment tax:** A Social Security and Medicare tax primarily for individuals who work for themselves

>> **Employer taxes:** Taxes that employers are required to withhold from employee wages, including Social Security and Medicare

>> **Excise taxes:** Taxes paid on the purchase of certain goods or services, such as gasoline or highway usage

If you're part of a large company, chances are you have tax accountants who know this stuff backward and forward. If you're just starting out as a sole proprietor or small business, a good place to start getting information is at the Small Business Administration (www.sba.gov). The Internal Revenue Service (www.irs.gov) also provides detailed information about business taxes.

Almost every state in the United States levies business taxes. Check your state government for details.

Regulations, such as tax liabilities, widely vary, depending on the type of business you're setting up and where you plan to do business. Some kinds of businesses must be accredited. Others require you to meet environmental regulations. Regulatory requirements for businesses vary so much, in fact, that we can't offer any better advice than checking with the Small Business Administration, your state government's business development office, your county or city government, and the local Chamber of Commerce for more information. If the regulatory landscape looks especially daunting, consider hiring a lawyer to help you navigate.

REMEMBER

If you're planning a business that must meet crucial regulations in order to operate, your plan should list the applicable regulations and include important details about what you'll need to do to meet them.

Forms

The following forms designed to help you examine your financial situation are online at www.dummies.com/go/businessplanskit.

Form 9-1	**Business Income Statement**	A template that helps you determine your business profits
Form 9-2	**Business Balance Sheet**	A template for calculating your business worth
Form 9-3	**Business Cash Flow Statement**	A template for tracking inflow and outgo of cash

3

Tailoring Your Plan to Fit Your Business

Focus your plan on your specific business situation, whether it's a one-person business, a small business or start-up, a virtual business, an established business, a nonprofit organization, or a business facing sweeping changes.

Assess whether you have what it takes to be self-employed and then plan a one-person shop that grows into a money-making business.

Plan a lean, agile small business with growth strategies that match your business goals.

Recognize the benefits, risks, regulations, tools, and technologies that affect the success of a virtual businesses and then tackle the nuts and bolts of planning, building, branding, and running a business with a remote workforce and likely no physical headquarters.

Take a serious look at how business planning can help your business through times of trouble, when a crisis strikes, or when it's time to pivot to a new focus.

Create a plan for a nonprofit that achieves its mission using social networking, online presence, grant proposals, and good old-fashioned fundraising events to raise the awareness and cash necessary to do good work.

Understand the forces that drive change in your area of business and create a plan that responds to the economic, technology, marketplace, and other disruptions and uncertainties.

Chapter 10

Planning for a One-Person Business

"Be Your Own Boss!" the advertisements beckon. What could sound better? No more punching a time clock. No more answering to supervisors. No more having someone else tell you what to do.

Almost everyone who's ever felt stuck on the corporate treadmill (or in a long commute) has dreamed of ditching the rat race, printing up business cards, hanging a shingle, and opening the smallest of small businesses — a SOHO or, spelled out, a *small office/home office one-person shop.*

More and more people are doing just that. Between 2000 and 2010, the number of self-employed workers increased 40 percent. One in five people are their own bosses, according to IRS figures. If current trends continue, one in four people will be self-employed within the coming decade.

As large companies shed jobs during the latest downturn, many people discovered that working for themselves was just about the *only* option available. A one-time bank analyst we know found herself running a Manhattan-based bicycle tour business. A former city manager in California set himself up as a booking agent for indie films. When home prices tanked, a real estate agent shifted gears completely and went into business developing an app the helps users estimate home repair costs.

But a lousy job market isn't the only or even the leading reason people go into business for themselves. Plenty of people want to escape the world of bosses and annual reviews and work for themselves, and a lot of businesses are by nature one-person enterprises. Plus, technological innovations — from accounting software to mobile payment systems to project management tools, cloud-based data storage, and web-based teleconferencing — have made it easier than ever to go out on your own in business.

But working for yourself isn't for everyone, as appealing as it may sound. One laid-off newspaper journalist we know tried to make it as a freelance writer, couldn't handle the solitude, and switched back to an office job in a university communications office.

Are you ready to take the plunge? Can you make a living? Can you keep yourself disciplined and focused?

This chapter helps you plot your strategy and create an effective business plan for a SOHO. It makes the case for why a business plan is important even if you'll be the only one who ever reads it. We offer tips on the parts of business planning that matter most to those who are self-employed and help you figure out what to charge and how to get paid for your products or services. This chapter includes advice on running your one-person enterprise as a profitable business. Plus, as proof that going it alone doesn't mean you're out there all by yourself, it directs you toward resources that make your job a whole lot easier.

Having What It Takes to Succeed in a One-Person Business

Going into business on your own definitely has its rewards. No boring staff meetings. No need for employee reviews. No interpersonal conflicts. But to succeed, you need to possess certain key strengths — qualities that not everyone has. To succeed as a one-person business, chances are you'll need to

>> **Focus on doing one thing well:** How many self-employed people have you met who shuffle through a stack of business cards as they explain the many ventures they're into, personifying the old line "jack-of-all-trades, master of none." See Chapter 3 as you focus on the purpose and strategic direction of your business.

>> **Establish pricing, billing, and collection policies:** From the get-go, you need to know what you'll charge and how you'll collect. Whether you're selling time or products, your pricing must be competitive, an accurate reflection of the value of your offering, and high enough to cover your production costs plus an adequate amount of profit to your business.

>> **Run your business like a business, not like an adjunct of your personal checkbook or a hobby that you pursue in your spare time:** Small business start-ups are often born at the kitchen table. But to succeed, you need to turn your idea into a formal business structure — complete with a designated workspace, a dedicated business bank account, and a written business plan that includes financial projections and reporting systems to keep your business on track.

WARNING

People who launch one-person businesses often make the mistake of thinking they don't need a written plan. Some set off without any kind of plan at all. We can tell you from personal experience that that's a bad idea. Planning is especially important if you want to succeed as a one-person business, which is what the upcoming sections are about.

Eyeing the pros and cons of a solo career

Here's the upside: When you work for yourself, no one else tells you when to start or when to knock off for the day. You have no salary cap, no performance reviews, no corporate politics, and no supervisors. And if you create a business doing something you love to do, you don't need motivational workshops to stay passionate about your career.

But here's the rest of the story: Solo careerists usually work longer and harder than salaried employees and require more self-discipline. And, although they don't answer to bosses per se, they do deal with clients, who sometimes make tough bosses look easy in comparison.

If you work for yourself, you get to

>> Be your own boss

>> Determine your own schedule

>> Control your own economic fate

>> Choose the kinds of work you want to do

But you don't get

>> A regular paycheck

>> Employer-provided benefits

>> Unemployment insurance and workers' compensation

>> Protection under labor laws

TIP

If you're not quite sure whether you're ready to go it alone, fill out the survey in Form 10-1, which you can find at www.dummies.com/go/businessplankit. If you answer yes to five or more of the statements, you probably have what it takes to be self-employed. If not, you may want to spend more time considering your options.

Planning for success

If you decide that the self-employed life is for you, the next big step is to craft a formal plan to guide your efforts.

Don't let the word *formal* scare you. When you're planning for a one-person enterprise, formal doesn't mean long or complicated. It just means putting a plan in writing to explain your business, your product, your market, your expertise, your goals, your growth plans, and what it will take to be successful.

REMEMBER

Naturally, as a one-person business, you're the primary audience for your plan. But after you have your plan down on paper, you'll find many reasons to be glad that you wrote it in the first place. Here are just a few:

>> **To seek business financing:** If you want help financing your business, bankers and potential investors will ask to see your business plan, and especially your financial projections, for proof that that you're serious about starting and running a successful business. Providing that proof in the form of a convincing business plan is more critical than ever during challenging economic times.

>> **To create marketing materials:** Your business plan, with its description of your products and services, your target markets, and your customer benefits, will guide what you say to potential customers.

>> **To hire an employee or outsource work:** When you want to describe what you do, what kinds of customers you serve, and how you run your business, your business plan is available as reference material.

>> **To work on the right tasks and objectives:** When you're doing all the work yourself, you can easily find yourself getting sidetracked. A business plan can help you focus on the jobs that really need doing.

>> **To identify the resources you'll need to succeed:** By formulating a plan, you'll have an opportunity to think through the office equipment, technologies, and other basic stuff you'll need.

WARNING

Don't try to keep your business plan in your head. Putting it in writing is important for the following reasons:

>> It establishes a contract with yourself by stating what you intend to do and how you plan to accomplish it.

>> It lists the resources you'll need to get your business underway.

>> It formalizes your goals and objectives.

>> It provides a road map that will direct your efforts and boost your confidence, two important keys to making a solo career work.

>> It creates milestones that allow you to chart your progress and gauge your success.

>> It helps you anticipate and address funding needs before they turn into funding crises.

Chapter 1 provides more detail about the benefits of a business plan. Read it if you still have any doubts.

Avoiding legal hassles

Big companies have legal departments. Medium-sized companies have lawyers on retainer. If you're a sole proprietor, we hope you never have to deal with lawyers at all. But there may be times when it's wise to seek legal advice before going into business for yourself. These include (but aren't limited to, as lawyers would say):

>> If you have signed a nondisclosure agreement with a previous employer. This agreement may limit your ability to do certain kinds of work.

>> If you have signed a noncompetition agreement with a previous employer. This agreement may prevent you from offering certain kinds of products and services or working with certain clients.

>> If your new business venture involves intellectual capital — that is, any kind of creative work that needs to be protected by copyright or patent.

>> If your business needs to establish a legal entity.

>> If your new business requires the use of contracts.

>> If your new venture offers products or services that may be the target of a lawsuit.

>> If your business will regularly engage the services of subcontractors or other people working for you.

>> If your business sells products or services that require multiple state permits.

The good news is that many lawyers are self-employed and can be hired to perform specific discrete services, such as preparing a stock contract or reviewing a nondisclosure agreement. Getting legal advice before you open the door of your new business can save you lots of trouble later.

TIP

Also be sure to check in with an insurance agent to make sure you have the necessary liability insurance. A liability policy is especially important if you see clients at your workplace. If your work involves expensive equipment, you may also want to check to make sure it is covered in case of loss.

Putting a price on what you do

For many sole proprietors, one of the toughest parts about being self-employed is putting a price on their products or services. Pricing is a balancing act that takes into account

>> The costs involved to provide your service or to make your product

>> The prices competitors charge for similar products or services

>> The pricing level that best reflects the value you offer and that your customers seek

>> The amount you need to receive to cover all costs and deliver an adequate profit to your business

WARNING

Here's the dilemma you face: If you charge too much, your customers won't buy. If you charge too little, customers may interpret your low price as an indication of low quality and choose to buy elsewhere.

So, how much should you charge? When determining your price tag, think about

>> **How customers perceive the value of your product or service:** Flip to Chapter 7 for information on establishing the position your business holds in the competitive marketplace.

>> **Whether to offer customer-responsive pricing:** If your customers seek a wide range of solutions from your business, consider charging a base price and adding costs for extra features and benefits, thereby tailoring prices to your customers' choices. Consider tacking on an extra charge for rush jobs, especially if they cost you more to deliver.

>> **How often you can adjust your pricing:** Retailers can shift pricing as they bring in new lines or offer new promotions, for example, giving them great pricing flexibility. To build in flexibility, many service companies provide project estimates based upon their current rates without actually stating hourly fees. This approach allows the service provider to maintain pricing flexibility. You can maintain flexibility in pricing by using the option of strategic discounting, which simply means reducing the prices of key products or services as a way to move inventory, attract a new customer base, match new competitors, or meet other objectives.

Knowing how to charge

Most self-employed service providers charge in one of the following ways:

>> **By the hour:** You establish an hourly rate, keep track of your time, and bill clients for hours spent on their behalf. This is the standard pricing approach for service businesses handling small-project jobs.

>> **By the project:** You and your client agree in advance on an estimated or fixed price for a defined amount of work. This is the standard pricing approach for service businesses handling large-project jobs.

>> **By the product:** You set a price for the products you make. You may build in discounts for large orders or offer other enticements.

>> **A combined approach:** A building contractor, for example, may bid on a set of plans and establish a fee for the project. But he may also stipulate that additional client-requested work over and above that covered by the estimate is to be paid at an established hourly rate.

Other businesses follow other billing approaches. For example, authors often receive a *royalty*, or a percentage of the cover price, for each book sold. Freelance writers and editors may charge by the page or by the word. A photographer might sell rights to photos based on the way the purchaser will use them. And some professionals are paid *retainers*, or upfront payments, in return for their availability to work on an as-needed basis.

EXAMPLE

A computer network expert might charge clients a monthly retainer. In return, he agrees to keep their computer systems updated and up and running. If a client needs him, he's available 24/7. If not, he enjoys his free time. The monthly fees provide him a steady month-by-month income, and his clients couldn't be happier because they view the monthly fee as a computer insurance policy that's always in effect.

Figuring out how much to charge

Whatever payment arrangement you settle on, you still have to figure out exactly how much to charge.

TIP

If you provide a service of some sort, begin by establishing an hourly rate. Even if you end up charging by the project or product, when you know your hourly rate, you can estimate the number of hours a job will take and multiply that number by your hourly rate to arrive at your project or product cost.

One way to establish an hourly rate is to find out what other people doing similar work charge. In some cases, you can discover this information simply by talking to other independent contractors or by looking at their websites or marketing materials. You can also check with professional organizations to get an idea of what people charge in different parts of the country. Rates do vary. For example, freelance editors may be able to charge $35 an hour in St. Louis or Cedar Rapids and $75 or more in pricey places like New York or California. To be competitive, set your rates within a similar price range. If you're just starting out, you may want to begin at the lower end of the scale. If you have a long list of credentials and have earned rave reviews from clients, you can shoot for the upper end.

Another way to arrive at your pricing is to consider the following:

>> How much customers will be willing to pay for your product or service

>> How many hours a year you think you can spend on billable activities and therefore how much money you can earn at various projected hourly rates

>> How many nonbillable hours a year you need to devote to running your business

>> How much it costs you to run your business

>> Whether your projected revenue minus expenses equals an adequate profit

EXAMPLE

Say that you're a consultant who wants to personally make $80,000 a year. Further, assume that your overhead costs total $22,000 a year, plus you want to earn at least $8,000 profit annually to fund future growth. That means your consulting business needs to bring in at least $110,000 each year.

Next, say that out of each 40-hour workweek, you'll spend 12 hours running your business (doing the banking, networking, making new business calls, working with accountants, and on and on). That leaves 28 hours a week 50 weeks a year (assuming that you give yourself two weeks off for a well-earned annual getaway) for billable activities — or a total of 1,400 billable hours a year. With all that information in hand, you can divide $110,000 by 1,400 hours to arrive at an hourly billing rate of $78.50.

If that's more than you think clients will be willing to pay, you have a few choices: You can reduce your overhead costs, you can reduce your earnings and profit expectations, or you can spend more hours on billable activities, which probably means working longer weeks.

To get a good idea of how you spend your working days, use the survey in Form 10-2. This information will be useful as you work to set your hourly rate.

Tasks and Time Survey		
Activity	**Estimated Hours Spent**	
	(Week)	**(Month)**
Developing new products and services		
Producing your product or service		
Marketing and business development		
Distribution or delivery		
Customer service or client management		
Office management		
Bookkeeping and accounting		
Other:		
Other:		

© John Wiley & Sons, Inc.

FORM 10-2: Complete this form to assess where you spend your business time so you can plan your hourly billing rates accordingly.

Here's another pricing example, using a slightly different approach to the calculations.

Say a custom jeweler wants to earn $42,000 a year. Working 40 hours a week 50 weeks a year, she'll put in 2,000 hours a year. Some of those hours, though, she'll spend on marketing, billing, and business chores not directly related to making jewelry, including an occasional sunny afternoon spent enjoying the great outdoors. That leaves her with about 1,500 hours a year to actually make jewelry.

To earn $42,000 in 1,500 hours, she needs to charge $28 an hour. On top of that, she needs her pricing to cover about $9,000 in costs involved to run the business — from overhead to the costs of raw materials that go into the jewelry. This adds $6 to her hourly rate ($9,000 divided by 1,500), bringing her total to $34 an hour.

But she still has more to consider, like profit — or extra money she can use to buy better equipment or expand to a bigger studio. To earn $4,500 of profit a year to support her long-term business goals, she needs to add $3 to her rates. That brings the grand total to $37 an hour if she wants to cover her salary, expenses, and profit in 1,500 hours of billable time a year.

Of course, a jeweler usually charges by the finished piece rather than by the hour. But by knowing her hourly rate, she can estimate the number of hours that go into a piece of jewelry and multiply to set its price. For example, a set of gold earrings that require ten hours of work will cost $370 plus the cost of the gold and materials. Knowing that figure, she can do a reality check: Given her market and her competition, is this price reasonable? If it is, great. If not, she's going to have to think a little harder about her business model. (For more information on business models and other strategies, flip to Chapter 5.)

Even if you're self-employed, plan to make and set aside a profit above and beyond what you pay yourself. Doing so allows you to expand and develop your business when times are good. It also provides an important safety net, should your business experience an unforeseen setback.

TIP

Take time to figure the hourly rate you need to charge to cover your salary, overhead, and profit projections. You may want to use Form 10-3 to make sure that your rate covers all your business expenses. Check all categories that apply to your business and enter the rough amounts you expect to spend.

Self-Employed Expense Checklist

Expense Category	Estimated Cost (Week, Month, Year)
☐ Rent	
☐ Utilities	
☐ Equipment costs	
☐ Maintenance costs	
☐ Office supplies	
☐ Postage and delivery costs	
☐ Automobile expenses	
☐ Travel expenses	
☐ Business-related meals	
☐ Advertising and marketing	
☐ Clerical or office help	
☐ Accounting and tax fees	
☐ Legal expenses	
☐ Information technology equipment costs	
☐ Health insurance and other benefits	
☐ Other	

© John Wiley & Sons, Inc.

FORM 10-3: Use this form to get a handle on your overhead expenses before setting your business pricing.

In your business plan, include specific information on how and what you intend to charge for your service or product. Show the calculations behind your pricing decisions. (Turn to Chapter 9 for information on managing the financial end of your business.)

Establishing billing policies

If you sell a product, you may get paid at the time you make a sale. If you provide a service, you may send out a bill and then wait — 30 to 60 days isn't uncommon — for your clients to hold up their end of the bargain and actually pay you. Most do. But sometimes things go wrong, and a business (or an individual) may be slow to pay. Worse yet, they may be unable or even unwilling to pay, so you have no sure-fire way to avoid trouble.

But the following tips may help:

>> **Discuss costs before you perform the work.** Put the numbers in writing and answer any client questions about the costs involved. Discussing fees can be uncomfortable, but it's way, way better to discuss them up-front rather than after the fact.

>> **Get the client's signature on your cost estimate or contract.** Doing so helps you later if you have trouble collecting what you're owed.

>> **Establish and explain billing policies.** Also include how you bill for work outside the scope of service covered by your estimate or contract and how you charge for client-requested changes.

>> **Put your billing and payment policies in writing, even if they just appear as fine print on the back of your estimate or contract.** By presenting them as established policies, clients are less apt to feel singled out when extra charges apply.

>> **Avoid billing surprises that don't show up until the client opens the bill.** Get additional costs approved, in writing, along the way.

>> **Send bills out on time.** The more promptly you bill, the more quickly you get paid.

Getting paid

As an independent businessperson, you are your own collection agency (unless a bill goes really delinquent). To nudge clients, use the following steps:

>> **Get personal.** When a bill is past due, pick up the telephone. Ask to speak to your contact for the project. Get the names of the people in accounts payable or purchasing and call them. Make appointments to visit in person.

STAY HOME AND GET RICH FAST 'N EASY

You've seen ads: Earn $5,000 to $10,000 a month working at home. *In your spare time,* no less. Most of these get-rich-quick schemes are bogus and even fraudulent. They seem to be cooked up by the same people who promise a 25-pound weight loss in a week with no dieting.

But that doesn't mean you can't make money working by yourself and from your own home or small office. In fact, according to *The Wall Street Journal,* independent contractors are typically paid 20 to 40 percent more per hour than employees doing the very same job. Why? Because the hiring firms don't have to pay them additional benefits, including health insurance, sick leave, workers' compensation, and so on. The companies also have absolutely no obligation to their outside contractors. It's no wonder they can afford to pay higher hourly rates. The only drawback to this plan is that if you're in business for yourself, you need to think seriously about providing yourself with the most important of these benefits, including a good health plan.

The ranks of the self-employed can also come out ahead by taking advantage of various business-related tax deductions. These deductions include necessary expenses related to your work — as long as the expenses are both reasonable and typical for the type of business you're in. You can even deduct the expenses of running a home office. Check out Form 10-4 to help you decide whether working out of your home is right for you and then take a look at IRS *Publication 587 (Business Use of Your Home),* which you can get from the IRS website at www.irs.gov. Also check out the IRS website for the new simplified option for figuring out the deduction for home businesses, called the "Simplified Option for Home Office Deduction." If you're self-employed, you can also establish your own retirement plan, which can offer significant tax advantages.

>> **Be persistent.** If a client is having financial difficulties and other creditors are trying to get money, the more persistent you are, the closer you'll get to the front of the line.

>> **Be pleasant.** Ask whether there is a problem with the bill. Your queries may uncover customer service issues or may even generate additional sales. Ask and then listen.

>> **Don't wait longer than 60 or 90 days.** If all else fails, take your case to court. Small claims courts resolve disputes involving small amounts of money — usually under $10,000. You can represent yourself, and the process is relatively quick and inexpensive.

Tailoring a Business Plan to Fit Your One-Person Enterprise

Chapter 1 describes each component of a business plan. Lucky for you, though, when you're self-employed, you can skip a few of the parts because they simply don't apply to your business or your business plan:

>> You can ditch the executive summary completely. Your plan is probably concise enough to read quickly and won't require a summary version.

>> You won't have much to say about your organization. It's hardly necessary to explain the chain of command when you're running a business with a staff of one.

>> Your business description can be short, so long as it's clear. Yours will probably describe your abilities, the products or services and advantages you offer, and the market potential you will tap into.

>> The financial review can be basic, as long as it provides thorough explanations of your projected revenues and expenses and how cash will flow in and out of your business.

TIP

When writing your business plan, don't worry about polishing your prose until it's perfect. The important thing is to get the key points down on paper.

REMEMBER

What your business plan *does* need to include is

>> An overview of your business

>> An analysis of your business environment

>> Your business strategy

>> Your financial review

>> A copy of your action plan

Together these five sections cover the nuts and bolts of self-employment planning. See Chapter 16 for how the pieces of the plan come together in a finished business plan. But first go through the following sections for tips on tailoring your business contents to the needs of your one-person operation.

Business overview

Before you wave off this section with the personal assurance that you know what business you're in and what you intend to do, realize that if your direction is even slightly fuzzy at the launch of your business, you'll pay the price for your lack of focus ever after. So don't skip these two steps:

1. **Write vision and mission statements.**

   These statements describe the purpose of your business and what you hope to achieve.

2. **Set goals and objectives.**

   Your goals and objectives define exactly what you want to accomplish and how you will go about achieving your aims. For most people, becoming self-employed is a venture into uncharted waters. For the first time, you're the captain, first mate, and crew all rolled into one with no boss calling the shots or evaluating your performance. Goals and objectives are essential because they serve as an important yardstick to measure your progress.

Chapter 3 offers help as you take both these steps.

Business environment

You can find out everything you need to know about assessing your business environment in Chapter 4. It helps you analyze your industry, your clientele, your competitive environment, and the economic and business trends on the horizon that can affect your success. All four are important even for one-person businesses. For example, you've probably looked around to see whether your regional economy has room for a number of construction contractors, self-employed accountants, freelance designers, or whatever other independent service you're offering. Even so, you want to look more closely to find out how many others are out there doing the same kind of work you do and decide what makes you a different and better choice — and whether there is, in fact, enough business to go around.

Just as important as assessing your competitive environment is the need to track key trends in your industry. If growth is booming in your area, business may be ripe for the picking. But if economic trends don't look so hot, you may need to dedicate time and energy devising strategies to attract new business in a slowing market.

As you study industry trends, be sure you read the indicators not just for the moment, but for the future as well. Include both a rosy forecast and a worst-case forecast. The cheerier version of the future should help keep you motivated. But the lesson from the recent recession is clear: Use the more conservative version for planning. It's better to be pleasantly surprised when business is better than expected than to be taken by surprise when the profit you'd hoped for doesn't materialize.

EXAMPLE

A tax accountant moved into a great new office space at a time when there was more work around than she could possibly take on. What she failed to pick up on, though, was that the local economy was actually slowing. What's more, many individuals and small businesses — the accountant's traditional clients — were beginning to rely on tax software programs rather than accounting services. Between higher office rent and a declining client base, she found herself in a financial crunch that she could have averted if she'd taken time to evaluate her business environment beforehand.

Business description and strategy

You're self-employed, so obviously you don't need much space to describe your organization. Instead, devote the effort to an explanation of how your business will operate — how you'll work with customers, deliver products and services, get new business, outsource work, and so on.

In this section of your business plan, also describe your strengths and weaknesses, both personal and professional. You *are* the entire management team and staff, so defining your own capabilities and how you'll compensate for shortcomings is an essential element of your business planning. For guidance, check out the section on company strengths and weaknesses in Chapter 5.

Financial review

The financial review section of your business plan doesn't have to be long, but it does have to be complete. Show how much you plan to make, how much you need to spend to get started, and how much you need on an ongoing basis to keep yourself in business. The earlier section titled "Putting a price on what you do" will help as you define your pricing and billing policies. To create financial statements, forecasts, and budgets, check out Chapter 9. If you plan to secure funding to launch your solo business, include the details in your written plan. For more on funding your plan, take a look at Chapter 8.

REMEMBER

Set money aside in case work slows down or a client doesn't pay on time. Decide how much money is enough to carry you through a month, two months, six months, or whatever time period makes sense for your business. Then build up a cash reserve — not in a personal bank account but in a business savings account where you're not likely to raid the money around the holidays or vacation time. We can't stress this point enough, especially during tough times. An adequate cash reserve can mean the difference between weathering a rough stretch and going bankrupt.

Action plan

Your action plan is just what the name suggests — a nuts-and-bolts plan of action, broken down step by step, to move your business ahead. Don't go forward without one.

TIP

Start by carefully looking at your personal strengths and weaknesses. If you know you're a strong service provider but a bit thin in the marketing area, for example, your action plan may include enrollment in a marketing class or arrangements for freelance marketing or agency assistance. If your accounting skills are a little wobbly, your action plan may be as simple as hiring an outside accountant. The reason the action plan is so important to a one-person business is because no supervisor or boss is telling you what to do next. You're the one who has to set the direction, steer a course, and measure your progress. Ultimately, your action plan is a good device for making sure your business stays on track.

Running Your One-Person Business Like a Business

Owning a business isn't a hobby. It's a job. It's how you make ends meet. People who go into business on their own thinking it's going to be a breeze are usually in for a shock — especially people who are trying to turn a gig that they love into a money-making operation. Being self-employed often means working harder and longer hours than if you worked for a company.

Creating a business plan for your SOHO is the first step toward taking the enterprise seriously. The planning process should consider everything you need to run your business like a business, starting with location. Keep these sections in mind as you put together your one-person plan.

Setting up a workspace

What kind of office, studio, workshop, or other workspace you need depends on the kind of work you do. To help get started, consider these questions:

>> **How much space do you need?** Take into account all the aspects of running your own business, including storing records, meeting with clients or customers, and doing the work itself.

>> **Will your space requirements change if your business grows?** The nature of your business will determine the answer. For example, an accountant can add clients without adding office space. A caterer may need a bigger kitchen.

>> **Can you work at home?** Working out of your house sounds great, but it isn't for everyone. Take time to assess your own working methods and temperament. Are you suited for working at home? Is your home suited to an office or studio?

>> **Do you thrive in the company of others?** If the answer is yes, consider sharing an office or studio space or apply for a spot in a co-working space like WeWork (www.wework.com). Shared worksites — offices or studies that are run cooperatively — are growing in popularity around the country. You can rent your own private space but share a reception area, break room, and equipment like photocopiers.

Avoiding the pitfalls of working at home

If a home office or studio makes sense for you, get off on the right foot by following these steps to form a strong business foundation and to separate home from work:

>> **Create boundaries between work and your personal life.** Set up a designated workspace with professional surroundings. Establish working hours that ensure personal time where business issues don't encroach on free time and family time.

>> **Keep finances separate.** Separating your home and business finances by establishing a bank account to handle your business funds is crucially important. Keep scrupulous track of which expenses are related to your business and which are personal expenses.

>> **Get out now and then.** Working for yourself at home can be a solitary pursuit. To stay connected, be proactive about meeting people for lunch, joining professional groups, or networking with other local business people.

Bossing yourself

When you're self-employed, you don't have to answer to the boss. You are the boss. And it helps to act like one. To remind yourself that you're the boss, consider doing the following:

>> **Review your performance.** Judge your performance against business goals and objectives. Make sure you involve your clients, where appropriate. Following major projects, discuss their satisfaction levels as a way to monitor how you and your business are performing.

THE NEW IDEA INCUBATOR

EXAMPLE

Shared workspaces have an important benefit that's hard to quantify but can spell success for many sole proprietors. Shared workspaces often bring together people who are pursuing very different kinds of businesses. Thus, they create far-reaching synergies that help promote problem-solving and creativity.

Here's a case in point. An independent software developer who was designing an audio recording program for iPads and other tablets set up shop in a shared workspace in Chicago. The developer knew everything about code, but not much about design. She happened to have a water cooler chat with a designer who shared an office, bemoaning how hard it was to figure out what to display on each page of the app. The designer, who worked in print, had lots of great ideas and had always wanted to expand into digital media. The two co-workers traded tips and critiques, and both their businesses benefitted.

>> **Reward yourself with praise, raises, bonuses, and retirement savings.** Some self-employed businesspeople tie their rewards to their business goals and objectives. If, say, you reach one of your more ambitious goals, give yourself a cash bonus out of the business profits. This strategy may sound a little silly — it's your own money, after all — but many freelancers and independent contractors say that these kinds of incentives are key to staying focused and on track.

>> **Give yourself a break.** One pitfall of being self-employed is that you end up working all the time, which is a recipe for burnout. Give yourself time off now and then. Employees at companies often get to go to off-site conferences or workshops, for example. Give yourself the same opportunities. Take a real vacation now and then with no work at all!

>> **Train yourself.** Employers know that improving workforce skills and education is crucial to success. Widening your expertise as a sole proprietor can be just as important. Seek out ways to expand your education and skills by attending training sessions, workshops, conferences, and other learning opportunities. If a workshop just happens to be in some lovely destination like Hawaii or the Bahamas, consider it a reward, as well.

Outsourcing

These days, self-employed business people can outsource a wide range of functions — from bookkeeping to print design — to make running a SOHO easier than ever. You can hire a lawyer by the hour to handle your legal work or a website developer to tend to your online presence. For more on outsourcing, check out *Micro-Entrepreneurship For Dummies*, by Paul Mladjenovic (John Wiley & Sons, Inc.).

REMEMBER

As you plan your solo business, identify key functions that you can't or don't want to handle yourself. Keep in mind: You don't have to do all the work in a one-person business, but you do have to be able to afford to bring in help when you need it. Estimate how much outsourcing is likely to cost and include those costs in your budget.

Developing a business network

When you're self-employed, business relationships you establish outside your company can be like lifelines. Your one-person business won't have a team to bounce ideas off of or to share concerns, ideas, or dreams. Instead, you'll want to develop a network of associates that you can count on for business contacts, ideas, and advice. So include in your business plan a discussion of how you will establish and maintain a business network. You can

>> **Keep track of your business contacts.** Use contact management software or keep lists manually but, one way or another, record names, numbers, and personal and business interests.

>> **Stay in touch.** Call associates from time to time just to say hello, see how business is going, and share insights. Send or forward useful news articles and call to congratulate them when appropriate. The bottom line is that you want to maintain contact, but also realize that friendly calls often yield new business. Every contact you make offers an opportunity to promote yourself and your business. Networking sites on the Internet have vastly expanded the ability to make and maintain contacts. Take advantage of them.

>> **Make contact with your competitors.** Chances are good that you have more to gain by networking with people in your industry than you have to lose. Minimally, you get to know each other, and the contact may well benefit your business. Competitors often refer clients to others when they can't or don't have time to handle a piece of business themselves.

TIP

>> **Join a business group to create an instant network.** Think Rotary clubs, chambers of commerce, and industry associations. You can find groups full of people involved in the same kind of business as yours or loose alliances of businesspeople working in the same geographic area. Some groups represent specific interest groups, such as women, minorities, or LGBT businesspeople. Your local chamber or economic development office may have lists, or you can look up "associations" online or in the Yellow Pages. The checklist included in Form 10-5 will jump-start your thinking.

Tapping into social networks

Social media networks have completely transformed the way businesses connect with customers, clients, independent contractors, and others. In fact, many sole proprietorships operate almost entirely by way of online networks. Photographers and designers post their work on Flickr or Tumblr, for instance, with links to their own websites, where potential clients can contact them for work. Many independent contractors use LinkedIn to connect to companies with jobs to fill.

TIP

Consider ways that you can use social networks to your own advantage to publicize your business, reach customers, or conduct business. One powerful strategy is content generation. Online content that promotes you and your business can reach a large audience at little or no cost. A New York musician we know posted a series of entertaining short tutorials on jazz improvisation on YouTube, with a link to his site, where would-be jazzers can purchase an instructional video or sign up for individual lessons conducted via Skype. Some business consultants have learned the same trick, creating and posting white papers or slide shows on business trends that attract potential clients.

TIP

Check out Form 10-6 for a checklist of great ways to promote yourself and your business — and get free publicity — using social networks and your online presence.

Checklist of Ways to Promote Yourself and Your Business through Social Media Content

Put a check beside social media marketing strategies that seem appropriate to your business. After you have identified potentially useful strategies, create an action plan for putting them into effect.

☐ **Start a blog.** WordPress, Posterous, and Tumblr make it easy to establish an online blog. Make sure to update your content on a regular basis, so prospective customers know that your business is active.

☐ **Go social.** Participate in social media by commenting on blogs. Ask and answer questions on LinkedIn. Watch for comments on your comments and start a conversation.

☐ **Generate news.** Send out email press releases to share news of interest. Press releases can sometimes trigger articles in local media, a great way to publicize your business for free.

☐ **Use surveys.** Sites like SurveyMonkey and Zoomerang allow you to survey customers and then share your results. Use the "Ask a Question" feature on Facebook to collect results you can then share on social media.

☐ **Share your expertise.** Post white papers (authoritative formal reports or analyses, usually based on research), video tutorials, or instructional blogs that demonstrate your talents and expertise. Direct interested individuals to a landing page where you can collect contact information. If you're worried about giving away your expertise, consider offering a limited free offering, accompanied by a premium paid version with more extensive content.

☐ **Create sharable graphics.** Create infographics, charts, or illustrations that demonstrate your areas of expertise and promote your company.

FORM 10-6: Use this checklist to identify ways to gain attention and customers.

Observing local and state regulations

Just because you're a one-person business doesn't mean you can run your business any way you want. Local and state regulations still apply. Many sole proprietors are surprised to discover that they are required to get a business permit to operate an office at home, for example. If you plan to meet with clients or customers, your home office may have to meet certain regulations for accessibility. A home-based bakery is required to get health inspections. Zoning laws often determine what kinds of businesses can and can't be operated.

For more information about local and state regulations that pertain to your business, check with:

>> Your local Chamber of Commerce

>> Your local county clerk's office

>> The appropriate state department

>> The Small Business Administration (www.sba.gov), which maintains a state-by-state listing of license and permit requirements

Putting your business plan to work

Getting absorbed by day-to-day business needs — whether collecting an unpaid bill or addressing a looming client issue — is easy to do. If you're not careful, you'll be so busy serving clients that you'll forget to run your own business. That's where your business plan can rescue you, keeping you focused on your goals and objectives and the deadlines of your action plan.

TIP

Because getting overwhelmed when you're putting together a business on your own is common, we have a one-person business checklist to help ease your worries. Keep Form 10-7 handy and make sure you've covered all your bases before opening your doors for business.

REMEMBER

Sole proprietors don't need to write out a long and formal business plan. But putting the key components in writing is important. It's equally important not to let that written plan gather dust. Post your mission statement in your office or studio. Many sole proprietors say they frequently get inspired all over again by looking at their mission and vision statement. Keep track of your goals and objectives, too. They can help guide and nudge you.

TIP

You can also assess your strengths and weaknesses, using Form 10-8. Every business, even a sole proprietorship, has its strong points and its liabilities. Recognizing your plusses and minuses can help you know where to put your energies as you plan and build your solo enterprise.

Strengths and Weaknesses Checklist

Use this form to analyze your own strengths and weaknesses when it comes to launching and running a business. Be honest with yourself. After you've completed an inventory of your strengths and weaknesses, use the last section of the form to consider strategies to work around your weaknesses.

List your five biggest strengths as a prospective sole proprietor:

1.

2.

3.

4.

5.

List your five weaknesses:

1.

2.

3.

4.

5.

List specific strategies that could help overcome your perceived weaknesses:

1.

2.

3.

© *John Wiley & Sons, Inc.*

FORM 10-8: Use this form to evaluate your strengths and weaknesses and to pinpoint strategies to help you address those weaknesses.

Forms

If you're self-employed, check out the following forms at www.dummies.com/go/businessplanskit to help you plan.

Form 10-1	Is Self-Employment Right for You?	A survey that helps you identify the traits needed to be successfully self-employed
Form 10-2	Tasks and Time Survey	A survey to help you estimate how much time you spend on each area of your business
Form 10-3	Self-Employed Expense Checklist	A checklist to help you get a handle on your business expenses
Form 10-4	Evaluating Your Home Office Options	A questionnaire to help you evaluate your home office options
Form 10-5	Checklist of Business Networking Resources	Resources you can turn to in order to track down business networking groups in your own industry
Form 10-6	Checklist of Ways to Promote Yourself	A list of strategies to use social media content to reach customers
Form 10-7	One-Person Business Checklist	A handy list of all the key things you need in place before you launch your solo career
Form 10-8	Strengths and Weaknesses Checklist	Questions to help you assess your starting positioning as a sole proprietor

Chapter 11

Planning for a Small Business

The big guys like Google, Toyota, Apple, Microsoft, and AT&T make the business headlines. But the real powerhouses driving the nation's economy are — you guessed it — small businesses, places like Giovanni's Pizza, Main Street Marketing, Woody's Custom Furniture, We-Fix-Phones, and Eye of the Needle Tailoring. Small businesses range from gardening maintenance crews to app developers. Together, these small businesses employ more than half of the US private sector workforce and create the majority of the nation's new jobs.

What qualifies as a small business? The official definition of a *small business*, brought to you by the Small Business Administration (SBA), a federal government agency dedicated to helping small businesses, is any enterprise that is "independently owned and operated and that is not dominant in its field of operation." If your company employs fewer than 100 people and has only a few locations, consider it a small business.

For the purposes of business planning, if your company is big enough to be publicly traded on the NASDAQ or the New York Stock Exchange, you're too big to be called a small business. On the other hand, if your business consists of you and you alone, you're a self-employed business owner — and you get your very own chapter (see Chapter 10).

Is your small business a start-up? Good question, and one that's not easy to answer. Everyone agrees that it's the trendy new term for a fledgling business, especially one involved in high-tech. Beyond that, there's no agreed-upon formal definition for a start-up. By the tech-oriented, commonly agreed-upon definition, a new restaurant isn't typically called a start-up. But a company developing an app that allows you to order from select restaurants in town would probably be called a start-up. Go figure. Asked to provide a definition, business gurus can begin to sound pretty silly. One of best tongue-in-cheek descriptions of a start-up that we've heard is a company with a cool new idea — and no guarantee of success.

Whether you call yours a small business or a start-up, we have one piece of important advice for you: The same rules for planning and running a successful business apply. This chapter helps you focus on the aspects of business planning most critical to small businesses –- especially those that are just starting up or ones that are playing catch-up and writing business plans for the first time. If your business is already in full motion, supplement the information in this chapter by turning to Chapter 13 to find out about planning for an established business.

Recognizing Why Your Small Business Needs a Plan

Business planning is critical to the success of every small business. In fact, according to the SBA, planning ability is one of the keys to small business success. (The others are sound management, industry experience, and technical support.)

Chapter 1 offers a complete description of the value of business planning. For small businesses, three key benefits really stand out. A written plan will help you

>> **Analyze your resource needs before you commit to a business idea.** One of the major reasons small companies go under is because they lack adequate resources to turn a good idea into a profitable venture. By writing a business plan, you detail your requirements for time, cash, and people and establish your equipment needs, location requirements, and the staff you'll have to hire. Together, these elements determine how much money you'll need up-front and how long you'll have to fund your enterprise while you wait for it to start turning a profit.

>> **Develop the information necessary to make the case for a business loan.** Unless you have a deep-pocketed relative waiting in the wings with a check to underwrite your business, you'll probably need to get a loan or attract the support of one or several investors. That means you'll need a convincing business plan. According to the SBA, a good business plan is a crucial part of any loan package.

THE LATEST LOOK AT ENTREPRENEURSHIP

As the economy has recovered in recent years, small businesses have boomed once again. About 14 percent of Americans are involved in starting or running a new business, according to a recent Global Entrepreneurship Monitor report, and 12 percent planned to start one — the highest rate since 1999.

Who's starting new businesses? Men are still more likely than women to start a company, surveys show, although the latest numbers show that the gender gap is narrowing. More than half of start-ups are created by partnerships of two or more people. Most owners are relatively young, as you may expect. But 11 percent are 55 to 64, proving that it's never too late to plan a new business. Also, as you'd expect, those who launch businesses tend to be ambitious and optimistic — convinced that their new product or service has what it takes to succeed. We heartily wish them luck.

>> **Shape a successful business strategy.** The business-planning process requires you to think clearly about your potential customers and your competitors. It also prompts you to assess your own strengths and weaknesses and the opportunities and threats that you face in your industry and marketplace. Your findings will lead to a business strategy that fits your market environment, builds on your business capabilities, and lays the foundation for your success.

Preparing the Contents of Your Small Business Plan

Right about now, because you're planning a small business, you're probably wondering whether you really need to put together a full plan, and if it really has to be a big deal.

Yes, you need a full plan, and no, it doesn't have to be a big deal. But if your business plan is going to help you succeed, it needs to cover all the bases, including the resources you need, your financial situation, and the strategy you'll employ to make it all work.

Your business plan should contain the following five parts:

>> A summary of your business environment

>> A description of your company

>> An outline of your business strategy

>> A summary of your financial statements and forecasts

>> Your action plan

The following sections cover these parts and the issues that deserve the most attention — and why.

Analyzing your business location and the surrounding environment

The very first section of your business plan summarizes how the environment around your business will affect your company's success. It examines the industry you're in, your customers, and your competition. For a thorough look at your business environment, check out Chapter 4, which guides you through such an assessment. As you consider location, weigh these points:

>> **Local business locations:** The first factor that affects the success of most small businesses is location, location, location. The reason: Many small businesses serve local customers. Especially if your business relies on foot traffic and spontaneous buying decisions, where you place your shop or office — on a busy thoroughfare or on a less-traveled alleyway — can mean the difference between success and failure. After you've decided on a prospective location and the geographic scope of your market area, you can evaluate the composition of your market area population, economic conditions, and competing businesses.

>> **Multiple-location businesses:** If your business serves multiple market areas, you need to assess these same issues in each area to arrive at a useful analysis upon which to plan your business.

>> **Target- or vertical-market businesses:** If your business serves customers far and wide who share specific wants and needs, assessment of your business environment will shift from a geographic focus to a focus on the customers who fit the unique profile of those in your target audience, called your *vertical market*.

>> **Online locations:** The Internet has given new meaning to location. Most brick-and-mortar companies also have website locations, and more and more companies are doing business entirely on the Internet. Driving traffic to a website is the key to their success. When you think of it, that's not all that different from a mom-and-pop store looking for ways to get people in the door. (For more information about marketing your business, no matter what your location, check out Chapter 7.) But many online businesses also need a physical location. Suppose that you're starting a small software company that will depend on highly trained software engineers. You have to locate your company in a place where these kinds of people live — or at least are willing to move. You're likely to find them in Seattle, Washington, or San Jose, California, for example. It may be a little more difficult, though, if you set up shop in Mountain Home, Arkansas. As you begin planning your business, make sure that you spend serious business-planning time weighing the pros and cons of your location and its business environment.

>> **Virtual businesses:** A growing number of businesses don't have any fixed address at all. The Internet has spawned the virtual enterprise, which not only doesn't have a brick-and-mortar storefront, but also doesn't even have a physical headquarters. Virtual companies are made up of an affiliation of employees whose only connection is online. For more on the benefits and challenges of running a virtual company, turn to Chapter 12.

Complete the business environment section of your business plan in three parts. Chapter 4 helps you arrive at your answers:

>> Describe your business or industry arena, including the trends you're seeing. Note whether the market is growing or shrinking; what it takes to enter the arena; and any technological, regulatory, or other changes you see on the horizon.

>> Describe your customers by stating where they're located; facts about their age, gender, income, marital status, and so on; and anything you know about why and how they buy products like yours.

>> Describe your competitive environment, including the strengths, capabilities, and growth plans of major competing businesses and how you plan to differentiate your business.

Describing your business and its purpose

Your *company description* is the component of your business plan that states what kind of business you're in and what you look like as a company. The company description tells exactly what your business intends to do, how it intends to do it, and what is going to make it unique and successful.

The reason this description is so important usually boils down to one word: money. Many small companies have to take out business loans, enlist the help of outside investors, or arrange for lines of credit to cover bills that need to be paid before revenues roll in. The first thing investors want to know is what your business does, and the best way to persuade them that your business idea is sound is to describe it concisely and convincingly.

TIP

As you describe your company, communicate the most important aspects of your business, including the kinds of customers you serve, the products and services you offer, and the capabilities that will underpin your success. Chapter 6 provides descriptions and forms to help you write your company description.

Plotting your business strategy

The *strategy section* of your business plan describes exactly how you intend to accomplish your business goals.

>> **If your goal is to get your business off the ground,** you need to outline your strategy for obtaining financing and launching your operation. See Chapter 8 for information on approaches for funding your business.

>> **If your goal is to expand your business,** you need to describe your growth strategy. Chapter 5 presents growth options and planning advice, and Chapter 13 helps set a plan for growing an established business.

>> **If your goal is to introduce a new product,** you need to detail strategies for research and development, production, and product introduction. Chapter 6 can help as you define and present your capabilities in each of these areas.

REMEMBER

In addition to all other strategies, this section of your plan needs to outline your marketing strategy, showing how you plan to reach customers and persuade them to buy what you sell. Your marketing plan is the blueprint you'll follow to achieve sales success. For more information on writing this section of your plan, see Chapter 7. For complete guidance on developing a plan scaled to your business size and needs, take a look at the most recent edition of Barbara's book, *Small Business Marketing Kit For Dummies* (John Wiley & Sons, Inc.).

REMEMBER

In the strategy part of your business plan, list your business goals and objectives and accompany each one with the strategy you'll follow to achieve success.

Staffing and outsourcing

One of the biggest challenges for many small businesses is staffing. The task of finding and keeping top-notch employees is toughest when a company is growing fast. But even if you're just starting out, planning your staff effectively can be a hurdle. To begin to tackle this task

>> Make a complete list of jobs and functions associated with your business. The more complete your list, the better prepared you'll be.

>> Identify which jobs or functions require full-time employees and which can be handled part-time or entirely outsourced.

>> List special skills or experience that particular jobs or functions may require.

>> Draw up a proposed staffing list, including full-time employees, part-timers, and outsourced talent.

TIP

Staff requirements are an important part of your business plan, so make sure you describe them in as much detail as possible. Go to www.dummies.com/go/businessplanskit to download and check out Form 11-1 and Form 11-2 for help on creating job descriptions and recruiting the best employees.

In your written business plan, describe your staffing plan. If your staffing model involves remote employees, you need to give attention to how you'll manage and monitor your workforce. Chapter 12 has plenty of tips.

REMEMBER

Temporary agencies have long been a great place to turn if you need to fill a position for a limited amount of time. Today, online sites like LinkedIn also offer an effective way to find people for specific projects. By hiring temporary or independent contractors, your company doesn't take on the responsibilities of a full-time worker. But be prepared to provide them the supervision they'll need.

REMEMBER

If you plan to use independent contractors, be sure to stay on top of all the relevant legal and tax requirements. According to IRS rules, an employer can't dictate exactly where and when an independent contractor works, for example. Independent contractors also may not use your company's equipment or facilities to perform their work. If the IRS determines that those whom you call independent contractors are performing their work too much like staff employees, you could be in for trouble. For detailed information, check out www.irs.gov.

Clarifying your financial situation

Your business plan absolutely has to include a complete financial picture of your company — including planned income, estimated balance sheet, and cash-flow projections. No ifs, ands, or buts. Your financial reports provide the navigational tools that you need to keep your business on track, plus they provide the essential information that bankers and other supporters need to see and monitor.

Whether you're starting a brand-new venture or expanding an existing enterprise, estimating how much money you'll need in the bank requires guesswork. But estimating how much you need gets a little easier if you focus on two kinds of spending:

>> **One-time start-up costs:** Every small business faces a long list of items that have to be acquired right from the get-go. *Start-up costs,* which are items you spend money on only once just to get up and running, include everything from a business license, start-up furnishings and equipment, and introductory marketing materials for that Grand Opening or Product Launch promotion you've planned.

>> **Regular monthly expenses:** After you're open for business, you have all sorts of ongoing expenses to deal with, from paying salaries to buying supplies. Over time, of course, you expect your sales revenue to cover these expenses. But that situation doesn't happen overnight, so you have to acquire or set aside funds with which to pay the bills in the early tough-sledding period. Having a three- to six-month cushion is a good place to start, but how long you'll need your funding cushion to tide you over depends on how long until your forecasted revenues kick in. Chapter 2 includes a section on how to calculate your start-up *runway,* or how much time you have before revenues need to take off.

For a good idea of what size bankroll you'll need to finance your small business start-up or expansion, download and use Form 11-1. To use this form:

1. **Fill in the blanks to detail your estimated start-up costs.**

2. **Estimate the ongoing monthly expenses you expect to incur and multiply by the number of months you think will pass before your business is bringing in sales revenue sufficient to cover its overhead.**

3. **Add the two totals together.**

   The resulting number is the financial cushion you need to start out with in order to have cash available when you need it.

   Use the figures you come up with in Form 11-1 as a starting point for developing the financial statements that you include in your written business plan. (For a step-by-step guide on how to put together your financial picture, flip to Chapter 9.) Be sure that you accompany your financial forecasts with descriptions of the assumptions you made as you put the numbers down on paper.

For more on funding your small business, take a look at Chapter 9.

REMEMBER

For the IRS's view on financial and tax matters, go to the horse's mouth. Check out *Business Expenses (IRS Publication 535), Tax Guide for Small Business (IRS Publication 334),* and *Small Business Tax Workshop Workbook (IRS Publication 1066).* All three publications are available on the IRS website at www.irs.gov.

Taking advantage of social media

Virtually every business has been transformed by the rise of social media, but perhaps none more completely than small businesses. The reputation of restaurants rises and falls on sites such as Yelp and OpenTable, for example. Beauty salons depend on being liked on Facebook. Photographers and graphic design firms can launch and grow their businesses through Tumblr and Flickr. Small businesses across the board have turned to online recruitment sites to hire employees.

REMEMBER

As you draft your plan, consider ways that your enterprise can tap the power of social media to publicize your offerings, connect with customers, conduct business, and get customer feedback. If social media is a key part of your strategy, provide specific details in your plan. For ideas on how to tap the growing power of social media, check out Chapters 7 and 15.

Establishing your action plan

Your business plan should include an *action plan* that outlines the sequence of steps you intend to take to implement your business plan, focusing first on the most immediate and pressing tasks you face.

TIP

A good way to approach your action plan is to look back at the strategies you selected to meet each of your goals and objectives. Break each strategy into steps and then prioritize which ones need to happen first, second, third, and so on. Follow these steps:

1. **Forecast your financial needs and the length of time your funding will last until revenues must take off.**

   Doing so guides the timeline in your action plan.

2. **Detail your staffing plan.**

   Especially if you're planning for a start-up, make sure your action plan addresses the process of putting together a top-notch staff.

3. **Define the actions you'll take to establish or grow your business, gain or increase name familiarity, and develop your reputation.**

   No doubt your business will face some degree of change over the time period covered by your business plan, so you also want to detail actions that can help you manage the change your business is likely to encounter.

TIP

To capture all the relevant information you'll need to include on job descriptions, use Form 11-2. For ideas on where to find employees who meet your requirements, look over Form 11-3, the Job Recruiting Checklist.

Determining a timeline

An action plan spells out the steps you need to take. To make sure you get your business up and running in a timely fashion, determine a timeline for every key step. A *timeline* lists the major milestones and has an assigned date for exactly when you intend to reach them.

When putting together your timeline, don't rely on wishful thinking. Give some thought to how much time each step is likely to take. The more realistic your timeline, the more apt you'll be to stay on track and the better prepared you'll be along the way. Make sure everyone involved in your business has a copy of the timeline. Check back now and then to assess your progress and to adjust your timeline if necessary.

Keeping an Eye on the Business Horizon

Change is an inevitable part of the economic landscape. And change is coming faster than it used to, especially for small businesses. Big companies are like luxury ocean liners. When they encounter a little squall, the passengers barely feel it. Large firms, in other words, can weather economic downturns or changes in the marketplace, though with the extent of change in today's world, even they're feeling the turmoil. However, small businesses are like small boats. The winds of change can bounce them around pretty hard and, sometimes, capsize them completely.

TIP

To succeed over the long haul, you have to navigate your small business through all the changes that are bound to happen. How? First, keep an eye on the horizon, watching out for what may be coming along. Second, be ready to change course or shift position to avoid trouble or to take advantage of good winds and strong currents.

REMEMBER

In the first section of your business plan, where you describe your business environment, make sure that you address changes that may affect how your company operates. Identify the trends and changes that are most likely to affect your business and describe how you will watch and respond to each of the specific issues and events that could play a significant role in the future of your small business. Such trends and changes may include a pending legal case, an emerging technology, or an upcoming regulatory decision. For more tips on how to master change, check out Chapter 15.

Growing — or Not Growing — Your Small Business

Many small businesses want to and always will remain small. Other businesses start small with the dream of growing big — sometimes very big. Take Starbucks, which began as a local Seattle coffee shop, and Apple, which was launched in a garage. Small businesses don't grow into giant corporations by accident, however. Behind that growth is a well-thought-out business plan along with the drive and the resources to get there. But becoming a big business isn't for everybody.

EXAMPLE

An entrepreneur who started a stereo shop in a small Illinois college town created just the kind of friendly, cluttered, slightly disorganized atmosphere you'd expect to see in such a place. But the salespeople who worked there really knew and loved audio equipment, and the business was stocked with great components at very competitive prices, thanks to the fact that overhead was so low. The unbeatable combination of quality, service, and price soon made the store a huge success — and the owner began to dream about expanding into a chain of stores throughout the Midwest.

The idea sounded good on paper. Unfortunately, the owner never put his business plan in writing. He launched right into action, building inventory and leasing storefronts without once thinking about how he would find knowledgeable sales teams, promote the new stores, or create an organization that could manage the jump from one shop to half a dozen. The laid-back, disorganized style worked fine for a single store with a garage-worth of inventory, but it turned out to be a disaster for the small chain. The losses from the new outlets soon eroded the original store's profits. Six months later, the owner closed up and went back to school, even though he'd already been through the school of hard knocks.

REMEMBER

A well-crafted business plan may have helped avoid disaster. But even before the planning, the owner should have asked one simple question: *Do I really want to grow my business?* Some small businesses are meant to remain small, and some business owners are meant to run small companies.

TIP

Whether you're growing your business or planning to stay small, holding on to valued employees will be critical to your success. You'll find useful tips on how to improve overall employee job satisfaction on Form 11-4. For many employees, satisfaction comes from knowing they're part of a team. For tips on promoting teamwork and team spirit in your small business, check out Form 11-5.

Before you make plans to grow your small business into something bigger, take time to ask yourself whether you really want to manage a larger company:

>> How will the day-to-day operations of the company have to change?

>> How will my own duties and responsibilities be different?

>> What additional skills will I need to make the growing business work?

>> What weak points or limitations do I have that may get in the way?

Don't be discouraged if your answers make you think twice about growing your business into something bigger. Not every business is suited to expansion — and not every small-business owner really wants to manage a big organization.

If your answers give you confidence that growth is a smart move, buckle down and really start planning. Turn to Chapter 5 for more details on the ways that companies typically grow and for a checklist of critical resources that you'll need as your company begins to grow. Then turn to Chapter 13 for information on how to write a business plan when you're working to grow an established business.

Keeping It in the Family

Family businesses can be very rewarding, but they can also be tricky to manage. Interpersonal relationships tend to play a bigger role in family businesses than they do in other small companies. Feelings get hurt, and when they do, the fallout affects both people's working lives and personal lives. Divorces can wreak havoc on a small family business. So can battles over succession, especially when several children are in position to take over the company when a parent retires.

Another challenge unique to family businesses is recruiting, rewarding, and retaining outsiders — key employees who aren't part of the family. Too often, outsiders may feel as if they can't compete with the special privileges accorded family members.

Fortunately, many of the special challenges of running a successful family business can be remedied. The first step, of course, is having a plan in place. A surprising number of small family-run businesses don't get that far. Along with the features of any business plan, a family-run company's planning efforts should include

>> Buy-in from all key family members in the business-planning process

>> Financial and governance policies that separate family issues from the business

>> A clear plan for succession

>> Compensation policies that treat all employees equally, regardless of whether they're family members or outsiders

>> Policies for negotiating disagreements should they occur

>> Regularly scheduled meetings attended by all key family members

Revisiting and revising the business plan, important for all ventures, is especially important for family-run enterprises. The process allows family members to raise and resolve issues that might otherwise fester. You can also use the planning process to boost morale and encourage a stronger sense of family — one of the biggest strengths of a family-run company.

Preparing to Sell Your Small Business

A successful business is often a valuable asset that you can sell when you're ready to retire or move on to the next big thing. If you're creating a business plan with a goal of selling the business in the near future, think through an exit strategy. You can find information on exit strategies in Chapter 5, and Chapter 13 has detailed information on planning for a merger or sale.

REMEMBER

Planning ahead can help you reap a bigger reward for the hard work you've put into launching and building your enterprise. Our advice: Don't wait until the last minute to begin to plan an exit strategy. Too many owner exits are prompted by unanticipated circumstances. And selling a business often takes time. Ideally, your business should be in sale-ready shape at all times, whether or not you have a sale in mind. That means keeping profits strong, maintaining a consistent record of success, and developing a growth plan that keeps the future of your business looking bright. Hit that trifecta and you're likely to sell your company at top dollar.

Forms

Go to www.dummies.com/go/businessplankit to view and download the forms for Chapter 11.

Form 11-1	**Start-Up Costs Worksheet for Small Business**	A worksheet designed to give you an idea of how much cash you need up-front to get a small business off the ground
Form 11-2	**Job Description Profile**	A template designed to capture all the relevant information that a job description should include
Form 11-3	**Job Recruiting Checklist**	Places small businesses can go to find qualified employees
Form 11-4	**Employee Retention Checklist**	Approaches to help you improve overall employee job satisfaction
Form 11-5	**Tips on Promoting Teamwork**	A list of ways you can promote a sense of team spirit and teamwork in your own company

Chapter 12

Planning for a Virtual Business

T he single most disruptive technological development of the past decades — by a long shot — has been the emergence of the Internet. Who would have imagined, just 20 years ago, that people would shop, read mail, send messages, watch videos, share photos, get directions, call a taxi, and even receive health advice on mobile devices? Along the way, the rise of the Internet has utterly changed how business is conducted. More and more employees are able to work remotely, a trend that is sure to continue as information technologies make it easier to stay connected almost anywhere you go. Today, designers can collaborate on projects without meeting in person. Lawyers can confer with clients on the opposite side of the globe. Software teams can brainstorm without ever being in the same room.

The result: the rise of a whole new form of *virtual business* (also sometimes called a *distributed business*). The most extreme example is a business that exists only online. No brick-and-mortar storefronts. No steel and glass headquarters. No conference rooms or water coolers. No employee cafeterias.

EXAMPLE

Consider the example of an editorial consulting business that offers the services of top-notch writers and editors for companies that need to develop print and website text. The business markets its services online. It consults with clients via email, chat apps, or Skype. All of its employees work remotely. Text is delivered via email, Google Docs, Dropbox, or one of dozens of other free file-sharing apps. The company's homepage lists no street address because there is none.

Other businesses may have some physical presence in the form of offices or warehouses, but much of their business is done online. The most famous example is Amazon. But plenty of other innovative companies are largely virtual, including Uber, Lyft, Airbnb, Mozilla, and many more.

Virtual businesses have become so popular that even national conferences are devoted entirely to running them. They're likely to become even more common for one simple reason: the flexibility and cost-saving benefits they offer allow businesses to compete more effectively in increasingly competitive marketplaces.

Virtual businesses are bound by most of the same rules that apply to traditional companies. Yet planning and managing a virtual business also poses unique challenges and offers special benefits, which are what this chapter is all about. Even if only part of your business is conducted virtually, you can find helpful tips here.

Understanding the Benefits and Risks of a Virtual Business

The most obvious benefit of a virtual business is tallied up in dollars and cents — the money saved by not having to maintain a snazzy suite of offices, a high-rent storefront, or other facilities. When a well-known business magazine headquartered in New York contemplated going virtual, it projected savings from rent alone at about half a million dollars a year — enough to give every employee a $16,000 bonus.

Even if you're not paying Manhattan commercial real estate prices, you can still save a bundle by creating a virtual office rather than renting a physical one. Here are some other benefits:

>> **Flexibility:** If your business uses independent contractors who are hired on a project basis or for limited periods of time, you can respond more flexibly to the ups and downs of the market, taking people on only when you need them.

>> **An edge in hiring:** Ask most people if they'd prefer to work at home and on their own schedule, and the answer is a resounding "yes!" Not everyone is cut out for working independently, of course, but for those who are, a virtual business can be attractive — making hiring top talent that much easier.

- » **Productivity:** A recent Stanford University study found that employees who telecommute or work remotely are 13.5 percent more productive. Maybe that's because they spend less time in meetings or hanging out around the water cooler.

- » **Employee retention:** The same Stanford University study found that employees who work remotely are half as likely to quit as office-based workers. That discovery speaks to the job satisfaction many people feel when they're judged by the work they do rather than the hours they put in.

- » **Creativity:** Creative solutions are the driving force behind many innovative businesses. Where creativity requires uninterrupted stretches of time and when the creative spark flashes at odd hours, a virtual business organization may be ideal.

TIP

If you're considering a virtual business operation, use Form 12-1 to check off the benefits that you hope to get. Highlighting the benefits you hope to enjoy by going virtual is important because it allows you to focus your planning to give you the best shot at attaining them. Go to www.dummies.com/go/businessplanskit to find and download the forms in this chapter.

Taking a cue from the first generation of virtual businesses

Many of the virtual businesses we've worked with are sold on the benefits of operating chiefly or entirely online. They love the cost savings, the flexibility, and the competitive agility they gain by operating as a virtual team. Businesses that depend on creative output are convinced that a virtual operation gives their employees the freedom to be more creative. Firms that employ young programmers say a virtual organization helps them keep and attract the best talent. Businesses looking for geographic reach say there's no better way to go after far-flung markets.

Check out the websites of many pioneering virtual companies and you can practically feel the excitement.

- » Automattic, which describes itself as "the people behind WordPress" is "a distributed company, democratizing publishing and development." All its employees, the website proudly proclaims, "work from their own home or office, and we're spread all over the world."

- » Mozilla, the nonprofit behind the web browser Firefox, has employees working in more than 30 countries. It describes itself to prospective employees as "a global pack of do-gooders, rabble-rousers, and passionate defenders of the web."

>> Upworthy, a fast-growing virtual media company, trumpets the fact that employees can work and live anywhere. "Work from home, from a coffee shop, from a coworking space," the company's website says. "Go move to Montana for a month and work from there if you want. (And if you already live in Montana, go on living there!)"

>> Fire Engine RED, a data solutions company that serves the education marketplace, boasts about the talent it has attracted as a 100% virtual company. "We're able to attract and hire top talent, no matter where they live."

>> Genuitec, a software company with a small home base in Texas, employs programmers around the world. With teams telecommuting in the United States, India, Mexico, Africa, and Europe, "we thrive in a full-time telecommuting environment," the firm's website proclaims.

WARNING

Sound great? You bet. But creating and managing a virtual business isn't all polka dots and moonbeams. Many of the companies we know had bumpy rides as they planned and launched their virtual businesses. Hiring people suited to working on their own can be tricky. Communicating with a remote workforce isn't easy, especially if you have employees scattered across many time zones. Creating a sense of teamwork and a shared commitment also can be a challenge in a company where people spend very little time face-to-face with one another. A virtual company can't easily take advantage of the synergy that comes from in-person meetings and the back-and-forth banter that goes with them.

The fact is, as cool as the idea of a virtual company sounds, not all business ideas are suited to operating without an office or home base.

EXAMPLE

Consider the example of several start-ups that are testing whether people will be willing to seek medical advice from remote teams of physicians. One new app provides dermatology advice (and prescriptions, if appropriate), on your smartphone. Instead of going into a brick-and-mortar clinic, you send a list of your symptoms and a photo of your skin problem. A remote dermatologist makes a diagnosis and provides a treatment plan without ever laying eyes on you. The jury is still out on whether this kind of virtual clinic will work. But almost everyone agrees that a virtual clinic is appropriate only for certain forms of medicine. Diagnosing and treating skin diseases may lend itself particularly well to a virtual format. Fixing broken bones, not so much.

Evaluating whether your idea is a good fit

Take time up-front to think through whether your business idea can succeed using a virtual organization. Ponder these essential questions:

>> Is the product or service you provide a good fit for a virtual business?

>> Can you effectively reach customers without a brick-and-mortar home base?

>> Which aspects of your operations are best suited to being conducted virtually?

>> Which aspects of your business would benefit from having an office or storefront?

>> What are the biggest challenges you'll face going virtual?

>> What strategies will you use to address those challenges?

If you find yourself struggling to make a strong argument for going virtual, you may want to rethink your plan.

TIP

To face up to the challenges that a virtual business organization can pose, check out Form 12-2. Tick off each of the items that are relevant to your business plan. Then take time to detail strategies that you plan to use to address these challenges.

REMEMBER

Very few businesses are entirely virtual. But more and more conduct key parts of their operations virtually.

Keeping up to date

Virtual businesses can be set up as sole proprietorships, S-corps, LLCs, and even nonprofit businesses. The same laws and regulations that apply to traditional businesses also apply to their virtual counterparts. But if you plan to create a virtual company, some points deserve special attention, among them:

>> **IRS rules regarding independent contractors:** If your remote workforce will include independent contractors, carefully review the rules to make sure your team members qualify. For detailed information, check out "Independent Contractor (Self-Employed) or Employee" at the IRS website, www.irs.gov.

>> **Nondisclosure and noncompete agreements:** Employees at virtual companies operate more independently than traditional punch-the-clock workers. If your remote workforce has access to vital competitive information about the company, be sure to have the appropriate nondisclosure and noncompete agreements in place during the hiring process.

>> **Tax laws:** If your business has a physical presence in a state — meaning a store, office, or warehouse — you're required to collect state and local sales tax. If you have no brick-and-mortar presence, you don't. Check with state revenue offices if you have any questions.

>> **Online marketing and advertising regulations:** The Federal Trade Commission oversees e-commerce rules and regulations. For detailed information, check out www.ftc.gov.

>> **Confidentiality rules:** Virtual companies that operate within particular industries — legal services and healthcare, for example — must take special care to protect the confidentiality of their clients when they exchange information online.

Running and Planning a Virtual Business

The business plan for a virtual business looks much like a traditional company's plan, but it may focus more attention on certain elements, such as management structure or hiring and retention. The plan should also take a close look at the technologies that will be used to keep a remote workforce connected. Read on for more guidance on the key considerations that go into planning and launching a virtual business.

Operating a company without an HQ

A headquarters or home office is more than a bunch of rooms and corridors. The space also reflects the hierarchy of a business and how it operates. For example, in the Washington, D.C., headquarters of a well-known magazine, one floor is devoted to editorial, another to photography, and another to art. One entire floor is devoted to captions that accompany the photographs. The top brass reside — you guessed it — on the top floor. The headquarters, in other words, reflects and reinforces the magazine's operational structure and priorities.

A virtual business must find other ways to establish and convey its management structure and its way of doing business. Several of the foundations of solid business planning — creating a strong mission and vision statement (see Chapter 3), setting a clear strategic direction (Chapter 5), and describing management and operations (Chapter 6) are especially important for virtual companies.

In our experience, successful virtual companies have the following in common:

>> **The right leadership:** Top managers are committed and even passionate about the benefits of a virtual structure.

>> **A strong team spirit and shared sense of business culture:** Everything the company does is aligned around common business vision, mission, values, goals, strategies, and brand (see Chapter 5 for more details).

>> **The right team members:** In the absence of face-to-face interaction, virtual companies succeed by developing detailed job descriptions and having systems and standards in place that cover everything from working hours and work quality to performance reviews. They hire people who work well with little supervision and who also have a clear sense of how they fit into the organization.

>> **Good communications systems:** Because people aren't running into one another in the hallway or at the water cooler, successful virtual companies institute formal ways for people to stay in touch. They make smart use of a variety of online communication and document-sharing tools.

REMEMBER

If operating as a virtual business is key to your competitive strategy, your plan should emphasize the benefits and challenges of operating virtually. Explain why a virtual organization is well suited to your goals and strategy, but also be up-front about the challenges of operating virtually, and detail how you plan to address them. If your business will combine some virtual operations with some traditional facility-based operations, describe how each will operate and interact. For more on business capabilities, take a look at Chapter 6.

Hiring and managing a remote team

At the heart of the virtual business model is a radical new relationship with employees. Instead of punching a clock or showing up at the office, employees work remotely, often when they want to, and their only contact with management may be via phone, email, videocall and groupchat apps, or other project management and digital technologies. The freedom and flexibility is a strong draw for many employees and can make it easy to tap top talent. But it also requires team members with the right temperament and talents.

From our experience, the best people for a virtual company organization are

>> Self-motivated

>> Well-organized

>> Good communicators

>> Flexible about their working schedules

>> Sold on the benefits of working virtually

>> Comfortable with evolving technologies

>> Willing to buy into the culture, mission, and goals of the business

TIP

Use Form 12-3 to rate prospective employees on the traits that are key to succeeding in a virtual organization.

Many virtual companies conduct the hiring process virtually, evaluating and interviewing applicants without ever having a face-to-face conversation. Traditional HR folks might see that as a disadvantage. But if prospective employees will be working remotely, it can actually be an advantage to interact with them during the hiring process in the same way you'll work with them — by email, videocall, chat rooms, and whatever other technologies you employ.

REMEMBER

Because employees in a virtual company work more independently than traditional employees, having a solid and detailed job description for each position is critically important. With a comprehensive job description in place, the job candidate will be clear about expectations. Having a detailed job description also provides the basis for reviewing an employee's performance.

TIP

Use the worksheet in Form 12-4 to begin the process of creating job descriptions for your key remote employees.

Using technologies to manage, motivate, and inspire

At the heart of every successful virtual company is a flexible IT network that allows employees, clients, customers, and subcontractors to interact smoothly and efficiently. Teleconferencing, videoconferencing, and groupchats allow participants from around the country or around the world to connect from far-flung locations. File-sharing programs allow group members to review and edit documents, passing them back and forth through digital transmissions instead of handing them off in person. Collaboration and project management apps provide a centralized place online where all project information is stored and accessible.

Supporting your virtual team with IT solutions

Technology is the key to virtual business success. If you're a small virtual company, you may be able to assemble the IT components for group communication and collaboration by yourself. Or, you can turn to a long list of readily available and often free collaboration tools and software solutions that you can stay on top of by opening your browser and searching for "virtual team collaboration tools." Among the many options, you can find the following tools:

>> **Collaboration tools** that direct group communications through a central hub, such as Slack, which is free, and Huddle

>> **Project management tools** for planning, scheduling, assigning, tracking, and managing tasks through a central hub, for example, Microsoft Project, Basecamp, JIRA, and Asana

>> **Document creation, file storage, and sharing tools,** such as Dropbox, Google Drive, and Box

>> **Virtual meeting tools,** for example, WebEx Meetings and GoToMeeting

>> **Videocall and conferencing tools,** such as Skype and Google Hangouts

>> **Realtime talk and chat tools,** for example, Skype, Facebook Messenger, Google Hangouts, and HipChat, to name a few

Plus, you can turn to experts for customized solutions, including companies that help artists or craftspeople build and manage retail websites, software programs designed to enable lawyers or other professionals to work virtually, and tech wizards who help you put together your own IT network.

The bigger your enterprise is, the bigger your IT component is likely to be. The specific technology tools you'll need will depend on the kind of virtual business you plan to run.

REMEMBER

Whether you're planning a one-person business or a sprawling international company with distributed workers around the world, your business plan should specifically address the kinds of technologies you'll use to conduct your business virtually.

Using technology as a team-building resource

One of the most difficult challenges for a virtual company is creating a strong sense of teamwork among employees who never lay eyes on one another. The chief complaint we've heard from people who didn't like working virtually is that they felt isolated and, well, remote. Successful virtual companies find clever ways to use technology to motivate and inspire employees.

EXAMPLE

One firm we know set up a group chat room, dubbed "The Water Cooler," which allows remote employees to interact informally, sharing personal stories and funny videos. Another company asked employees to create online bios that combined both professional information and personal stuff like favorite hobbies and most embarrassing moments. Another encouraged remote employees to interact by creating a virtual book club and an intranet travel site that allows employees to post photos and descriptions of their vacation outings and take advantage of group discounts.

Other strategies to inspire and motivate remote employees and to foster teamwork include

>> Posting your mission statement and values statement prominently on your website and on key internal communications with employees (Chapter 3 explains why both are critical to a business plan)

>> Creating an online newsletter or blog that includes vignettes of remote employees

>> Offering awards and contests that allow remote workers to compete against one another, either individually or in teams

>> Holding in-person or virtual annual retreats or summits where remote employees get together — in real-life if possible and in real-time if not.

Branding an enterprise with far-flung virtual partners

Your brand is the set of beliefs that people associate with your business name. It mirrors the overall image and tone of your company, your employees, your product, and your customer service. Branding is reflected through everything from your name and logo to your business offerings to how product manuals are written and how employees interact with customers. (For more on branding, check out Chapter 7.) Branding requires consistency in message, tone, interactions, and the promise you make and keep with customers. And branding can be a challenge in a virtual enterprise, with far-flung employees operating independently. To insure consistency across all areas of your operation:

>> Draft a clear and concise brand statement and communicate it to everyone.

>> Design a logo and establish exactly where and how it should appear.

>> Create stationery, business cards, and a format for the block of text used in email signatures and make sure all virtual team members know to use them in any official business communications to project a consistent company look.

>> Establish style guidelines for all formal written communications. (Search online for "brand style guidelines" for plenty of examples.)

>> Consider hiring an editor who oversees all official company documents, from instruction manuals or product FAQs to marketing materials. A poorly written document reflects badly on the quality of the products or services you offer.

>> Develop a set of customer service guidelines to establish the quality of customer interactions you expect your employees to provide.

>> Ask your customers and clients for feedback. Follow a sale with a customer survey or telephone call, for instance, in order to get a sense of how your remote team is performing.

Because branding is so important to a company's image — and because it's a challenge for many virtual companies — your plan should specifically describe how you intend to develop the communication consistency that's essential to strong brand management.

Establishing standards and policies across a virtual enterprise

The virtue of a virtual company is that employees have tremendous freedom in their working lives. Managed well, a virtual company can be more flexible and efficient than a traditional nine-to-five, office-based enterprise. But with employees working as free agents distributed around the country — and sometimes around the world — virtual companies must establish specific standards and policies for operations and procedures, so that employees know how the business runs and what is expected of them.

REMEMBER

The specifics will depend on the kind of business you plan to run. In the area of human resources, policies range from how prospective employees are hired and trained to how and how often their performance will be reviewed. If your business involves contracts with clients or customers, you need policies in place to establish who is authorized to sign on behalf of the company. Plus, you'll need policies for how products are produced, how and when outside supplies or services are purchased, how timelines are created and tracked, and more.

EXAMPLE

The online company Etsy provides a marketplace for artists and craftspeople to sell their wares. Sellers are essentially distributed employees who create the products sold on the company's website. Etsy's claim to fame is that it is a marketplace for handmade or individually designed products. Recently the company came under criticism because some people were hiring others to make the products and in some cases even selling (and sometimes reselling) manufactured goods. In response, Etsy established specific standards — "Our House Rules," the company calls them — for what constitutes "handmade" goods and manufactured products.

REMEMBER

Your business plan won't include every standard and policy relating to how you do business. But definitely give some thought to the most important standards and policies you'll need in place to run your operation. Those that are essential to defining your business and how it will operate should be described in your plan.

Staying One Step Ahead of a Fast-Changing Business Model

Many observers, ourselves included, are convinced that virtual companies will become increasingly common as advances in technology make it even easier for employees to work wherever they are. Transformative innovations will continue to yield new opportunities and new virtual business models.

To take just one example, virtual reality is already making inroads in the information and entertainment sector. Chances are good that virtual reality will soon be used for hiring and training remote employees and as a tool for allowing potential customers to try out a product or service before buying it. No one — not even so-called futurists — can accurately predict where technological change will lead. But if you're already on the cutting edge as a virtual business, it's smart to stay as informed as you can about new breakthroughs and changing trends. Our advice:

>> Keep an eye on business and technology news.

>> Attend technology conferences relevant to your business, such as QCon, AppSphere, CIO, ITEXPO.

>> Listen to your virtual team members (as remote workers, they're often the first to hear about some cool new file-sharing or teleconferencing platform).

>> Schedule regular sessions with key managers to review your IT operations and suggest areas for improvement.

For more ideas, check out Chapter 15.

Forms

The following forms are online at www.dummies.com/go/businessplanskit and can help you explain your company's strategy in your business plan.

Form 12-1	Checklist of the Benefits of a Virtual Organization	Use this form to prioritize the advantages you hope to gain by operating as a virtual business.
Form 12-2	Challenges of Managing a Virtual Organization	Use this form to identify the most significant challenges your business will face.
Form 12-3	Remote Employee Hiring Checklist	Use this form to rate prospective employees for their ability to succced in a virtual business organization.
Form 12-4	Job Description Worksheet	Use this form to create job descriptions for your remote employees.

Chapter 13

Planning for an Established Business

When you start a new venture, business planning feels essential. After all, you need to have all the answers at your fingertips when bankers, investors, or others ask you details, so you write a plan. But after your company is up and running, you may be tempted to assume that business planning is behind you.

It's not. Or at least it shouldn't be, if you want your business to succeed in the face of change.

REMEMBER

If you don't have a process in place to fine-tune your business to meet the realities of today and the forecasts for tomorrow, you're apt to get overtaken — by technology, by competition, by market conditions, and by the changing world around you. Never has that been truer than today. Companies without an ongoing planning process in place, one that allows them to respond quickly and strategically, run the risk of finding themselves out of business.

Whether you want to grow, seek financing, prepare for a sale, or plot a business turnaround, this chapter helps you take stock of your business situation today and develop a plan that steers you clear of trouble and toward opportunity in the days and years ahead.

Purpose-Driven Planning

If your established business doesn't have a business plan, you're on a trip without a road map, and that's reason enough to start writing one today. Odds are you already have a plan, but it needs to be updated. If your business is like most established businesses, you're getting ready to write or rewrite your business plan to address one of the following situations:

>> You're raising capital or seeking new rounds of financing.

>> You're positioning yourself for a sale or merger.

>> You're preparing for business expansion.

>> You're working to overcome business downturns or disruptions.

The upcoming sections deal with what's involved in planning for each of these purposes.

Planning to Raise Capital

Entrepreneurs in need of money to get their businesses started or to fund expansion plans can finance their business plans in many different ways. (Chapter 8 explores how to find funding in detail.) Of the alternatives, most established businesses focus on two options: bank financing and investor capital.

Bank financing

If a primary purpose of your plan is to obtain bank financing, bankers are your primary audience, and the bank where you have established relationships is likely your best starting point.

REMEMBER

Bankers need to see your complete business plan, for sure, but be aware that your executive summary — the part they'll flip to first — is where they expect to find a succinct overview of your business purpose, situation, finances, goals, and the strategies you'll follow to achieve success. (Refer to Chapter 1 to see what goes into an executive summary.)

Plus, bankers want to see the specifics of your loan request, such as:

>> How much do you want to borrow? Naturally, potential lenders want to make sure that the amount you hope to secure is reasonable in light of your business's bottom line.

>> How will you use the loan funding? In reviewing a loan request from an established company, a banker will want to see how the funds will be used for positive purposes that will contribute to business growth and profitability, and thus to the certainty of loan repayment. Will you use the funds to hire new employees, fund a major marketing effort, purchase equipment or a business building, or pay off debts? Be specific.

>> What positive impact do you expect the loan funding to have on your business? What goals or objectives will it help you achieve? Lenders are more confident forking out money if you give them reason to believe the loan will improve your business and boost its profits.

>> What repayment terms are you requesting? Business loans come in many shapes and sizes, from short-term bridge loans to long-term loans, each with its own terms.

>> How can you demonstrate your ability to meet the payment terms? Show financial statements, forecasts, and cash-flow projections to prove that you'll be able to repay the loan on the schedule that you're proposing. See Chapter 9 for help assembling your financial statements.

>> What collateral or assets will you pledge to secure the loan? As you seek loans, refer to Chapters 8 and 11 to review different types of loans and visit the Small Business Administration website at www.sba.gov for information on government-backed loan programs.

Investor capital

Major capital investors fall into two categories:

>> *Venture capitalists* are professional investor groups whose major motivation is return on investment.

>> *Angel investors* are successful and wealthy entrepreneurs who invest in up-and-coming companies with their money and also with their expertise and guidance.

Both types invest in established companies with proven products, markets, and business models, but angel investors are more willing than venture capitalists to entertain smaller investment requests and to invest at an earlier stage in a company's life cycle.

Whichever approach you decide to pursue, when you're trying to raise capital through investors, you need to present much of the same information that bankers require — and then some.

Whereas bankers want to know how you'll repay them, investors want to know when and how they'll see not only a repayment, but also a sizeable return on their investments. As you make a proposal to investors, be sure to cover the following points:

>> The amount of funding you're seeking

>> How you'll use the funds and what impact the investment will have on your success

>> What return on investment the investors can expect to receive

>> When the investors will get their money back

>> What the investors will receive for their backing (equity in the company, for example, or a role on your board)

>> What reporting you will provide to keep investors informed about how you are spending their money

Now more than ever, venture capitalists and angel investors need to be convinced that your idea will provide a return on their investment. Don't waste your time or theirs unless you're certain that your executive summary and business plan can convince them that your business idea is unique and timely with a large and growing market, that you have proven personal leadership abilities, that your management team has strong and relevant expertise, and that your strategy is capable of delivering impressive sales and profit margins.

New equity investment approaches

The Internet has opened up new opportunities for funding, mostly by making it much easier for people who need money to connect with people who have bucks to lend. A growing number of online sites bring lenders and borrowers together. Some pool money from groups of investors. Others, like Kickstarter, reach out to individuals interested in helping promising start-ups — which can range from eco-friendly businesses to filmmakers hoping to raise the cash they need to shoot a movie. Called *crowdsourcing*, these new approaches have traditionally offered investors a reward, such as membership or a discount, in return for their financial help. But some crowdsourcing efforts now offer equity in return for money. For additional information, check out Chapter 8.

Planning for Business Growth

Chances are good that you want to see your business grow — a little or a lot. To do so, you probably want to win new customers or earn more business from your existing customers. To achieve your goal, you may need to

>> Open new market areas

>> Introduce new products

>> Offer new services

>> Initiate new customer-service programs

>> Enhance your competitive position so that more customers choose your business offerings over those of your major competitors

TIP

If you want to grow, your business plan needs to set and describe such growth strategies. See Chapter 5 for information on the major ways that companies plan for growth and then complete Form 13-1 to consider approaches you may want to pursue. You can find all the forms in this chapter at `www.dummies.com/go/businessplankit`.

Planning to Lock in Customer Loyalty

Assume that you have a crackerjack product or service to offer and a clever marketing team that knows how to grab the attention of potential customers. Your business is out of the gate and already ahead of expectations. So what could go wrong?

WARNING

If you're like many of the companies we've consulted for, trouble comes in the form of customers who buy something, like what they get — and then for some reason don't come back for more. Here's why that's a big problem: most businesses spend a lot of time and money reaching customers and convincing them to make that first purchase. The only way to amortize that customer-acquisition investment is to win repeat business. You may actually lose money on the customer who only buys from you once.

To retain customers, you have to continue to offer them top quality and great service, while adapting what you offer to meet changing needs, of course. But these days, you may also need to set up a customer loyalty program to give them an extra incentive to come back. Checkout Chapter 4 for more on planning a customer loyalty program.

Planning in Times of Trouble

As the saying goes, stuff happens. The economy tanks. A big client takes its business elsewhere. A product that looked really good on paper doesn't appear nearly as attractive in real life. A regulatory ruling abruptly alters your business landscape. A competitive assault blindsides your business. Key employees stage a mutiny.

You get the drift. In business, sometimes the going gets tough, and your strategic plan is reduced to tatters as a result. That's when you need to revisit your business plan — in a hurry.

Maybe your business model — your plan for how you make money — isn't quite what it was cracked up to be. (See Chapter 3 for information on business models.) Maybe your financial projections were a little too rosy. Maybe your analysis of your strengths, weaknesses, opportunities, and threats (see Chapter 5 for the lowdown) missed some key points. Instead of throwing up your hands in despair, use these sections to pinpoint what went wrong and to begin planning a way to turn the situation around.

Diagnosing your problems

Most companies don't land in hot water overnight. Warning signs usually precede disruptions, even if they're not always easy to see.

TIP

So how do you know if your company is headed for trouble? Use Form 13-2 to scan some of the early warning signs. If you see items that hit close to home, check out those issues as they relate to your company. If none of the warning signs apply to your company, congratulate yourself for passing the test but keep the list handy and return to it from time to time, just to be on the safe side. If you check three or more items on Form 13-2, however, definitely revisit your business plan and the assumptions behind it.

Suppose that customers aren't flocking to your new location the way you thought they would. Go back to your original market analysis to see what assumptions you made at the outset. Next, look at how the current situation differs from the way you envisioned it to be. Do you face unanticipated competition? Have your customers' wants and needs changed? Was your promotion inadequate? Pinpoint the problems and redraft your business plan to accurately address your business situation.

WARNING

Don't play the blame game or look for scapegoats. Even if you ultimately decide that you need to make personnel changes, the first step isn't to place blame; you need to figure out what went wrong and how to get your business back on track.

Getting a second opinion

Sometimes getting an outside opinion about a difficult business situation can be helpful. When your company faces a crisis, you can bring in *turnaround profession-als* to help determine what's wrong and how to revise your business plan to address the situation. To find consultants, start at the Turnaround Management Association website (www.turnaround.org).

Before you enlist outside help, you may want to bring your own management team together to assess the damage and to attempt to find a solution. Done right, this meeting of minds can create a stronger sense of teamwork and inspire the troops. And, with any luck, you'll come up with good, creative, strategic solutions.

REMEMBER

Keep in mind that your own management team may not see critical issues objectively. Vested interests, assumptions, and emotions can get in the way. Outside consultants, such as turnaround professionals, don't carry the excess baggage. They can take a clear-eyed and unemotional look, pinpoint what's wrong, and help arrive at a solution — even if it's a painful one. Most are available to guide the redirection of your business plan and to help steer the turnaround process.

Analyzing your current situation

To begin shaping a plan to get your business back on course, you need to know exactly where you stand — with an emphasis on the word *exactly*. When your company is in trouble, focus on three parts of business planning:

>> **Financial review:** Business troubles usually boil down to a simple, painful fact: Money is flowing out faster than it's coming in. Now you have to assess your current financial picture, focusing on cash flow and revised financial projections. (Check out Chapter 9 for details.)

>> **SWOT analysis:** The opportunities and threats your business faces today may have changed since you last analyzed your business situation. Even your relative strengths and weaknesses may be different. Take time to revisit your last SWOT analysis and direct your attention to the strategic issues that are most likely to have an immediate, positive impact on your situation. (Refer to Chapter 5 for assistance.)

>> **Business model:** Your *business plan* describes how you plan to build your business. Your *business model* defines how your business will make money. If your business plan isn't working, or if your finances are askew, a shaky business model is very likely to be part of your problem. Revisit your notions about how your company expected to make money. Spend some time thinking about ways to revise or expand your model to bring in more revenue as you work to turn your business around. (Again, Chapter 5 helps out.)

BACK TO BASICS

For years, Moe's Music did okay renting and selling musical instruments. Then, the California music shop decided to expand into music education. The plan made sense on paper because many junior high and high schools were dropping music education programs, and Moe's Music hoped to pick up the slack.

The company's plans hit a sour note, however, when it had trouble recruiting and retaining qualified music teachers. It also struggled to find ways to control the quality of music instruction. On top of those problems, expanding its facilities to accommodate practice and rehearsal rooms proved more costly than projected. Within two years, the company was singing the blues.

Fortunately, the management team moved quickly to refocus the company's strategy. Instead of trying to run a music school, Moe's invited selected music teachers in the community to work as independent contractors, teaching in the rehearsal rooms for a small hourly fee. The shop began to stock music books and other instructional aids recommended by its independent teachers, making a small profit on each sale. Local bands were also invited to rent rehearsal spaces after hours. Within a year, Moe's business was back up to tempo.

Charting a Turnaround

If your company is facing a business downturn or even a crisis, create a revised business plan that reflects your new realities and sets out a step-by-step action plan to address them.

In crisis planning, don't start the whole process of business planning from scratch. Your mission and vision statements are likely still intact. Your company overview probably hasn't changed all that much. In fact, you can probably focus your immediate attention on the following four areas of your plan (the rest you can tend to later, after the heat is off):

>> Modify your goals and objectives.

>> Revise your company strategy.

>> Update your financial review.

>> Revise your action plan.

The steps you take are pretty much the same as those involved in assembling any other business plan. (See Chapter 16 for information on putting a plan together.)

The big difference when you're trying to orchestrate a turnaround is to keep the most urgent issues front and center. Focus your goals and objectives on resolving your direct threats and getting your company back on an even keel. The same goes for your revised strategies and action plan: Make sure that they specifically address the immediate problems you face and that they can achieve the solutions you propose within the time frames you set.

WARNING

Desperate times sometimes call for desperate measures. If you're awash in red ink or burning through resources faster than you can say venture capital, you have to take bold actions like slashing expenses, letting people go, or shaking up your management team. Doing so isn't easy or pleasant, but remember: If you can't do it, your investors will find someone who can. In fact, when turnaround professionals are brought in from the outside, one of the first steps they often take is to order a change at the top.

Keeping an eye on the clock

When you're creating a turnaround plan, time is critical — and not just because your money may be running out. When times get rough, employees grow restless, morale slides, and your company's reputation — both inside and out — begins to suffer. Over time, your relationships with suppliers, distributors, bankers, and even clients can deteriorate.

REMEMBER

The faster you turn things around, the smaller the impact this rocky period will have on your business and its future. As you draft your revised goals and objectives, keep one eye on the clock. Set precise deadlines by which to complete steps and make sure that everyone takes those deadlines to heart.

TIP

You want to set aggressive but not unreasonable time frames. Meet with the people who will actually be doing the work to discuss exactly what it's going to take and to agree on the quickest deadlines that make sense. Get ironclad commitments all around. Your No. 1 goal must be to reassure everyone around you that your company can make good on its word — and that means making promises that you can keep.

Focusing on what's doable

When your company is in trouble, you're looking for bare bones, no-nonsense planning. You have to focus on what you *can* do, not what you *want* to do. Don't make the mistake of turning your goals and objectives into a wish list. Sure, developing a new technology to streamline your manufacturing or expanding into international markets would be nice — and maybe someday you will — but, when times are tough, focus on what you can afford to undertake with your strained budgets and time frame.

Getting the right people in the loop

If your business is in trouble, you'll hear from plenty of unhappy people: unhappy investors, unhappy vendors, unhappy employees, and unhappy customers. You can't order smiles back onto their faces (they will come when the company's back in the black again), but you can follow this good advice: Whatever you do, keep on talking. Keep everybody continuously informed about exactly what's going on.

Turnaround professionals advise that you

>> Meet with your management team

>> Meet with your senior advisers

>> Meet with your employees

>> Meet with your customers

>> Meet with your suppliers

>> Contact the tax authorities

>> Contact your bank

TIP

In other words, stay in close communication with everyone who has any stake in your company and the turnaround you're working to accomplish. Don't pretend that business is better than it is. Be honest about what people can expect and when they can expect it. The more straightforward you are, the better the odds are that you'll keep people on your side. Remember, people are often your biggest asset, especially when your company experiences hard times.

Using your plan to communicate

You won't find a better way to convince people that you can change the fortunes of your company than by putting together a solid turnaround plan. In fact, make your revised plan the basis for communicating with all your stakeholders. Your investors and lenders will probably insist on seeing the plan. (In some cases, they may even play a role in shaping it.) Your suppliers aren't likely to clamor for it, but fill them in on the details anyway, especially if you can't pay them on time. At least you can give them the confidence that your good intentions are supported by a solid plan.

REMEMBER

Make sure that you also share your turnaround plan with employees — every last one. Teamwork is always important, but never more so than when a company is in trouble. If your whole staff is in on the plan, you enlist all employees' support along with their loyalty, plus you make it clear that everyone is on the same team.

Sharing your plan boosts morale at a time when people must work harder, often under difficult circumstances.

Pivoting Your Business

Business conditions can sometimes change in such a way that a business needs to make a 90-degree turn to stay profitable, dramatically shifting its business model, its core products and services, its target market, or even its corporate image. We don't mean crisis management. We mean having to make a cool-headed decision to turn the company in a different direction to ensure long-term success.

If the strategy behind your business plan involves a pivot, careful and detailed planning is particularly crucial.

The following section will help you decide if you really need to pivot your company and then guides you through the steps of planning and executing a change of course.

Defining the problem you want to solve

Companies typically decide to pivot their focus because they've run into trouble. If your company faces some problems, the best way to focus your efforts is to zero in on the one big problem you hope to solve by pivoting. Of course, everything in a company is interconnected, so identifying the root problem can sometimes be daunting. But the more sharply you focus on a single problem, the more successful you'll be in finding a solution.

EXAMPLE

When the latest economic downturn hit, a San Francisco-based landscape artist saw sales of her paintings dry up. When she bemoaned her situation with a business consultant friend, he suggested that maybe the real problem was her business model. She loved to paint. In fact, she created far more paintings than she could place in galleries. Selling paintings in galleries took time, and the galleries took a substantial cut. Because each painting didn't cost very much in terms of materials, he suggested that she drop the price for each painting and sell them directly on the Internet. She pivoted her business by adopting a new business model — dropping the price in order to increase volume of sales. Within months she was selling two or three paintings a week and earning way more than she ever had by exhibiting in galleries.

Assessing the benefits and risks

Whatever the reasons behind your decision to steer your company on a new course, make sure you carefully assess the benefits you hope to gain by making a big change. Then, weigh them against the risks by following these steps:

1. **Begin by stating clearly, in a sentence or two, the problem you face.**

2. **Outline your basic strategy for addressing the problem.**

   Be as specific as possible about the strategic steps you intend to take.

3. **For each of the strategic changes you list, write down the benefits you hope to gain.**

   Zero in on measurable results here, such as "increased online sales" or "greater customer loyalty."

4. **For each of the strategic changes you propose, list the potential risks.**

   Again, be as specific as possible.

After you've considered both the hoped-for benefits and the potential risks, strategize ways to maximize the benefits and minimize the risks. Put your strategies in writing in your plan.

EXAMPLE

Toyota made its name in the 1970s with reliable, low-cost automobiles. In the late 1980s, the Japanese car giant decided to enter the luxury car market with a new brand, Lexus (the name itself a melding of luxury and excellence). The pivot offered the obvious benefit of an expanded market. But the move had risks. The most serious: Car buyers might view the new Lexus as nothing more than a gussied-up Toyota with a few fancy extras thrown in and a much higher price. To keep Toyota's image as a reliable economy car maker from diluting the luxury appeal of the new line, the company sold the new cars in independent Lexus dealerships and advertised them independently. The strategy succeeded. Lexus soon became one of the world's most successful luxury automobiles. Many people weren't even aware that the two very different lines were manufactured by the same automaker. In 2005, Lexus separated from the parent company Toyota. It now has its own dedicated design, engineering, training, and manufacturing centers.

Taking advantage of synergies

Undertaking a sweeping change of direction can be overwhelming. But pivoting your company doesn't mean that you have to re-invent the wheel. Often, you can take advantage of synergies that will make the process both more efficient and more effective.

To do so, keep these steps in mind:

1. **Take a look at the strategies you've proposed to execute your pivot and break each one down into a list of detailed action steps you need to take.**

   This list should be as specific and comprehensive as possible.

2. **Review the action plan you've created by putting a check beside the items that you can accomplish using company resources or staff, thus taking advantage of existing synergies.**

3. **Put an X beside the items that really do feel as if they'll require you to re-invent the wheel — or in this case, do something the company has never done before.**

4. **Look at the items marked with Xs and consider how your company's existing strengths can be used to make the change as efficiently and effectively as possible.**

   Think about resources outside your company, too, that might create synergies that can make the task a little easier — good relationships with vendors, for instance, or a stable of independent contractors you already work with.

5. **If you think there may be synergies you haven't tapped, consider sponsoring a brainstorming session with a cross section of the company's staff.**

   During the session, identify synergies that will help you implement your action plan.

Getting everybody on board

Any big change in a company's direction ultimately affects almost everyone. Unfortunately, not everyone will be happy with the change at first. A lot of people may feel threatened — just at a time when you need their cooperation and commitment. That's why looking for every opportunity to keep people informed and motivated is so important. To get everyone on board, consider these points:

» Make sure everyone on staff understands why the changes are being made.

» Explain the benefits as clearly as possible.

» Keep employees informed about how the changes are likely to affect them.

» Give employees a chance to air their concerns and offer suggestions.

Balancing decisiveness with flexibility

After you make the decision to pivot your business, be decisive. To succeed, you have to be convinced that the change is the right one to make, and you have to convince your employees.

REMEMBER

But being decisive isn't enough. At the same time, you must remain flexible enough to adjust your course. Even the best-laid plans encounter unforeseen obstacles. In our experience, the most effective way to build flexibility into your plan is to establish metrics that allow you to measure your progress, along with a review process tied to a specific timeline. If you begin to fall short on an important metric, brainstorm ways to get back on track.

Using your customers as a guide

Don't get so caught up in the details of planning to pivot your business that you lose track of one essential fact: You're in business to provide customers with something they want or need. Your customers are your ultimate metric. If they're happy with what you provide, you're in business. If not, you're in trouble. You can check in with customers before, during, and after a pivot in several ways, including the following:

» Use customer focus groups to test new ideas and strategies.

» Check out what customers are saying about you and your offerings online.

» Use surveys to find out what customers think of the new direction you're taking.

» Check back with customers frequently to make sure your strategy is reaping the benefits you hoped for.

Turn to Chapter 4 for more tips on how to keep the lines of communication open with your customers.

Planning for a Merger or Sale

The time may come when you're ready to hang up the reins and call an end to your involvement in your company. In that case, your business plan needs to include an exit strategy that defines how you'll reap the value of your business upon your departure. Even for businesses just starting out, having an exit strategy in place is important. Knowing how you plan to leave your business will help you make the right decisions in starting and growing your enterprise.

TIP

If your exit strategy involves selling your business or merging it with another company in the near-term, business planning takes on a whole new urgency. Before contacting a business broker or approaching likely buyers, use Form 13-3 to ready your business for presentation. The following section guides you through all the important steps you need to take as you plan to sell or transfer your business.

Assessing your company's transferability

Even if your business is in great shape, you still have to convince prospective buyers that it can transfer into their hands and still stay strong. The issues of most concern are

>> **Whether customers will stay with the business even after a change of ownership:** A buyer wants to be convinced that clients are more loyal to the business than they are to you, the business owner. Be ready to show the number of clients who have long-standing relationships with your business and explain why they'll stay customers when the new owners take over. Also be prepared to explain how customer information is kept in databases that can be transferred to the new owner.

>> **Whether the company's key capabilities and processes will remain intact:** A prospective owner must be convinced that the company will go on doing what it does well. Take time to assess whether your business has developed systems around your capabilities and whether those systems are easy to adopt, thanks to business and marketing plans and production and policy manuals.

>> **Whether legal contracts can be transferred:** A buyer wants to know that contracts for client, supplier, distributor, and other key business relationships exist and are transferable or assignable. The same goes for building and equipment leases. Especially in the case of your building lease, if your business success is reliant upon its location — as is the case with most restaurant and retail establishments — be sure your lease extends at least five years into the future.

>> **Whether the workforce will stay:** Key employee contracts, profit sharing programs, employee benefit plans, and other employment incentives help bind employees to a business, as do programs that inspire employee development and morale. Be prepared to explain your employment programs, plans, and policies to a buyer.

TIP

Form 13-4 helps you assess the transfer-readiness of your business in each of the four preceding categories. The owner of a sale-ready business will answer the questions with Yes answers. If you answer many of the questions with the answer No, consider actions you can take to remedy the situation so your business will be ready to transfer more easily to a new owner.

Planning for a change in leadership

When the head honcho of a big company becomes too closely associated with its success, the Board of Directors and investors begin to get nervous. No wonder. Unexpected things can happen, from illness to a defection to another company. If a firm's products and success appear to be the result of one individual — think iPods and iPhones — everyone gets jittery. Even in small companies where everyone pitches in, an unexpected change in leadership can cause major disruptions reaching all the way to the bottom line. Indeed, a lack of succession planning can be devastating in a small business caught by surprise when the top leadership departs.

REMEMBER

Planning for succession or a change in leadership is critical. Your blueprint for passing the torch doesn't necessarily have to be part of your written plan. But succession plans should definitely show up there if a change at the helm is imminent. You may also want to address your back-up plans for other top people on your management team, depending on the size of your company.

Forms

To help your established business meet new goals, check out the following forms, which you can find at www.dummies.com/go/businessplanskit.

Form 13-1	**Growth Strategies Worksheet**	Approaches to consider as you chart a growth strategy for your business
Form 13-2	**Checklist of Common Warning Signs**	Common danger signals that may mean your company is headed for trouble
Form 13-3	**Selling Your Business Worksheet**	Issues to address as you prepare your business for sale
Form 13-4	**Business Transferability: Assessing Your Sale Readiness**	Issues to consider if you plan to transfer your business

Chapter 14

Planning for a Nonprofit Organization

You may have heard the joke about the company that lost money year after year until it finally decided to become a nonprofit organization. The joke offers a good punch line, but people in the world of philanthropy know it's a long way from the real reason that organizations become nonprofits.

To nonprofits (also known as *not-for-profits* and *NPOs*), the bottom line isn't and never was about making money. Sure, fundraising is essential to underwrite programs, but to nonprofits, the ultimate motivation isn't the dollar but the good deed. To industry associations and business groups, doing well means helping others succeed. To charitable organizations, it means making the world a better place by aiding disaster victims, protecting the environment, offering childhood vaccinations, enhancing the arts, preserving history, protecting individual rights . . . the list goes on and on.

Nonprofits don't seek to make a profit, but they still need a business plan. Here's why: Business planning makes nonprofits more businesslike in how they operate and how they achieve success. A business plan provides a clear mission and vision. It helps you zero in on the people you plan to serve and what you aim to accomplish. And by doing all that, you put your organization in a position to raise more funds to devote to your good work. This chapter leads you down the nonprofit business-planning road.

Running a Nonprofit Like a Business

Every organization, whether for-profit or nonprofit, needs to manage its staff, set goals, market, deliver products and services, maintain budgets, and measure progress. The business rules are pretty much the same whether you're providing meals to shut-ins or turning your mother's cookie recipe into a million-dollar enterprise. Business fundamentals matter — no matter how lofty your mission.

Ditto for business planning. The same steps apply whether your venture is big or small, service or retail, for-profit or nonprofit. But to nonprofit organizations, certain steps require special attention. The following sections show you where to focus your efforts when writing your business plan.

Before launching a nonprofit organization, test your idea by asking these questions:

>> **Is this idea something you really believe in?** A driving passion isn't the only qualification for success, but it sure helps. Having that passion helps balance the fact that most people who start, run, or work with nonprofit organizations earn less money than they would working in the private sector. What motivates them isn't the money but doing something that they really care about.

>> **Does the nonprofit fill a need?** The process of planning is to make sure that your venture — for-profit or nonprofit — is likely to succeed. One indicator is whether it addresses a real market need. You probably don't think of nonprofits as competing in the same way that for-profit companies do, but in many ways they do. They often compete for scarce grant monies. They also need to check out what other similar nonprofits are doing to make sure that they aren't duplicating efforts. They have to convince donors that their work is worthwhile, and they have to reach clients who can use their services.

TIP

To test your idea, fill out the Nonprofit Planning Worksheet in Form 14-1. You can find it and the other forms in this chapter at www.dummies.com/go/businessplanskit. Don't agonize about how you word your answers; just give your responses serious consideration. Your findings will be useful when you write your mission, goals, and business plan.

Fine-tuning your mission and vision

Be sure that your business plan describes exactly what kind of a future you're working to create (your organization's *vision*), backed by a description of the purpose of your organization, what you do, whom you serve, and how you intend to achieve your vision (your organization's *mission*). Although mission and vision statements are important to all business planners, they're absolutely essential to the people running nonprofits. Here's why:

» The vision and mission statements define your organization's entire reason for being. Look at these two examples:

- A pharmaceutical company may work to find cures for diseases, but the real reason it's in business is to make money. In contrast, a nonprofit organization that's dedicated to providing breast cancer treatment to uninsured patients follows its mission to assist women in need.

- Bookshop owners do what they do because they love books, but they also sell books to earn income. A lending library, on the other hand, exists solely to encourage reading and promote knowledge.

» They describe reasons why others should believe in and support your efforts.

» They convey a compelling sense of what your organization is and what it does.

» They communicate the value your organization delivers and why its work is important.

» They appear in every grant proposal and fundraising request, and they need to be compelling enough to attract and persuade contributors — who make all your good works possible.

In addition to your vision and mission, you may want your business plan to include your organization's *values* by listing the underlying beliefs and principles that guide all your business decisions. Chapter 3 outlines all the steps involved in creating mission, vision, and values statements. It also features 12 mission statements from both the for-profit and nonprofit worlds.

REMEMBER

Don't be reluctant to "go for the heart" when you're crafting your vision and mission statement. Donors open up their wallets in part because of that heart-warming feeling that *they're* doing good by contributing their hard-earned cash. Make your case an emotional one, and you'll underscore the importance of your mission — and improve your fundraising success, as well.

TIP

For more examples of mission statements from a variety of nonprofit organizations, check out Form 14-2. Evaluate what you like and don't like about each one as you work on your mission statement.

DOING GOOD IN TIGHT TIMES

Nonprofits, like almost all other enterprises, are affected by downturns. But surveys show that the effects of an economic slump vary widely depending on the nature of the organization. Some charitable organizations, such as food banks, may see an increase in volunteers and donations. But others, including many cultural organizations such as volunteer orchestras and art programs for children, may experience a shortfall. Surveys suggest that the nonprofits that fare well have a few things in common:

- **Good communication:** Especially when the need is great and money is in short supply, nonprofits need to make the case for their critical importance as persuasively as possible.

- **Strong leadership:** It's easy for both paid staff and volunteers at nonprofits to get discouraged when they have to struggle for support to do the work they believe in. When funding falls short, morale can slump. A strong leader helps keep the troops focused and inspires everyone to make the extra effort.

- **Ambitious plans:** When times are tight, many organizations are tempted to reduce or eliminate programs. Sometimes cutting back is essential. But cutting too many programs too close to the bone can cause donors to wonder what they're donating for. Surprisingly, the nonprofits that did well during the last big downturn were typically groups that expanded their efforts, adding new programs and reaching out to help more people.

- **Diversified support:** Nonprofits that weather economic turmoil are typically those that get their support from a wide range of donors, including individuals, foundations, public sources, and others. Nonprofits that manage to diversify their support also find themselves in a stronger position during economic expansions.

TIP

Work with your board of trustees to review your organization's mission statement on a regular basis to see that it accurately reflects your organization's current situation. If the profile of the clients you serve or the causes you champion change over time, revise your mission statement accordingly.

Creating the appropriate structure

The United States has more than 1.5 million nonprofit organizations, ranging from small groups like Mentor Me Memphis to one of the largest, the Bill & Melinda Gates Foundation, endowed with more than $30 billion. In 2014, nonprofits accounted for more than 10 percent of all private-sector employment in the United States.

As you organize your nonprofit venture, you want to choose a legal structure appropriate for your situation. The following represent your basic options:

>> **Informal nonprofits:** As the name implies, these organizations are loose-knit groups of like-minded people who get together for activities or to be of service to the community. Examples include local book clubs, self-help support groups, or graffiti cleanup patrols. Informal nonprofits have no legal structure and typically raise and manage only small sums of money. They aren't big enough to fall under the watchful eye of the IRS.

>> **Nonprofit corporations:** Incorporation allows a nonprofit organization to protect its directors and staff from certain types of liability, similar to the protective shield offered to for-profit companies. Incorporation also ensures that the organization will be able to continue its activities even when the founding members are no longer around. To get the details on incorporation in your state, check with the office of your Secretary of State, Division of Corporations, or Attorney General.

>> **Tax-exempt nonprofits:** Nonprofit corporations with charitable, educational, scientific, religious, or cultural purposes can file for tax-exempt status under section 501 of the Internal Revenue Service Code. The major types of tax-exempt organizations include

- Charitable organizations (religious, educational, scientific, and literary organizations, for example)

- Social welfare organizations (civic leagues and community groups)

- Labor and agricultural organizations (labor unions and farm bureaus)

- Business leagues (trade associations and chambers of commerce)

- Social clubs (country clubs, fraternities, and sororities)

- Fraternal organizations (lodges and other clubs)

- Veterans' organizations (armed forces groups)

- Employees' associations (employee-benefit groups)

- Political organizations (campaign committees, political parties, and political action committees [PACs])

>> **Qualified nonprofits:** Donations to qualified nonprofits may be tax deductible — a distinction that can matter a great deal to contributors. Qualified organizations include religious, educational, scientific, and literary groups, as well as child and animal welfare organizations, certain veterans' organizations, fraternal societies, and more.

TIP

For information on whether your organization qualifies for tax–exempt status, check out *IRS Publication 557*. For a current list of qualified nonprofits, look at *IRS Publication 78*. Both publications are available on the IRS website at www.irs.gov.

Setting goals and objectives

How do you spell success? That's really what a discussion of goals and objectives is all about. To for-profit companies, the answer is easy: M-O-N-E-Y. To nonprofit organizations, however, the answer is far less tangible. You measure success not in dollars, but in how well your organization serves those in need or how well it advances the causes it champions.

Goals and objectives provide a road map that helps keep your organization on track; they keep your efforts focused on providing the greatest possible value to the clients you serve; and they help convince contributors that you're making a real difference in the world by stating in measurable terms the outcomes you deliver.

Think of it this way: Because your goals and objectives define the real bottom line of your nonprofit organization, they're the keys to unlocking support from donors and foundations. Without gifts and grants, you can't achieve your purpose. It's that simple.

TIP

Make sure that your written plan includes your organization's goals and objectives. If you don't already have them down on paper, turn to Chapter 3 for some easy-to-follow goal-setting tips. Also, be sure to think about your goals from the standpoint of your clients and your contributors by considering these questions:

>> What goals are most meaningful to the people you serve or the cause you're fighting for? How can you best meet those goals through a series of specific objectives?

>> What goals would best persuade your contributors that the work you do is important and makes a difference? What specific objectives would help convince them that you're meeting those goals?

REMEMBER

Even the highest ideals don't substitute for clearly stated goals and measurable objectives. Funders need more than an assurance that you're working to make the world a better place. They want to know for whom, in what way, and exactly how you'll measure your impact.

Sample goals and objectives

EXAMPLE

Take the example of a nonprofit group, Jobs For All, that matches unemployed people with employers who have entry-level positions to fill. One way to gauge its effectiveness would be to count the number of clients served each year or, better yet, the number of clients who were actually placed in jobs. If the organization's mission involves preparing people to work by teaching them job skills and helping them deal with issues like childcare, an even better measure of success would be to track how many people were placed in jobs that they kept for a reasonable length of time.

Measuring the nonprofit's results may lead the organization to set a goal to increase the number of clients successfully placed in long-term job situations. Another goal may be to increase funding in order to expand services.

Knowing their goals, the staff's next step is to write objectives that detail the measures they'll take in order to achieve each goal. For example, to increase the number of clients successfully served each year, objectives may include the following:

>> Enlisting ten new employers into the job-placement program over the next six months

>> Finding jobs for an additional 75 unemployed people in the coming year

>> Increasing the percentage of clients who actually remain employed for at least six months from 60 percent to 85 percent

A sample solicitation based on goals and objectives

After you establish your goals and objectives, use them as powerful motivators in fundraising campaigns. Take a look at this funding solicitation letter from the job-placement organization featured in the previous section:

EXAMPLE

Last year, Jobs For All placed 350 unemployed people in productive and meaningful positions in our community. This year, with your help, we plan to make that number 425. What's more, we're committed to increasing the percentage of our clients who remain on the job for at least six months from 60 percent to 85 percent.

How will we do it? First, we plan to expand our job-placement program. But that's only the beginning. We're working with the community college to offer basic computer-skills classes. And we're creating a job-assistance hotline to provide immediate help to our clients when they encounter problems at home or on the job.

But to do this, we need your help. Our fundraising goal of $500,000 represents a 20 percent increase over last year's target. We know that's ambitious. But we also know that with your generosity, we can change lives for the better.

Organizing to Do Good Work

Even though nonprofits don't have a profit motive, they still have to be efficient and accountable. If your organization relies on charitable contributions, donors will weigh your organizational capabilities in much the same way they weigh the capabilities of a for-profit company. Whether they're directing charitable funds or nest-egg dollars, investors want to ensure that their money goes into ventures that will succeed.

They want to be convinced that an organization has the capabilities to turn ideas into reality. We describe the qualities they look for in detail in Chapter 6, and you need to summarize them in the company description section of the business plan. As you write the plan for your nonprofit organization, pay special attention to these four qualities:

>> Strong and streamlined operations

>> Efficient organization

>> Experienced management

>> Innovative ideas based on R&D expertise that's capable of designing, developing, and enhancing distinctive products, services, and technologies

The following sections take a look at the aspects of these four qualities that are particularly important to nonprofit organizations.

Operations

The term *operations* typically refers to how companies carry out their business — that is, how they handle day-to-day activities and how they produce products and provide services efficiently and cost-effectively in order to maximize profits.

OPENING HEARTS, MINDS, AND WALLETS

Fundraising will probably play a starring role in your business plan for the simple reason that it's crucial to the health and well-being of most nonprofit organizations. In your plan, be sure to describe who will head your fundraising effort and how you will organize activities. Include your strategy for targeting and communicating with likely donors, who most often come from one or more of the following sources:

- Individuals

- Corporations

- Private foundations

- Community foundations

- Government agencies

Individuals represent by far the largest contributor group. In fact, most nonprofit fundraising campaigns receive 70 to 80 percent of their money from individuals:

- People who have given in the past are the most likely candidates to give again — so long as they have a sense that their money is being well spent.

- People who somehow benefit from your programs are usually receptive contributors.

- People who know firsthand of your good works are likely to support your work by writing checks. For example, a person who knows someone with Parkinson's disease is more likely to support related medical research than someone who knows very little about the illness.

What's the best way to reach individual donors? The answer depends on the nature of your organization and the kinds of contributors you plan to target. Door-to-door solicitations are great for local nonprofits or for large organizations with strong grassroots networks. If you can tell your story clearly and compellingly in print, a direct-mail campaign can be a cost-effective way to generate results.

As you craft your fundraising plans, use the questionnaire in Form 14-3 to gather information about your ideal individual donor.

To nonprofit organizations, efficient operations are just as important, but for different reasons. In your world, efficiency means that your organization does more with less. It means that you leverage maximum value out of every donor dollar by spending as little as possible to deliver quality services and support for your causes. And that means you end up reaching more people, doing more good, and, as a bonus, having an easier time raising funds in the future.

See that your business plan includes a discussion of how you'll address the following four areas that comprise your operations:

>> **Location:** As an example, an organization providing food to homeless people needs a location close to homeless shelters and social services.

>> **Equipment:** For example, if you plan to enhance online donor communications, you'll need the appropriate computers, a server, donor management software, and other tools.

>> **Labor:** No matter what your mission, you need a plan for recruiting and training paid staff and volunteers.

>> **Process:** You need to describe how you'll operate your organization. A food bank, for example, needs a process for gathering food contributions, sorting them in a central location, and delivering them to those in need.

As a nonprofit, your operations are important for another reason, too: Your organization will likely apply for grants, and grant applications require a detailed description of operational procedures in order to assess your ability to serve your constituents, recruit and keep necessary staff, and do your good work efficiently and effectively. Successfully managing these areas allows you to achieve a positive return on the grant dollars being invested in your organization. The good news is that you can probably cut and paste directly from your business plan — or at least borrow from the main points.

Organization

Some nonprofit groups manage to do their work entirely through the services of unpaid volunteers. When the groups reach a certain size, however, most organizations add a core staff of paid employees who work closely with the volunteer corps.

Often, the person who heads the professional staff is called a Chief Executive Officer (CEO) or sometimes a Chief Professional Officer (CPO). Some nonprofits also appoint a senior volunteer to the position of Chief Volunteer Officer (CVO). The CEO or CPO manages paid staff, and the CVO oversees volunteer activities.

TIP

In your business plan, include your organizational chart, indicating which positions are paid and which are opportunities for volunteer assistance. Assign titles — director of programs, for example, or director of fundraising — and include a summary of key job descriptions and responsibilities.

REMEMBER

Because the overriding purpose of most nonprofits is to promote worthy causes or serve people in need, salaries and compensation can be delicate issues. It's easy but inaccurate to view money spent on staff salaries as money not available for investment in your mission. Well-selected professionals make your organization efficient and effective and make achieving your mission possible. Although most people who choose to work for nonprofits are in it for reasons other than money, they still want to be compensated fairly for what they do.

If you're not certain how much to pay staff members, start by finding out what professionals in similar positions in for-profit and nonprofit organizations in your market area get paid.

Management

Most states require incorporated nonprofit groups to have a *board of trustees,* or a group of people who serve as the organization's official governing body, providing oversight and direction while also helping to raise funds, guide the organization, and shape its programs. (Contact your attorney or the office of your state's Attorney General for details.)

Even if your organization isn't incorporated, consider creating an informal advisory board to help steer your organization. As you select nominees for your board, look for people who are

>> Passionate about your nonprofit's mission

>> Ready, willing, and able to raise money

>> Experienced in the for-profit world of business

TIP

Form 14-4 provides a checklist of major duties that nonprofit boards of trustees often assume. Check the ones that are relevant to your organization and its requirements. Filling out this worksheet provides an idea about the kinds of capabilities you seek in board members, and it helps as you evaluate the overall makeup of your board.

In your written plan, list the members of your board of trustees along with their affiliations. If you don't yet have a board, describe the kinds of people you hope to recruit and how you plan to go about approaching them.

Research and development (R&D)

In the nonprofit arena, R&D rarely involves technological breakthroughs or science and engineering feats. For nonprofits, R&D usually means researching issues that affect the clients and funders of your organization and developing programs that fit the changing realities of the world around you.

In the for-profit marketplace, the consequences of change are pretty hard to miss. When customers stop buying a company's products, the firm adapts or goes under.

Nonprofits, on the other hand, are a bit more insulated from competition, and that's precisely why research is so important: It helps your organization stay a step ahead of change, which, in turn, helps ensure that your services are responsive to real and current needs.

Large nonprofits hire outside specialists to conduct studies and write reports on the key issues they address, but you can take steps on your own, too. For example, you may conduct a survey of your client groups, obtain and pore over government reports, or analyze statistics that apply to your organization's work (like the regional rate of domestic abuse, the continuing loss of regional open space, or the changing face of local homelessness).

Whatever the focus of your research and whoever carries it out, the goals of your research should include the following:

>> Understanding basic issues

>> Tracking major trends and external changes

>> Identifying unmet program and service needs

>> Weighing the pros and cons of alternative solutions

>> Evaluating the effectiveness of existing programs

REMEMBER

In the company description of your business plan, include key research to underscore the importance of the work you do. Also, describe how you plan to conduct ongoing research in order to stay abreast of the changing needs of your clients, your causes, and your organization.

Gathering Grants and Courting Donors

Unless you're lucky enough to have a bottomless endowment that pays all your bills, your nonprofit is likely to depend on money from grants and donors. Fortunately, if the work you do matters, you should be able to find groups and individuals ready to open their wallets. These sections help you locate sources of donations and grants and plan fundraising events.

Finding funding

Because fundraising is so crucial to many nonprofit organizations, your written plan needs to explain exactly where you intend to get the money to support your efforts and how much you expect to raise.

Typically, nonprofits take in the money they need to operate from the following sources:

>> Donations from companies and individuals

>> Government or private foundation grants

>> Income from endowments and trusts

>> Income from products and services, such as proceeds from the museum shop, concert tickets, and door-to-door cookie sales

>> Special fundraising events (check out "Planning fundraising activities" later in this chapter)

Most nonprofits rely on a combination of these funding sources. National Public Radio (NPR), for example, relies on donations from listeners like you, corporate sponsors, and a little bit of help from Uncle Sam.

One common source of funding for nonprofits is grants, which come in just about every shape and size imaginable, from small local grants to large grants from international foundations. Whether you're going after a modest grant or a major one, you can expect to have to write a grant proposal. Most foundations provide detailed directions about the information they want in order to consider making a grant.

TIP

For an overview of the typical parts of a grant proposal, take a look at Form 14-5. A solid written business plan provides most of the information you need to fill out a grant proposal.

TIP

If grants are likely to be a significant source of your funding, consider hiring a grant writer. Yes, you're likely to have to spend a little money up-front. But professionals with experience in grant writing often pay for themselves in the grants they manage to land for nonprofits. Top-notch grant writers may be able to steer you to grants you weren't even aware of.

Wherever your dollars come from, be sure you establish a detailed record-keeping system. If your nonprofit is incorporated, official corporate documents, board-meeting minutes, financial reports, and other records must be preserved over the life of the organization. For more information, check with the office of your Secretary of State or state Attorney General.

All kinds of new Internet-based and mobile technologies make the job of raising money and managing donors and donations easier than ever. Check out sites such as DonorSnap, Causes, Crowdrise, FirstGiving, FundRazr, Givezooks!, and Givlet to compare the tools and services offered to nonprofits. Mobile payment systems like `Square` make it much easier to accept payment by credit card during fundraising events. `Paypal` offers nonprofit organizations reduced transaction charges.

Tailoring your plan to big donors

Ideally, a nonprofit, like a good investment portfolio, will be diversified. That means it gets its support from a wide range of donors. But some nonprofits, because of the kind of work they do, rely very heavily on one or two major foundations for their support, which is okay. However, if you plan to get the majority of your funding from one or two foundations, make sure you know everything you can in advance about the criteria they use.

Fortunately, most major charitable foundations have very specific guidelines posted on their websites. After all, they want to make sure that nonprofits with a good idea do their homework before submitting a grant application. Review those guidelines very carefully as you craft your business plan. You may be able to lift chunks of your plan into the grant application, saving you time and speeding the process of getting money.

EXAMPLE

The Bill & Melinda Gates Foundation, for example, is best known for its efforts to improve global health. But the foundation also offers a variety of grants to promote education and other issues in the United States. What are they looking for? The foundation's website answers that question in detail. The scope of its grants is so wide today, in fact, that the foundation guides prospective applicants in part by listing what it *doesn't* fund. That list includes

>> Direct donations or grants to individuals

>> Projects addressing health problems in developing countries

>> Political campaigns and lobbying efforts

>> Building or capital campaigns

>> Projects that exclusively serve religious purposes

If a nonprofit's good cause doesn't get tripped up by one of these exclusionary criteria, it may have a shot.

Planning fundraising activities

Most small- and medium-sized nonprofits raise at least some of their money from fundraising events, which range from silent auctions and dance-a-thons to special presentations and events. Some nonprofits depend almost entirely on fundraisers. If your group plans to raise a chunk of its cash from such activities, your business plan should address the details — including both how much the fundraisers will cost and how much you plan to raise. If the fundraiser is a very big part of your revenue, it deserves a business plan of its own.

TIP

Successfully running a big fundraiser is a lot like running a small company. In fact, if you're a small nonprofit planning a big event, you may need to hire an event–planning professional. The more carefully your organization thinks through all the aspects of a fundraiser, the more successful it's likely to be. Consider the following points when planning a fundraiser:

>> **Know your purpose.** Besides raising funds, fundraisers publicize what your nonprofit does, help enlist new volunteers, and win community support. Outline your goals and objectives thoroughly as part of the planning process.

>> **Pick the right venue.** Seek out a spot that's conveniently located, comfortable, and an appropriate size for what you plan to do.

>> **Think like your guests.** Spend time brainstorming about what your guests are likely to want and what will encourage them to donate. Think through what a typical guest's experience will be from arriving to leaving the event.

>> **Plan advance sales.** Selling tickets in advance helps you know how many people are likely to attend your fundraiser and also gives you cash up-front to produce the event.

>> **Keep them entertained.** Speeches may be an essential part of your fundraiser, but keep them short. Provide entertainment, when appropriate.

>> **Offer multiple ways to donate.** Don't just rely on entrance tickets. Include a silent auction, a raffle, games of chance, or other moneymakers. Provide a way for people who can't attend the fundraiser to donate, such as an online auction.

>> **Give something back.** Consider offering attendees a little something as a way of saying thanks — a tote bag, T-shirt, or wine glass embossed with the name of your nonprofit, for instance. Make sure the thank you gift is appropriate to the nature of the nonprofit and the fundraising event.

>> **Account for all donor levels.** Some of your support may come from very deep pockets, but chances are you also depend on small donors. Make sure a fundraising event allows donors at all levels to participate.

>> **Get the word out.** Start publicizing your event well in advance. Contact local media (newspapers, radio and TV stations, community websites, and blogs), put up posters, post social media announcements and updates, and send out email blasts to make sure people know about your event.

>> **Say thanks.** You may be amazed at how many nonprofits stage an event, count the proceeds, and never say thanks to their donors. Thanking people individually helps ensure that they'll be back next year. Be sure to thank donors big and small. Today's small donor could well become a much bigger supporter next year.

Keeping the Books

Nonprofits aren't in business for the money, but if they don't keep track of the money they handle in a businesslike way, they may find themselves in hot water — or even out of operation entirely. You can find everything you need to know about the basics of business accounting in Chapter 9, and the same rules pretty much apply to for-profits and nonprofits alike. However, a few special financial considerations apply specifically to nonprofits, and that's what this section is all about.

Managing overhead

Imagine if a nonprofit organization spent 80 percent of its revenue on fundraising events and 20 percent of its revenue on supporting its causes and clients. Donors would quickly question whether they were contributing to a charitable group or to a fundraising engine.

As a nonprofit, you need to keep your expenses in line. Whether you're talking about office rent, supplies, advertising and promotions, or the budget for your next fundraising event, watch your costs like a hawk:

>> Be sure your overhead matches the standards that donors expect from charitable organizations.

>> Keep your spending to the lowest possible percentage of your organization's income, aiming for a number under 25 percent.

WARNING

>> Let your expenses climb at your own peril. Organizations like the Wise Giving Alliance (formed when the National Charities Information Bureau merged with the Council of Better Business Bureaus Foundation) provide donors with reports on the charitable performance of soliciting organizations. Their guidelines stipulate that member organizations must spend at least 65 percent of funds raised on program activities, keeping overhead to less than 35 percent. Even small organizations are wise to adopt similar ratios. For more information on the Wise Giving Alliance, visit www.give.org.

Putting working cash to work

Just like for-profit companies, nonprofits need a cushion of cash or other liquid assets on hand. The question is, how much? The answer depends largely on the nature of your nonprofit's mission. For example, a relief agency that responds to unforeseen disasters needs a large bank balance ready to draw upon when the unforeseen need occurs. A nonprofit that runs a community food bank, however, probably doesn't need anywhere near as great a reserve.

You can imagine why cash reserves are a touchy subject: People donate money to further a good cause, not to see their money sitting around in a bank account somewhere. (The exception is endowment funds, which are set up specifically to generate interest income to fund nonprofit programs.)

REMEMBER

If you do keep a sizeable reserve fund, be sure your donors understand why the reserve is necessary. Also be sure that your organization has a procedure in place to protect the funds for the appropriate programs and against erosion from administrative or operational expenses.

Staying accountable

Nonprofit organizations are founded on trust. Donors trust that you'll use the money they give wisely, and grant makers trust (and usually verify) that you use the funds they provide for the purposes described in the grant application. The members of the board of trustees are responsible for making sure that the organization lives up to its pledges, and that means maintaining accountability by keeping track of where, when, and how the organization spends each dollar.

REMEMBER

In your business plan, include provisions for an annual audit of your organization's finances.

Many nonprofits hire professional accounting firms to conduct an audit in order to make sure it's independent and objective. But if your nonprofit is small or relatively new, you may opt to create a volunteer committee of people with experience in accounting to review the records, verify bank balances, and produce a written report of their findings. In order to ensure that the committee has no conflict of interest, it should operate completely independently of the board of trustees.

Marketing and Promoting a Nonprofit

All you have to do is watch the public service ads on television to see that some of the biggest and most high-profile nonprofits spend a lot of time — and money — trying to get their message out to the public. The big reason is to attract financial support, of course. But nonprofits also want people to know what they're doing in order to develop a strong image and to make sure that the people they serve are aware of their offerings.

REMEMBER

Your nonprofit may not be ready to produce its own television spot, but even the smallest nonprofit organization should have a marketing strategy in its plan. Your strategy may be as simple as producing a website or brochure or as complex as sending volunteers door-to-door. Whatever your strategy for attracting dollars and donors, it should be spelled out in the plan.

Social media networking sites offer creative ways to get the word out about your good work and to enlist support. Many nonprofits have discovered that their web presence is key to keeping donors informed and to raising cash. Donors are often willing and grateful to receive periodic email messages and newsletters with updates about how their money is being spent.

TIP

Check out Form 14-6 for a checklist of what effective marketing materials should include. Don't be reluctant to toot your own horn. If you really believe in the work you're doing, you should be proud of it. Let the world know.

Forms

If you're part of a nonprofit organization, take a look at the following forms at www.dummies.com/go/businessplanskit to help you plan:

Form 14-1	**Nonprofit Planning Worksheet**	A worksheet that helps you develop your nonprofit idea
Form 14-2	**Examples of Real-World Nonprofit Mission Statements**	A selection of nonprofit mission statements along with space to record your impressions
Form 14-3	**Ideal Individual Donor Questionnaire**	Questions that help you gather information about your ideal individual donor
Form 14-4	**Checklist of Responsibilities for a Nonprofit Board**	A list that helps you determine the capabilities you seek on your board of trustees
Form 14-5	**Checklist of Typical Grant Proposal Sections**	The typical sections you should think about including in your grant proposal
Form 14-6	**Checklist of Nonprofit Marketing Strategies**	A list of items to consider including in your marketing strategy

Chapter 15

Planning in a Transformed World

C hange is the factor you can most count on as you plan for business success in this early part of the 21st century. Products have always moved through life cycles and markets have always evolved, but today's changes sweep wider and faster. Technological innovations alter how businesses operate and compete. Digital communications reshape customer relationships and competitive landscapes. Global, economic, and political upheaval shake up business environments. Disruptive innovations upend industries. Consider the following:

>> It took nearly a generation for people to switch from buying long-playing vinyl albums at record stores (remember them?) to downloading MP3s — but it took only a few years for consumers to shift from owning music to listening through streaming-music services.

>> Seven years after the 2007 iPhone introduction nearly two-fifths of American households had cut the home phone cord, disrupting the century-old landline telephone network. By 2017, analysts predict the number of mobile devices will exceed the number of people on the planet.

>> As of 2015, 100 billion Apple apps had been downloaded — from zero in 2008 — making apps more ubiquitous than pencils.

>> Since the 1970s, data storage migrated from floppy disks to CDs to DVDs to USBs. Today data has moved online and into in the cloud, vaporizing previous solutions and cratering businesses that failed to forecast the future.

Next up? Self-driving cars, in-home 3D printing, robotics, augmented reality, rapid expansion of everyday devices connected through the Internet of Things (IoT), transformations in healthcare, and, no doubt, innovations not yet imagined.

For business planners, change presents huge opportunities or, if unanticipated, considerable upheaval. That's why this new edition of *Business Plans Kit For Dummies* helps you plan for change through every step of your business plan development.

>> Chapter 2 includes a section on testing your business idea against changes in marketplace conditions.

>> Chapter 4 helps you analyze how changes affect consumer tastes and purchasing trends.

>> Chapter 5 guides you through a SWOT analysis to assess your business strengths, weaknesses, opportunities, and threats in light of the changes it faces.

>> Chapter 6 has a section on aligning business capabilities with changing conditions. It also describes how to pivot your business strategies, if changes in your business world make a complete course correction necessary or opportunistic.

>> Chapter 8 sheds light on important changes that affect how and where to get funding for your business.

>> Chapters 10 through 14 include tips on adapting to change when writing a business plan, whether for a one-person business, a start-up or small business, a virtual business, an established business, or a nonprofit organization.

This chapter focuses entirely on proactively planning for change as a fundamental step in the business planning process. It helps you identify the drivers of change in your business arena so you can anticipate the likely impact and devise strategies to avert trouble and gain competitive advantage.

Recognizing the Drivers of Change

When events or situations within or outside your company positively or negatively influence how your business operates and succeeds, they're considered *driving forces* or *drivers of change.* They take many forms, and more often than not a number of change drivers combine to shape a company's fate.

Take into consideration the solar energy industry. Only a few years ago, rapid technological advances made solar panels more efficient and economical at the same time that regulatory incentives and tax credits made installing solar panels far more attractive for many households. Add in regulations designed to lower carbon emissions, and at least three distinct drivers of change contributed to growth, resulting in more solar panel installations over the past several-year period than over previous decades combined.

But change is an ongoing condition, and today the solar energy industry continues to transform. With so many solar panels installed, with installation warrantees expiring, with investment incentives declining, with utility companies fighting for solar-usage surcharges, and with new methods for storing solar-generated electricity, solar business planners face a new round of change drivers. They're anticipating and responding to changes with revised pricing, a shift of emphasis from installation to maintenance contracts, operational changes to enhance technical performance, collaborative partnerships with energy storage innovators, and new efforts to influence tax incentives and regulatory policies.

The transformations facing your business may be less glaring, but you can be sure that when it comes to change, your business isn't immune. Read on for help diagnosing the factors affecting your business, assessing the impact, and planning proactive change-management strategies.

The first step in successfully navigating around change is recognizing the key drivers of change in your business and your industry. Most fall within these categories:

>> **External drivers** are forces outside the control of your business. They include such wide-ranging factors as changes in technology, the fluctuations in environment, access and cost of resources and raw materials, political trends or movements, rules and regulations, industry outlook, competition, disruptive innovations, and market conditions, including changes in demographics, consumer behaviors, and purchase preferences.

>> **Internal drivers** are forces within the control of your business. Common factors include changes in leadership, business mission, branding, products or product lines, product pricing, systems, operations, technology, equipment, staffing, morale, and financial condition.

Go to www.dummies.com/go/businessplanskit to view and download Form 15-1, which lists the main change drivers in most industries. Put a check beside those that are most likely to have an impact on your business. Give this form some thought. Your answers are the basis for anticipating and managing change and overcoming the disruption it can deliver to even the smallest business.

EXAMPLE

Consider the example of a self-employed artist. Shifts in economic conditions and art collection trends reduced the number of people willing to plop down a thousand dollars or more for a piece of original art and, as a consequence, put a number of small galleries where artists show their work out of business. Fortunately, Internet sites where artists could market and sell art offered alternate opportunities for reaching customers, although they quickly became a crowded and competitive environment. At the same time, though, other factors opened entirely new opportunities. For example, forward-thinking artists realized that the aging Baby Boom generation included hobbyists willing to plunk down money for online courses, instructional videos, and books about painting and drawing. Artists who saw and seized upon the opportunity found themselves subsidizing their art with revenue from instructional online courses, videos, and educational workshops. Even though other artists struggle, those who spotted the trends early, and planned accordingly, have weathered the turbulence.

Proactively Planning for Change

As part of your business-planning process, assess the major changes your business faces and devise a response plan for each area, using the advice in the following sections.

Planning around economic uncertainties

Anticipating future economic conditions will always be a guessing game. By doing some research, however, you can arrive at informed guesses. Take a few minutes to think about which of the following four main drivers of economic change might affect your business.

>> **Economic policy and regulatory changes:** New regulations and taxes can dramatically change the economic climate for companies. For example, a dramatic adjustment in interest rates can make business borrowing and expansion easier or much more difficult. New environmental regulations can pose challenges for some companies and offer huge opportunities for others. Returning to the solar power example from the preceding section, consider that a phase-out of tax rebates can slow panel installations or, if anticipated and used as a marketing lever, can speed decisions to purchase while rebates are still in force.

>> **Manufacturing and material costs:** For companies dependent on materials and commodities, changing prices can have a big impact on the bottom line. When coffee prices soar, for example, chains like Starbucks

and Peet's have to figure out how to make a profit without raising their prices so high that customers balk.

» **Environmental disruptions:** Mother Nature can overturn the best-laid plans. Today and for the foreseeable future, one issue that confronts many businesses around the world is global climate change. Increased flooding, more intense storms, and extended droughts come with significant economic consequences. Certain industries are more exposed than others. If yours is one of them, don't wait to begin to plan how your business will respond.

» **Political instability:** Wherever you do business, you may have to deal with shifting political winds. A change in government, a new economic policy, or political unrest can all affect your ability to do business and make a profit.

TIP

Take time to identify key economic uncertainties that confront your business. Then begin to think about how you can address potential changes proactively. For instance, a business with overseas operations can limit its liability to political instability by avoiding countries that represent high risk. Farmers concerned about reduced rainfall can choose crop varieties that require less water. A mom-and-pop store in a neighborhood that has begun to experience problems with crime can consider heightened security or moving their store to a safer area.

REMEMBER

If your business faces significant economic uncertainties, your written plan should spell them out in detail. It should also describe your plans to address potential disruptions.

Creating a technology plan

New technologies create opportunity, but they can also cause disruption.

EXAMPLE

Just ask the guy who used to run the successful video rental shop around the corner, before a start-up called Netflix came along. Or the taxi driver whose fares were eroded by app-enabled Uber and Lyft drivers. Even those with businesses that are helped rather than hurt by technology need to stay alert for advances that can take away their technology advantage — or present opportunities to further leverage technology to their competitive advantage.

The challenge of staying a step ahead of evolving technologies never ends. Netflix may have made a killing from the evolution of entertainment technologies, but the company had to be nimble to survive. From its DVD-by-mail beginnings, Netflix spent heavily to transition into on-demand streaming of movies while also maintaining its DVD distribution systems. Then, as competition from other on-demand video companies heated up, Netflix again transformed, adding content production to its offerings and releasing the original TV series *House of Cards* in 2013. The lesson for tech adopters, as a Netflix manager told *The New York Times*, is always to "embrace change."

View or download Form 15-2 for a list of questions that can help you evaluate how technological innovations may alter your business. Your answers can help you anticipate innovations and point you toward new ways to compete.

Technology is such a powerful driver of change that a growing number of companies and organizations draft stand-alone *technology plans* that focus solely on technology implementation. Many libraries have technology plans, for example. The reason: the Internet and the rise of e-books are radically changing how people use libraries and therefore how libraries do business. Healthcare systems have also adopted technology plans, originally in response to the move to electronic medical records and more recently to address trends in patient communication and personalized healthcare solutions.

A technology plan has many of the same components as a business plan. These three are worth zeroing in on:

>> **Clear goals and objectives:** New technologies can easily dazzle you. But all those bells and whistles have to be useful; if not, you're throwing away money and wasting time. Be specific about your technology requirements and what you hope to achieve so you can set and plan around measurable goals.

>> **A carefully thought-out budget:** Implementing new technologies can be costly and involve unexpected expenses. Defining your technology needs and establishing a budget grounded in reality can help you avoid potentially disastrous surprises.

>> **An implementation plan:** Introducing new technologies into your operation takes time and training. By creating a detailed implementation plan you can anticipate challenges, plan for initial and ongoing training, monitor for technology improvements and advancements, and chart a smoother path to success. For ambitious implementation plans, assign staff members to specific responsibilities and schedule periodic reviews of your progress.

If you're planning for a one-person business or a small business, you can address technology as part of your overall business plan. But if new technologies are a major force in your business, consider creating a separate technology plan.

IS THERE AN APP IN YOUR PLAN?

With 1.6 million apps available to Android and Apple users, your app is entering a crowded environment. Factor these 2015 findings from www.thinkwithgoogle.com into your plans:

- The average user has 36 apps and uses only one out of four on a daily basis.

- More than half of all apps are downloaded based on a personal recommendation; the next highest source of app discovery is an app store followed by online search, company website, and advertising.

- Most people download an app because it sounds interesting or fun, because they're familiar with the business or brand, or because they want discounts or rewards, in that order.

- Most people expect apps to be free; the apps they're most willing to pay for feature technology, finance, and local information. Most revenue comes not from downloads but from freemium-to-premium upgrades and in-app purchases.

- A quarter of installed apps are never used or quickly abandoned due to loss of interest, which can be overcome by discount offers, exclusive content, use by friends and family, and notification of new features.

Whether your established business is planning to introduce an app or whether building an app is the idea for your new business idea, follow all the steps for developing a business plan, paying extra attention to the following:

- **Goal setting:** Be clear about the market niche and purpose of your app, whether it's for business productivity, business-to-customer interface, entertainment, shopping, or other uses. Then set clear usage and revenue objectives to guide your planning.

- **Marketing:** Next to designing a great app and user experience, marketing is the make-it-or-break-it factor that affects app success. Create an all-important pre-launch plan to enlist beta testers, attract early champions and word-of-mouth marketers, direct interest to an app landing page, and pitch media contacts for launch-day coverage. Then be ready post-launch with a plan for ongoing marketing to build awareness, prompt installations, heighten retention and usage, inspire user interaction, and develop reviews and high ratings. As part of your marketing program, include your plan for facilitating *user onboarding* by developing an entry screen that provides an app walkthrough and allows you to collect user data for follow-up messages that encourage ongoing usage.

(continued)

(continued)

- **Budgeting:** The answer to the question "How much does app development cost?" is similar to the old question "How long is a string?" There's no single answer. About the only clear-cut line item is what the app stores charge you to submit and sell the finished app you produce. Beyond that, costs for design, development, software, testing, marketing, hosting, and maintenance range widely. Use the forecasting and budgeting forms in Chapter 9 as you plan for all the costs involved.

Responding to changing customer expectations

The customer is always right, right? If only it were that simple. These days, customers are also connected and empowered in ways that few imagined, even a decade ago. When they like something, they turn to social media and review sites to let everyone know. When they're not happy, watch out. Negative rants can go viral and spell big trouble. Just ask any restaurateur who has experienced a string of complaints about food or service on OpenTable, Yelp, or UrbanSpoon.

REMEMBER

The way customers communicate and how their opinions can impact the reputation of businesses has changed dramatically, and it's likely to go on changing. However, one change seems set and irreversible: Customers expect immediate access to, interaction with, and responsiveness from the businesses they choose to buy from.

The following sections help anticipate and plan around their changing demands and desires.

Improving your business-to-customer online interface

People expect businesses of every kind to have a website. If people can't quickly find a business online, chances are good they'll assume it has gone out of business. Yet, even in the face of that reality, one in four businesses are still without a website. On the slim chance yours is among them, don't wait to develop one. Even if you're among the majority of businesses with a site, take time to be sure it meets the requirements of today's users. Here's what you need:

>> **A site your business controls and can easily update.** You want a site where people can get a sense of your brand and its reputation, access facts and news about your business, and find out how to reach you, preferably with a single click on a button large enough for a fat finger to touch.

>> **A site findable by a search for your business name.** If it's likely that people will also search for your business using your product names or your personal name, optimize use of those names throughout your site so that your site will be discovered and rank well in any of the searches.

>> **A site that loads quickly and displays well on any size screen.** Templates for *responsive website designs* that show well whether on the smallest phone or the largest screen are available through most site-building services. If you're planning a complicated website, one that involves accepting orders and payments from customers, for instance — or if you just don't have time to develop your own — hire a website designer experienced in building sites that adapt or respond to all screen sizes.

TIP

In your business plan, summarize how customers find, reach, and interact with your business online, and how your business-to-customer interface will change over the business plan period.

Responding to changing customer demands and desires

Changing customer attitudes, expectations, and shopping and purchasing patterns call for revisions to long-standing marketing patterns. If your company depends largely on advertising in print and other media, for example, take note. Be aware that today's customers are more likely to trust peer reviews on sites like Amazon and Travelocity over messages in your paid advertisements. Responding to this reality, major ad agencies are closing their print ad departments and beefing up their digital communication and social networking divisions. The take-home message for you and your company's marketers: cultivating satisfied customers who speak up in great online reviews and posts may be more effective than print ads.

If you don't know what your customers expect or how satisfied they are with your offerings, make it part of your business-planning process to find out. Read online reviews and comments about your business, product, or service, but also read reviews of your competitors and others in your business category. Keep a list of the key things customers are saying they like and dislike. If online reviews aren't available, consider sending out customer surveys, either by mail or email. (For advice to follow when conducting customer research, see Chapter 4.) Above all, find out more about your customers' desires and demands so you can adapt your business to address their shopping and purchasing preferences, including:

>> Personalized service

>> Immediate service and faster delivery

>> Responsiveness to social and environmental values

>> Prompt interaction and responsiveness to customer input

>> Round-the-clock online access with seamless interface between online and in-person communications and transactions

>> Self-service options

>> Preference for user-generated messages over business-generated marketing and for authentic and personal communications from businesses

TIP

Managing changing customer expectations is an ongoing process. Use Form 15-3 as a guide. Then use Form 15-4 to brainstorm ways your customer knowledge can lead to changes in your products and services.

As you receive customer input or identify changes in customer expectations, carefully consider how best to respond. Three questions can help guide you:

>> **Is the comment, preference, complaint, or suggestion reasonable?** Your business can't be everything to everyone. Assess whether you can and should respond with business changes. A sports bar that gets dinged in an online review because it's too noisy may decide that being noisy is the nature of its business. On the other hand, a software developer that gets repeated customer suggestions for a new feature may be want to seriously consider adding it. After Nissan's electric car, the Leaf, was first released, customers harped about the way the onboard software calculated and displayed miles left on the battery. The company wisely responded with a software update that addressed the issue.

>> **What's the best way to respond?** Consider your options for addressing a change in what customers want or desire. You may discover that there are several ways to respond. For example, a company that gets a lot of complaints because its product is difficult to assemble can decide to redesign the product or simply improve the assembly directions.

>> **What specific steps do you need to take?** After you settle on how to respond, list the action steps to take. Establish a response timetable so that you address your customers' expectations in a timely fashion.

Becoming a Change Master

Keeping one step ahead of fast-changing markets and technologies is a challenge. Even the biggest players with the bulkiest research budgets have stumbled by misreading the tea leaves. For example, a growing market for biofuels once seemed like a slam-dunk, until favorable changes for other renewable resources, coupled with concerns about land use, began to dim the high hopes for ethanol. Blockbuster Video got tripped up when it didn't anticipate the shift to online movie rentals and then video streaming.

REMEMBER

As you develop your business plan, challenge long-held business approaches by posing a simple question: *What if?* What if new competitors emerge? What if the materials you use for manufacturing soar in price? What if the economy slumps big time?

If you're operating a one-person business or a small business, you can ponder these questions on your own or with a mentor or advisor. Put your answers in writing as a way to organize your thoughts. If you're writing a plan for a large company, consider convening a committee to assess the impact of change and to brainstorm scenarios for how you can respond with changes to your business strategies. Your futurists should base their assessments on known trajectories of change. But they should also be encouraged to think outside of the box as they consider conditions — from transformative technologies to environmental shifts — that could rock the foundations of your business.

The following sections explore ways to identify and deal with major changes in your business environment stemming from disruptions in your marketplace, your customer base, or the regulatory environment in which you operate.

Strategizing for turbulent times

In our experience, companies that successfully navigate swiftly changing currents use these five basic strategies.

>> **Testing assumptions:** Most predictions about the future are based on assumptions. Consider a restaurant chain that offers low-calorie fast food, assuming that a certain customer segment will choose its eateries for its menu of healthy, nutritious offerings. However, the chain's leaders are assuming that customers will agree on what comprises a healthy choice. If the public begins to perceive that fresh versus frozen ingredients or locally sourced versus imported food is healthier than low-calorie choices, one of the pillars on which the chain is built begins to wobble. In planning for an uncertain future, take time to test assumptions to find out how sturdy they are. Look for facts that verify the accuracy of the assumptions. Observe customer reactions to offerings that were designed based upon assumptions. Seek customer and expert feedback. Above all, remain open to adjusting the assumptions on which your business plan is based.

>> **Bracketing expectations:** Business planning is based on expectations. A company that uses copper in manufacturing expects the price of copper to

remain within a certain range. A company that makes souvenir pens expects to sell a certain number of pens each year. But during uncertain times, smart companies bracket their expectations, for example, thinking about what would happen if sales or material availability fell off or soared beyond the norm. The bracketing strategy is exactly the same process professional photographers use when they take the same picture several times at different exposures, just to make sure they get the perfect shot. By bracketing expectations, business planners can foresee the impact of unintended circumstances.

REMEMBER

>> **Having a Plan B:** Your business plan spells out what you hope to achieve if all goes according to expectations. If you're competing in a rapidly or even a moderately changing marketplace, also sketch out a Plan B that includes the steps the company will take if something unexpected happens. Your Plan B doesn't have to go into great detail. Instead, it charts the steps you'll take to redirect your business plan if the assumptions or expectations you've planned around don't pan out. To identify the changes most likely to trigger the need for Plan B, refer to the earlier "Recognizing the Drivers of Change" section in this chapter.

EXAMPLE

For example, a Chicago-based fine art photographer produced images that sold well in galleries in vacation spots like Santa Fe and Sarasota. He decided it was time to open a gallery in Chicago, where he could sell his work directly to the public. He found just the right location and crafted a business plan, including reasonable estimates of operating costs and sales revenue. But he also developed an alternate plan, in case his revenues didn't quite match his expectations. His Plan B included subletting gallery space to other fine art photographers and using the space for studio photography classes to help pay the rent.

>> **Seeking reliable sources of information:** Predictions are most likely to prove correct if they're based on the best available information. Check out industry-based journals, trustworthy business reports, and assessments from reliable sources in your market area and business arena.

>> **Tracking changes:** Transformations that change markets or technologies may seem to come out of nowhere, but early signs often suggest that change is coming. To scan the horizon, search online for recent-year business or industry trends, flip through magazines you might not usually read, look over the titles on best-seller lists, and note anything interesting that pops up to indicate changing conditions. It could take the form of results from a technology pilot project or a report on changing customer trends. Watch for headlines in the business sections of major newspapers that can tip you off to something brewing. Every time you come across changes that surprise you or pique your interest, ask yourself: How could this affect the business we're in or the customers we serve?

Changing from within

Responding to external changes, such as emerging technologies, environmental disruption, or shifting customer expectations, often requires internal changes in what your business does and how it operates. Some business plans are based specifically on making moderate-to-dramatic changes to respond to evolving circumstances.

WARNING

If you're planning to make big changes to an established business, move carefully and strategically. Handled badly, internal changes can cause morale to plunge and even affect your bottom line. Handled well, internal changes can strengthen competitiveness and boost morale. Take these steps:

>> **Do your homework.** Make sure you've explored all your options before instituting sweeping changes. Ask yourself: Is this the best approach for us? What are the benefits? What are the drawbacks? How will these changes be implemented? Finally, spell out the changes, positive and disruptive, in detail.

>> **Identify everyone who will be affected.** After you outline the changes, consider how they'll affect everyone in your business. Thinking ahead about the impact on your employees and customers can help you anticipate problems and speed implementation.

>> **Communicate at all levels.** Make sure everyone knows what the planned changes are and why they are essential. Spell out the benefits and how the changes will be implemented. If appropriate, plan meetings where employees can ask questions and voice their concerns.

>> **Assign a change manager.** If the plans are substantial, consider assigning a manager to oversee the implementation of the changes. Libraries that implement technology plans often assign one person to be in charge, for example.

>> **Gauge your progress.** Making far-reaching changes in how a company does business can be very disruptive. As you move forward, set milestones against which you can gauge your progress. Then leave the door open for employees to communicate concerns, complaints, and constructive ideas.

>> **Stay flexible.** Be decisive when you introduce a big change and allow time for changes to take effect and gain acceptance. But also stay flexible. Even the best-laid plans sometimes need to be fine-tuned as they move forward. Commit to the change you're making but don't be so wedded to the details of your plan that you can't adapt tactics as implementation proceeds.

Taking risks

Starting a new business is always chancy. Even managing a successful business through times of accelerated change poses risks. If you're not taking chances, chances are you're not growing as a business.

EXAMPLE

Some entrepreneurs are willing to take on big risks in hopes of reaping even bigger rewards. One such risk-taker, who made a fortune in financial services, bought dozens of distressed properties — and we're talking skyscrapers — in downtown Detroit. When the once-great city's streets were lined with abandoned businesses and pockmarked with empty lots, when the municipal government declared bankruptcy, this brave entrepreneur maintained his vision. He sunk more than one billion dollars into revitalizing the downtown area, trusting his assumptions and expectations that his plan would contribute to a turnaround. His efforts represent the biggest private redevelopment effort in US history. Will he succeed? Detroit emerged from bankruptcy after 18 months, which is a good first step on its road to recovery.

TIP

Every business plan involves a degree of risk. Some risks threaten established strategies; others provide new opportunities with big upsides. Take time to consider the risks your business may encounter and the way you'll address them, should they arise. Start with a SWOT analysis of your business strengths, weaknesses, opportunities, and threats (Chapter 5 outlines the steps to follow). Then, look in this chapter for help considering the driving forces of change that could present risks to avert or seize upon.

In your business plan, describe the risks involved with the opportunities you're pursuing and your strategies to manage risk without compromising your goals and objectives.

Forms

Go to www.dummies.com/go/businessplanskit to view and download these forms that help you identify, plan for, and manage changes in your business world:

Form 15-1	Identifying Key Drivers of Change	This form identifies the key drivers of change that could impact your business.
Form 15-2	New Technology Questionnaire	This form can help you assess the role that changing technologies might play in shaping your business.
Form 15-3	Managing Changing Customer Expectations Questionnaire	This form can help you explore what your customers want and how that's likely to change in the future.
Form 15-4	Adapting to Customer Demands and Desires Questionnaire	These questions can lead to customer-inspired business changes.

4

Making the Most of Your Plan

Draft a clear and concise business plan that effectively spells out your strategies for turning a good idea into a successful enterprise, with step-by-step advice and tips for locating additional resources to guide you through the process of putting your plan down in writing.

Customize and create your plan using a downloadable *Business Plans Kit For Dummies* business plan creation template.

Identify the key audiences your plan addresses and make sure the plan answers all the questions readers may have in a clear and understandable way.

Create a brief executive summary of your plan that you can use to give investors, clients, customers, or new employees a quick and compelling idea of what your business is all about.

Put your business plan to work by organizing your company around the plan, using your plan to develop employee skills, and monitoring success using metrics and milestones set out in your plan.

Make a commitment to review your formal business plan on a regular schedule in order to see how well you've achieved your goals and objectives, how your business situation or environment may have changed, and how to revise your strategy as necessary.

Chapter 16

Putting Your Plan Together

You've reached the point where you actually *write* your business plan. If you're arriving at this chapter sequentially (every author's dream!), the business-planning groundwork is behind you. By now, you've defined your business purpose (Chapter 3), assessed your business environment (Chapter 4), charted your strategy (Chapter 5), detailed your company capabilities (Chapter 6), designed your marketing plan (Chapter 7), and taken the measure of your finances (Chapter 9). The next step is to assemble the raw materials into a formal written plan.

If you rank the idea of writing right up there with paying taxes or find putting one word in front of another as excruciating as rolling boulders up a hill, take heart. The following pages keep the process easy. Plus, the effort you make now will pay off in many ways:

>> **Making good ideas even better:** Putting your plan into writing makes it easy to see which ideas don't hold water and which ones look even better when you take time to develop them.

>> **Developing a plan of action:** Like many entrepreneurs, you may have dozens of ideas rattling around in your head. Organizing them into a written plan forces you to think about how they fit together and which ideas should receive priority status in your action plan.

>> **Avoiding unnecessary mistakes:** Your written plan is the first serious test of your business venture. If your business doesn't make sense on paper, what are the odds that it will pass muster in the fiercely competitive world of business?

The upcoming pages help you review the components of your plan, put together your planning team if it's a joint effort, target your audience, and assemble a plan that creates a cohesive sense of what your business is and how it will achieve success.

Making a List and Checking It Twice

Putting together your written business plan is a bit like building a house: Before actual construction begins, you need to be prepared with accurate blueprints and the right equipment and supplies. With a business plan, you also want to make sure that you're well prepared and that you have all the resources you need at your fingertips.

TIP

As you organize your effort, use the checklist in Form 16-1. It lists all the items you may want to include in each of the major components of your business plan. Check off the items that you already have in hand, at least in a rough form. (Don't worry about the table of contents and the executive summary at this point. You put these two pieces in place last, and we cover them in the "Addressing more than one audience" section later in this chapter.) Go to `www.dummies.com/go/businessplanskit` to find the forms in this chapter.

Business Plan Components Checklist

Use this form to help you and your planning team keep check of the components to be included in your business plan. Remember, not all business plans need to contain all the following parts. Consider crossing out those that do not apply to your business plan.

☐ **Table of contents**

☐ **Executive summary**

☐ **Company overview**
- ○ Business description
- ○ Mission statement
- ○ Vision statement
- ○ Major business goals
- ○ Values statement
- ○ Listing of key products and/or services
- ○ Business model summary
- ○ Business structure
- ○

☐ **Business environment**
- ○ Industry overview
- ○ Barriers to entry
- ○ Market overview
- ○ Customer profile
- ○ Competitor analysis
- ○

☐ **Company strategy**
- ○ SWOT analysis
- ○ Business model
- ○ Business goals
- ○ Marketing plan
- ○ Plans for growth
- ○ Exit strategy
- ○

(continued)

FORM 16-1: Use the checklist as you prepare the pieces of your business plan.

☐ **Company description**
- ○ Introductory highlights
- ○ Products and/or services offered
- ○ Research and development
- ○ Operations
- ○ Sales and marketing
- ○ Distribution and delivery
- ○ Customer service
- ○ Management
- ○ Organization
- ○ Key strengths

☐ **Financial review**
- ○ Income statement
- ○ Balance sheet
- ○ Cash flow statement
- ○ Financial forecasts
- ○ Master budget

☐ **Action plan**
- ○ Short-term goals
- ○ Immediate objectives
- ○ Next steps

☐ **Appendices**
- ○
- ○
- ○

© John Wiley & Sons, Inc.

PAGE 2 OF FORM 16-1.

Not every business plan will contain every item on this list. Still, take a good look at the items you *haven't* checked. Make sure that the omission is intentional and that you're not leaving out important information.

If you still have some homework to do before sitting down to write your plan, here are the main topics and where to turn for help:

» Company overview: Chapters 3, 5, and 6

» Business environment: Chapters 4 and 15

» Company description: Chapter 6

» Company strategy: Chapter 5

» Marketing plan: Chapter 7

>> Financial review: Chapter 9

>> Action plan: Chapters 3 and 5

In addition, you can use the chapters in Part 3 to tailor your plan to your specific business. Make use of Chapter 10 if you're self-employed, Chapter 11 if you're planning for a small business, Chapter 12 if you're planning a virtual business, Chapter 13 if you're growing or revamping an established business, and Chapter 14 if you're involved with a nonprofit organization. Check out Chapter 15 if your business is confronting a particularly turbulent period of change.

Locating Additional Resources

As you put your business plan together, you may discover that you need additional resources. The following sections offer suggestions on where to go and what to look for if you need to fill in any blanks.

The bookstore and library

Okay, we're partial to the book you're holding, but you can find dozens of other useful titles in the marketplace — particularly ones that concentrate on specific areas, such as marketing or financial planning, or ones that focus on particular kinds of businesses, such as nonprofits or sole proprietorships.

For additional background on general business-planning issues, pick up a copy of the most recent edition of *Business Plans For Dummies,* by Paul Tiffany and Steven Peterson (John Wiley & Sons, Inc.). For help preparing your marketing plan, check out *Small Business Marketing Kit For Dummies* by Barbara Findlay Schenck (John Wiley & Sons, Inc.).

WARNING

Although the basic principles of business planning may be timeless, certain subjects — marketing via social networks, for example — change rapidly, and a book that's more than a few years old may reflect ancient history. If you want timely information — details about tax considerations for a small business, for example — be sure to check when the book was published.

TIP

Magazines, newspapers, and journals offer another way to track what's happening in the world of business in general and your industry in particular. Identify titles of interest and become a subscriber so you can routinely scan the business environment for trends or new developments. Spend time in your local library to review recent issues of magazines and journals to find those relevant to your business.

The Internet

Plenty of websites offer useful tips on business planning. In particular, the federal government provides heaps of solid information on planning, starting, and operating your own company through its Small Business Administration site (www.sba.gov). Even the IRS presents helpful planning tips in its handbooks, which are also available at www.irs.gov.

TIP

Spend a couple of hours online looking for useful resources on your own. To avoid being overwhelmed, enter the keywords *business plan* along with keywords specific to your business area (*nonprofit, retail, travel, financial services, app development,* and so on) in your favorite search engine.

You can also use the Internet to uncover information about competitors, markets, business trends, and new technologies — all the factors you need to account for to put together a complete picture of your business environment. Going to the home pages of your competitors is another good starting point. Reading reviews posted by customers offers invaluable insights. From there, you can enter online press-rooms with current news announcements, executive bios, recent publicity, and other information.

WARNING

Unlike magazine articles, which are typically checked and rechecked for accuracy, online content isn't always validated or confirmed by anyone beyond the person who posts it, so follow three simple rules when you use the Internet for business research:

>> **Check the date.** Many online documents aren't dated, so you may not know whether you're reading the latest scoop or dated material. Look for a publishing or posting date. If you can't find one, dig a little deeper to see whether or not the information is still relevant.

>> **Verify the source.** Especially if you're relying on critical information, make sure you know where it comes from. An article about energy trends from a respected business magazine is likely to be more reliable than a similar article from a PR company hired by the petroleum industry, for instance.

>> **Double-check key facts and statistics.** If you use specific pieces of information — about business trends, markets, competitors, technology, or whatever — as the central building blocks of your business plan, make darn sure that the facts you gather from the Internet are correct. If your financial projections are built on the fact that the market for online lingerie is growing at 40 percent a year, for example, verify that you're dealing with a fact and not some online entrepreneur's fantasy.

Business software

Software programs allow you to assemble all the components of a business plan automatically, turning them into a polished, ready-to-print document. The best programs also make easier work of the financial parts of business planning — creating income statements and cash-flow statements, for example, or making financial projections (see Chapter 9). Most software programs also allow you to add graphics, such as tables and charts, into your plan, providing an easy way for your audience to see at a glance what you're describing in the written document.

WARNING

Business-planning software programs can make the job of business planning almost *too* easy. With all the software bells and whistles, newcomers can inadvertently skip the serious (that is, difficult) work of creating and writing an effective plan. Remember, the best software-planning tools guide you through the important aspects of business planning and then keep track of your words, sentences, and paragraphs — they don't think for you. You still have to do the serious mental work yourself.

TIP

Investors and bankers who review and fund business plans are all too familiar with the look and feel of the most popular software-generated business-planning documents. When using one of these programs, customize your plan to make it unique. The last thing you want is for your business plan to look exactly like the others that cross a venture capitalist's desk.

Expert advice

No one knows the ins and outs of planning and running a business better than someone who has done it before. If you have questions you can't answer, or if you run out of ideas on ways to get your company off the ground, turn to someone with tried-and-true expertise for advice.

The first place to look for expert advice is from someone you know on a personal or professional basis. If that tactic doesn't pan out, ask friends and colleagues for suggestions. Other good places to look for help are the chamber of commerce and the business section of your local newspaper. You may end up paying for some of this advice, but when you really need help, it's worth the investment.

Decide exactly what kind of assistance you need. After all, you can't ask someone to plan your whole business for you, but you can ask for help fine-tuning your marketing strategy, for example, or reviewing and critiquing your financial projections.

Consider contacting the Service Corps of Retired Executives (SCORE), a nationwide organization that works with the SBA to provide help to business owners. SCORE has a free online newsletter and provides free email counseling. The group also has local chapters around the country, with retired business people ready and willing to help. It also sponsors small business awards. For more information, check out www.score.org.

A retired schoolteacher came up with a business idea that promised to keep her busy while helping out some of the hardest-working people in town. She wanted to start an online agency to represent the dozens of women who were cleaning houses in the area. She planned to help them organize their schedules, communicate with clients, and do the bookkeeping. She also wanted to offer them benefits such as health insurance. In return, she would take a small percentage of the money they earned. But how much? How should she organize her business? How should she market it?

With so many questions, she quickly felt overwhelmed. Then, she happened to read about a local businessman who was retiring from a high-tech business he started. On a whim, she wrote to him, asking whether he had time to help her put together a plan. He called her immediately; they met a few times, and within a month, she had a solid business plan in place. With it, she was also able to get a small business loan for the start-up money she needed.

Self help

Many local communities have organizations of businesspeople who get together to share ideas, exchange contacts, help each other out, and just plain socialize. Some of these groups are comprised of people with like interests or needs, whereas others are made up of local people from across the business spectrum. You can also find virtual business groups that regularly schedule online meetings to support one another. To get started, check out www.meetup.org, which posts meetings of all kinds within certain distances of where you live or do business. Rotary, the international service organization, is another helpful resource for bringing people together. (Check out www.rotary.org for details.)

Starting with a template

No two business plans are alike. In fact, one reason we deliberately don't include sample business plans in our book is that they're not usually very helpful, and often steer people in the wrong direction. Your business plan should reflect your business, your goals, your strategy, and your specific action plan. Cutting and pasting from existing plans usually results in a stitched-together plan that lacks the specifics that make good plans effective.

TIP

Still, having some guideposts is helpful. So we put together a comprehensive template that we think is far more useful for most business planners. Use the template in Form 16-2 as a guide to what your business plan should include.

TIP

If you're writing a business plan for a small company or a sole proprietorship, you may be shouldering most of the work yourself. Form 16-2 will be especially helpful as a guide. We can't emphasize enough the importance of putting your plan in writing, even if you're among the few people who will read it. The process of writing can help you refine and test your ideas. Also, a written plan is something you can turn to both as a reminder and a way to gauge your progress.

If you're writing a complex business plan for a larger enterprise, the task may require teamwork. The next section can help you manage your team and the project to make the planning process more efficient and effective.

Assembling Your Planning Team

The size of the team you bring together to develop your business plan depends on the size and structure of your company and on the complexity of the business plan you're developing:

>> If your company is small, you don't need to worry about who's in charge of each piece of your written plan. Lucky you: You're in charge of it all! However, that doesn't mean you have to develop the plan alone. Your plan will be stronger if you bounce your thoughts around with someone who's willing to serve as a sounding board. Also, enlist someone you trust to read and critique your final draft before you print the final copy.

>> If your company is moderately sized to large, the process of creating your written plan requires a certain amount of organization. Before you sit down and fire up your planning software or your word processor, consider the advice in the following sections.

Read on for tips on how to organize your planning team and how to get the most out of their efforts.

Delegating responsibilities

If your company has a management team, divvy up the work of putting together your written business plan. Delegating makes your job easier. Plus, different perspectives prove helpful as your team reads and reviews drafts, offers suggestions, and fine-tunes the document. The group will arrive at a stronger plan, and you'll win group support and improve morale at the same time.

How many people you involve depends on the size of your company and how big and complicated your plan is. Here are some tips to help you create a team that's both efficient and effective:

>> **Keep your team lean.** Involve only as many people as you need to get the job done. Too many planners — like too many cooks in the kitchen — can spoil the recipe for successful planning. A bloated team can mean endless meetings and too many points of view.

>> **Choose people who want the job.** There's no point in assigning a planning task to someone who really doesn't want to do it. To help win team interest, take time at the beginning to explain why creating a written business plan is so important. Select managers who really want to help and who are willing and able to complete the tasks you assign.

>> **Organize your team around the plan.** By organizing your team around the major components of your business plan, you make sure that all team members know their tasks and how their work fits into the larger picture. Some of the assignments are pretty straightforward: Your financial person should take charge of the financial review, and your marketing head should put together the business environment and marketing sections. If certain pieces of the plan are more complex than others, think about assigning a small group to work on them.

>> **Put one person in charge.** Every team needs a leader, and that's particularly true when putting together your business plan. Keeping track of the whole process can be a job in itself, especially if you have a larger team or a complicated plan. Name one person as project director, and make sure everyone on the team understands that he or she has ultimate authority.

>> **Appoint a wordsmith.** If you're lucky, someone on your team is good at putting words down on paper. Name this person your senior plan editor. Among the tasks: Writing key sections of your plan, such as the executive summary; checking grammar and spelling; and making sure that the writing style is clear and consistent throughout the plan.

>> **Consider using collaboration software.** A growing number of software programs are available that help people work together on a common task, such as developing a business plan. Some enable remote employees to meet via the Internet. Others allow working groups to share and exchange documents.

Setting the ground rules

As soon as you've selected your team, establish procedures that spell out exactly how the team will work together. The clearer the ground rules, the smoother the process. Make sure that your ground rules address these three points:

>> **Identify key steps.** The process of writing a business plan usually includes five steps: research, first draft, review, revised draft, and final review. Make sure you specify the steps that fit your situation and spell them out up-front.

>> **Establish a schedule.** The process of writing a business plan shouldn't be long and drawn out. A business plan has to be timely, which means it needs to respond to the business environment as it is — not the way it looked six months ago. To keep your project on track, set due dates for each component of the plan and each step in the process. Give the members of your team as much time as they reasonably need — but no more.

>> **Assign duties.** Make sure that all team members know exactly what you expect of them, including which components or sections you want them to assemble and when drafts and reviews are due.

Putting first things last

Issues of timing are bound to come up as you try to put your plan on paper. How can you put together the executive summary, for example, before you have the rest of the business plan in place? And don't you need the company strategy written up before you can tackle the action plan?

Each component of your written business plan has to be in sync with the sections around it. For example, if you talk about the need to increase the subscriber base for your investment newsletter in the company strategy section, but you fail to say a word about it in your action plan, anyone reading your plan is bound to wonder if you really know what you're doing.

Follow these steps to make sure that everyone is working on the same page:

1. **Sit down with your team and hammer out an outline containing the key points that each section of the plan will address.**

   Refer to the checklist in Form 16-1 as a guide. You may need more than one meeting to create your outline, but consider it time well spent.

2. **With the outline in hand, make sure team members understand what each section should include and how the information relates to the other plan components.**

   Doing so allows team members to spot discrepancies or omissions early on.

3. **Write your executive summary last, because you can't summarize a plan you haven't written.**

   You'd be amazed at the number of business planners who've anguished over the executive summary simply because they tried to write it first. Save yourself the agony: The executive summary may come first in the finished plan, but it should be the last component you write — usually after your team completes and reviews the second draft of each of the other components.

   When you write your executive summary, don't worry about repeating yourself. The whole point of the opening section is to capture the key points of your plan — using the same language you use in the plan. Don't grab a thesaurus hoping to find some colorful new way to express your mission or your strategy — you'll only confuse your readers and your team. Say what you mean the same way, only shorter.

Keeping track of it all

Two simple tools can go a long way toward streamlining the business-plan assembly process — and keeping everyone involved calm and happy. One tool is a simple tracking sheet that shows at a glance where every part of the process is at any given time. The other tool is a loose-leaf notebook.

The master tracker

Use a master tracking sheet to track every piece of the plan, who's in charge of each piece, the key steps involved in completing them, and where each piece stands at any given moment. This is especially important when your plan has a large number of sections and appendices.

You can create your master tracking sheet online, on a blackboard, or on paper. Whatever you choose, make sure you make it readily available to every member of your planning team and that you update it regularly.

Use the tracking sheet in Form 16-3 to customize a tracking sheet that matches the contents of your plan.

The old-fashioned loose-leaf notebook

All the razzle-dazzle online resources and state-of-the-art software tools are great, but you should also consider using an old-fashioned loose-leaf notebook to keep your project organized. You have to juggle a lot of information — versions of your mission and vision statements, biographies of your key managers, financial statements, charts and graphs, product specifications, and more — so each time you revise and reorganize, pop open the rings, slip an old section out, and pop a new one in.

A loose-leaf notebook is also one of the best — and most cost-effective — tools to capture the big picture of your plan, because you can easily and quickly page through all the sections.

Targeting Your Plan to Key Audiences

Immediately after you decide who's going to write your plan, you need to think about who's going to read it. After all, your business plan should communicate your vision and strategy — what you plan to do, and how you intend to do it. But it can't communicate if the people who read it can't understand it. You wouldn't speak French to someone who only speaks Chinese, right? For the same reason, you don't want to fill your written business plan with technical jargon that your audience won't understand.

Read on for advice on how to identify the various audiences your business plan intends to address. If you hope to reach several very different audiences, you can find tips on creating alternate versions of your plan geared for each specific group.

Identifying your stakeholders

Your *stakeholders* include everyone who has a vested interest in your company, what it does, or how it operates. That includes employees, customers, suppliers, outside consultants, lenders, investors, shareholders, regulators, competitors, and other interested parties.

Some of these groups may have direct stakes: You owe them money, for example, or they own a piece of your company. Others have less tangible interests: suppliers who want to continue selling to you or civic organizations that want to make sure you remain a good corporate citizen. Obviously, not all your stakeholder groups share the same interests or values:

>> Someone who owns shares in your company is probably most interested in whether, when, and how you plan to grow.

>> A local environmental group may want proof that you're following environmental regulations.

>> Bankers look at your plan with a focus on your financial health — studying your cash flow, business assets, and forecasts to determine your prospects for solid, stable growth. They have to decide whether to finance your business, so they look for proof of your long-term prospects along with assurance that you're a good risk when it comes to repaying loans.

>> Investors are interested in the factors that predict growth — especially rapid growth — so they turn a sharp eye to sections that describe your business opportunity, your management team, and your plan of action.

TIP

Form 16-4 lists various stakeholder groups along with the parts of the business plan and specific issues that are of special importance to each audience. Go through the list and put a check beside the groups of stakeholders you want your plan to address. Circle the issues that you think are of greatest concern to each group. This form can help you address all the key topics as you tailor your business plan to the interests of various audiences.

Addressing more than one audience

The following three parts of your business plan help different audiences to quickly access information that addresses their unique interests.

Table of contents

A well-designed table of contents offers a map that leads readers to the sections of your plan that most interest them in no time flat.

TIP

If your business plan is more than ten pages long, consider including a table of contents that lists sections and subsections. Include page numbers so that you and your readers can quickly locate specific sections in the plan.

Executive summary

A solid, well-written executive summary gives a clear and concise description of your company and the key issues that the body of your business plan will describe. Some of your readers may find out all they need to know in this summary. Others will decide to read the rest of your plan based on what they read in the executive summary. Either way, the executive summary is a critical piece of all but the briefest written plans.

To decide what to put into your executive summary, go through the revised draft of your plan and highlight all the critical points that you want everyone — including those who read only the executive summary — to know. Be ruthless here. Choose the one or two elements in each section that are absolutely essential. Remember, the executive summary is meant to give a very quick overview — the rest of your plan fills in the details.

After you highlight the critical points, organize them into the first draft of your executive summary. Try to express major ideas by using the same words that you use in the plan itself.

TIP

As you start, think about the short speech you'd give if one of your stakeholders — a banker or potential investor, for example — asked you to describe your business on an elevator ride from the lobby to the 25th floor of a high-rise building. In those few seconds, how would you describe your business idea, your strategy, and how you intend to achieve success? Right now, write down your answer. (If you have a digital recorder or voice recognition software handy, start talking.) Chances are good that you'll instinctively hit all the key points. (If you need help writing your "elevator speech," see Chapter 6.) Make sure that your executive summary hits all those same important points.

Ideally, you should keep the executive summary of your business plan to a page or two. This section is a summary, after all. If it runs long, try tightening up the language or pruning out the least essential points.

TIP

If your business idea is based on something brand new, be sure your executive summary and your plan's business overview section explain your new technology in terms that anyone can understand. Include all the technical details in an appendix.

The appendices

Unlike your appendix, which sits in your body and does nothing, the appendices in your business plan range from useful to absolutely essential — especially if you want your business plan to address several audiences at once. The appendices are where you can stuff all the nitty-gritty details that flesh out your market analysis, your technology, or your product specs — details that may be essential to a full understanding of your business plan but are of interest to only a small number of your readers.

REMEMBER

No one judges business plans by the pound, so don't fill your appendices with absolutely everything you know just to make your plan look heftier. The material they contain should relate directly to your business plan and should provide important details about your markets, your strategy, your management team, your technology, or other key aspects of your business.

EXAMPLE

In fact, you should reference all documents that appear in the appendices at some appropriate place within the main body of your plan. Here are two examples:

> *Our advanced Internet platform offers many competitive advantages over existing software, including higher speed, lower cost, and greater reliability. (For technical details, see the "Technical Specifications of ISP Version 6.1" in Appendix 2.)*

> *Our market analysis shows that many IT professionals are concerned about the speed and bandwidth of existing Internet software platforms, and they're willing to pay more for next-generation technology. Their chief concern is reliability. (For details, see the "Market Data Analysis Summary" in Appendix 3.)*

References alert readers to where they can find additional information. By putting supporting documents at the end, you ensure that the main body of your written business plan doesn't become bogged down with details.

Creating alternate versions of your plan

You may find that a single written plan can't cover all the bases — especially if you need to communicate specific information to a number of different audiences. Don't worry; no law limits you to just one version of your business plan. In fact, many companies write versions specifically targeted to different audiences — for example, one aimed at employees, another toward potential lenders or investors, and a third for more general interests.

Developing several versions of your business plan is basically an assembly job. Follow these steps down the line:

1. **Create a complete and comprehensive master plan — one that includes everything that's likely to be important to all your stakeholders (see Form 16-4).**

2. **Zero in on which special audiences you want to address.**

3. **Decide which parts of your master plan are important and which ones aren't relevant to each specific target audience.**

After you know your audience and its requirements, putting together an alternate version is as simple as cutting and pasting the relevant parts of the master plan together.

If you or your staff makes business presentations, consider creating a set of slides using PowerPoint or another commercial presentation software program to highlight key parts of your business plan. Make sure each slide zeros in on a single point; too many words and ideas on a slide are a turn-off. Choose a graphic style that remains consistent throughout the presentation. Use charts, graphs, and other images to help convey key ideas whenever possible. Make sure that your presentation is consistent with your business plan. And if you significantly revise parts of your business plan, update your slides and make sure everyone involved is alerted to avoid using out-of-date information in presentations.

When creating alternate versions of your plan, make sure that they all mesh with each another. For example, don't write one mission statement for one audience and another for a second group of readers. And whatever you do, don't create different sets of goals and objectives for different stakeholders. At the very least, you'll confuse everyone — yourself included. At worst, you'll anger audiences if they discover that you're saying one thing to one group and something different to another.

The job of creating a targeted version of your business plan is really one of deciding which parts of the master plan to include and which to leave out. The wording should remain the same in all versions.

Fitting the Pieces Together

When you have a working draft in front of you, look at the document as a whole to make sure that all the pieces fit together. For example, your company overview should reflect your mission statement, your assessment of the business environment should be in sync with your business strategy, and your company strategy should support goals and objectives.

If your plan is a team effort, devote extra effort to a review of the overall document. Sometimes the right hand doesn't know exactly what the left hand is doing, even when you have a solid outline for everyone to work from. The best way to catch inconsistencies or omissions is to have all the members of your planning team read your draft plan in its entirety.

TIP

After you have a polished draft, enlist the help of people who haven't been involved along the way. Outside readers will see the document with fresh eyes and are more likely to catch discrepancies or places where the language isn't crystal clear. Invite people who aren't afraid to be completely candid, even if that means giving you a thumbs-down on parts of your plan. Be clear that the plan is a working draft and that you welcome any and all comments, positive or negative. But ask your critics to provide constructive help, as well. If something in the plan is unclear or needs further explanation, ask them to suggest ways to fix the problem.

TIP

To help with the review process, use the Working Draft Checklist in Form 16-5. The checklist covers key questions that you and other reviewers should ask when reviewing your written business plan.

Don't panic if your reviewers come back with all sorts of suggestions or constructive criticism. This just means that they're doing their jobs and helping you identify problems so you can address them now — before your plan hits the desk of a banker, investor, or business partner. A little criticism won't hurt; it will make your business plan much more effective.

Working Draft Checklist

☐ **Is your executive summary clear and compelling?**

☐ **Do the major pieces of the company overview — your mission statement, values and vision, major business goals and objectives — work together to explain who you are and what you believe in?**

☐ **Does the overview provide a strong sense of the nature of your business and the products and services you plan to offer?**

☐ **Do your goals and objectives match the company's mission?**

☐ **Does the plan offer a convincing analysis of the market you intend to enter?**

☐ **Does the plan give a clear description of who your primary customers will be?**

☐ **Does the plan adequately and objectively assess your strengths and weaknesses?**

☐ **Does the company's strategy make sense in light of your analysis of the business environment?**

☐ **Does your action plan match up with your strategic direction as outlined in the plan?**

☐ **Does the plan's financial review reflect your business strategy and action plan?**

☐ **Does your action plan include enough specifics to create a road map for the near-term?**

☐ **Is the plan clearly written and easy to understand?**

☐ **Is there anything missing from the plan that should be added?**

☐ **Is there anything that should be cut from the plan?**

☐ **Are there other changes that would strengthen your written plan?**

© *John Wiley & Sons, Inc.*

FORM 16-5: When reviewing drafts of your business plan, use this checklist.

TIP

Before you finalize your written plan, put together a timetable for when you'll begin the process of reviewing and revising your plan. Our suggestion is to re-evaluate your plan once a year. If your business hits a rough patch, however, or if it's growing very fast or undergoing great change, you may need to revisit your plan more often. In that case, remember that you don't have to undertake the entire process. You can focus on the relevant sections of the plan — marketing, for example — and leave the rest in place.

Forms

The following forms at www.dummies.com/go/businessplanskit can help you put your written business plan together:

Form 16-1	**Business Plan Components Checklist**	A list of the major components of a business plan along with the elements that go into each section
Form 16-2	**Business Plan Template**	A detailed template you can use to draft your written plan
Form 16-3	**Master Plan Tracking Sheet**	A tracking form that shows at a glance where you are in the process of writing your business plan
Form 16-4	**Business Plan Target Audience Guidelines**	A form that helps you tailor your business plan to various target audiences
Form 16-5	**Working Draft Checklist**	Questions to ask when reviewing the working draft of your business plan

Chapter 17

Implementing Your Plan

A sk successful entrepreneurs how they made it, and they'll usually list two reasons. No. 1: They had rock-solid business plans in place. No. 2: They stuck to them. Okay, well maybe there's a third reason: They had a process in place to recognize when their plan wasn't working and the flexibility to quickly and effectively revise it. These days, in the face of fast-evolving technologies and plenty of economic uncertainties, No. 3 is more important than ever.

This chapter helps you use the business plan you've created to steer a course toward success. It's packed full of ideas for ways to put your plan to work. It shows how you can use your plan to organize your business, and it helps you choose the best organizational structure and the most effective procedures for getting the job done. It offers tips on how to use your plan to get all you can out of your most important resource: your people. Finally, it contains ideas for reviewing and revising your plan to keep it fresh and vital.

Organizing around Your Business Plan

A business plan is like a blueprint. It tells exactly what you're working to achieve, but the end result happens only if you hammer it into reality.

A blueprint for a new house guides every construction step down to a fraction of an inch. A business plan is more of a framework for success. It helps you organize your business around your mission and vision, your goals and objectives, and the strategy you've outlined to achieve success. It provides milestones along the way to measure your progress. Plus, it keeps everyone on the same page and working toward the same positive outcomes. These sections outline how to organize your business, assign duties and responsibilities to employees, and set up systems and procedures based on your business plan. By aligning your company and your business plan, you'll stand the best chance of achieving your goals and objectives.

Form meets function

The first step in putting your plan to work is to configure your company to reflect your plan in every part of your organization, from the structure of your management team to the procedures you put in place to make your company work. As you shape your organization, pay particular attention to these three parts of your plan:

>> **Business description:** Look at your company's capabilities and resources (see Chapter 6 for more information) and then develop your organization to fortify strengths and overcome weaknesses.

>> **Business strategy:** Build programs and systems that support your plan for reaching, serving, and satisfying your customers.

>> **Action plan:** Detail all the steps necessary to implement your business plan, including the priorities and timelines you'll follow as you make it all happen.

As you organize your company, know that most businesses are built around one of four common organizational models (see Chapter 6 for details):

>> **The pack:** In this model, one person runs the show, and everyone else is an equal member of, well, the pack.

>> **Function:** This model divides people into groups based on the functions they perform in the company.

>> **Division:** This model divides distinct parts of the business into separate divisions, each with its own management structure.

>> **The matrix:** Here, employees can wear more than one hat and report to more than one supervisor, encouraging team members to share talent, expertise, and experience.

REMEMBER

The most effective organization depends on the kind of business you're running — big, small, formal, informal, online, manufacturing, retail, service, or a dozen other considerations. But most of all, it depends on your business plan.

Consider these questions and pointers as you shape the organizational structure that's best for your company:

>> **Is one individual responsible for the vision and strategic direction of your business?** If so, you may want to use the pack model, with one leader and a pack of team members. This model works best for small businesses built on one person's vision. Even big companies like Apple have thrived with one very strong and visionary leader. Just be sure you have a succession plan in place in case leadership needs to change.

>> **Is employee creativity crucial to the success of your business?** If so, you may want to consider a loose organizational structure with relatively few management levels, giving your staff the freedom to be creative. Companies like Google have built their success on unleashing the creativity of their employees. They also have won employee loyalty and created a corporate image that resonates with customers.

>> **Are speed and flexibility crucial to your ability to remain competitive?** If so, think about a flat organizational structure with as few management levels as possible. This kind of organization has challenges, of course, one of which is directing the activities of employees who don't report to a manager. But many small- to medium-sized companies make this structure work by creating effective lines of communication among employees.

>> **Does your business consist of several distinct functions, each with its own culture and kinds of employees?** If so, consider a functional organization. One group handles product development, for example. A separate group leads marketing efforts. This kind of structure requires a level of management to oversee the efforts of the various groups.

>> **Is much of your work conducted on a project basis, moving people and resources from one job to another?** If so, a matrix organization may work best for you. You may even decide that a virtual organization structure makes most sense. (Check out Chapter 12 to explore the benefits — and challenges — of a virtual business.)

REMEMBER

You can alter your organizational structure at some point down the road, especially if your business is growing rapidly or your business environment has changed significantly. In fact, maintaining the flexibility to reshape how your business works has become one of the keys to success in today's fast-changing business world.

EXAMPLE

A San Francisco-based design firm began as a small operation, working out of a loft space with three employees who collaborated on each project. As the business grew, the company added more designers and account managers and eventually moved to a much bigger space south of the city. As it expanded, however, it maintained a flat organizational structure, mostly because no one thought to change it. Eventually, the team was so big — and the meetings to discuss new projects grew so long — that the company changed its structure to a functional organizational structure with teams devoted to print design, web design, and video development. Workflow efficiency improved dramatically.

Duties and responsibilities

After you've structured your organization, your next task is to assign duties and responsibilities to your key people. You may have made many or most of those assignments already, at least for your top management team. Even so, take time to review your assignments against your business plan. Be sure these assignments are closely aligned with your major goals and objectives, because if the work of your key employees isn't directly tied to your company's goals, those goals won't get accomplished.

Figure 17-1 shows how an executive-services company matched the duties and responsibilities assigned to key employees with business goals and objectives.

By assigning responsibility for major goals and objectives, a business significantly improves the odds that its action plan will be carried out. What's more, the assignment chart confirms that senior managers will work closely together to accomplish the plan — supporting the company's decision to adopt a relatively flat, flexible management structure. As a bonus, the assignment chart provides guidelines the company can follow as it writes detailed job descriptions for key managers.

TIP

As you create your assignment chart, use the template provided in Form 17-1, which you can find at www.dummies.com/go/businessplanskit. Form 17-1 helps you align assignments with your major goals and objectives to keep your plan on track.

Goals and Objectives Assignment Chart

GOAL • OBJECTIVE	WHO'S RESPONSIBLE	NOTES
Enhance staff expertise	Director, H.R.	Must work closely with Director of Sales to determine key skills required by clients
• Schedule regular training seminars (by 5–1)	Training manager/ outside training consultant	
• Have all staff certified (by 12–15)	Director, H.R.	
Increase brand awareness	Marketing/Sales VP	Must work closely with direct reports to shape marketing strategy
• Create customer referral bonus program (by 6–15)	Director, Sales	
• Begin monthly newsletter (by 8–1)	Director, Marketing Communications/ outside contractor	Consult with Information Technology to determine feasibility of an online version
Improve customer service	Marketing/Sales VP	High priority — should involve input from all senior management
• Hire two new employees (by 7–15)	Director, H.R.	Consult with marketing
• Install new job-tracking software (by 9–15)	Operations VP/ outside consultant	Work closely with marketing staff to determine requirements

© John Wiley & Sons, Inc.

FIGURE 17-1: Use an assignment chart to make sure management duties and responsibilities align with major business goals and objectives.

Systems and procedures

In order to put your business plan to work, you must know how your business will operate on a day-to-day basis. Your knowledge leads to the development of systems and procedures for everything from product development to sales and customer service.

A rational set of procedures and well-defined systems can mean the difference between business success and failure. They ensure efficiency, quality control, employee productivity, and customer satisfaction. And, in the end, they protect your bottom line.

TIP

You don't have to reinvent the wheel to install systems and procedures. Consider these steps:

>> Inquire with industry groups about standard operating procedures or basic business systems that may be well documented or available as prepackaged software.

>> Read trade publications and investigate third-party providers who may offer software or other packaged solutions that meet your operational requirements.

>> Talk with people who run companies similar to yours outside your direct competitive arena. They likely have time-tested sets of procedures and resources they can discuss with you.

>> Hire managers with experience in businesses like yours. With these old hands comes expertise with procedures and systems that you can replicate to build an efficient operation and reliable quality control.

As you build your systems and procedures, look back over the company description, strategy, and action-plan sections of your business plan. Jot down all the systems and procedures you think you need to get the job done.

REMEMBER

Even small businesses and sole proprietorships need to have systems in place for tracking customers, monitoring workflow, and keeping those invoices moving along. By taking the time to write out your operations and procedures you'll identify any gaps and ensure that you don't spend more time than you need on the business of doing business. It will also help you get new hires quickly up to speed.

TIP

You may not need to address every item on Form 17-2, but it's worth looking all of them over to see which ones are relevant. Form 17-2 lists the business systems and procedures common to most businesses, along with slots for you to fill in procedures specific to your company. After you go through the checklist, circle the two or three procedures most critical to your business strategy and plan. Break each down into a series of steps in order to identify potential gaps before they cause problems.

Getting Team Buy-In

Business buzzwords tend to have plenty in common with Hula-Hoops and pet rocks: They achieve wild popularity one day and become clichés the next. But one buzzword has never gone out of fashion, and that's teamwork. Whether your company is a small shop or a sprawling multinational, if more than one person is responsible for the work, you need teamwork in order to succeed.

REMEMBER

When your employees feel like they're part of a team, they have more incentive to work hard and work together instead of cruising on parallel tracks or even working against each other. As a result of teamwork, one plus one can actually equal three because team players often produce results that are greater than the sum of their individual contributions. Teams are inherently strong, so a business culture that encourages teamwork can help carry you and your employees through the bad times as well as the good. Teamwork also strengthens and advances the brand image of your business, because everyone is working to present the same brand message and keep the same brand promise.

Read on to discover the many benefits of distributing your business plan to everyone on your team, including employees throughout the company and independent contractors and team members who may work remotely. Because teamwork depends on a strong leader, this section also covers choosing the most effective leadership style, based on your business plan, as well as ways to use your plan to develop employee skills.

Distributing your plan

Your plan lays out your company's mission, vision, and values (see Chapter 3). It also sets the ground rules and establishes your game plan, so you should share it with the people you count on to help you achieve victory. See that everyone on your team is familiar with your plan, clear about the strategy, comfortable with his or her role, and in tune with exactly what has to be done to be successful.

TIP

Give each member of your management team a copy of your plan to read carefully. Distribute the most important parts of your plan to your entire staff — at meetings, in a newsletter, or on your intranet. By doing so, you

>> **Promote teamwork:** To do their part to make your business plan work, all members of your team need to know what's in the plan, so they're clear about the business mission, basic strategy, major goals, and plan of action.

>> **Create a sense of ownership:** Your business plan serves as a blueprint for what the business aims to become. By sharing this information with

employees, you show them how their personal involvement contributes to making the plan a reality.

>> **Link individual and company performance:** By evaluating team members in relation to key goals and objectives in your business plan, you underscore why their performances really matter.

>> **Generate feedback and new ideas:** At all levels of your organization, employees are a great resource — whether they offer new ideas or provide a reality check. Make sure that everyone is familiar with what you're working to accomplish together. Encourage everyone's input.

You don't need to spring pop quizzes to test staff knowledge of your business plan. (Although it would be interesting to try one out on your top managers: "In 25 words or less, describe our ideal customer. Which of the following best describes our action plan? What is our mission, anyway?") But by giving the plan to employees and encouraging them to read it, you cultivate organization-wide understanding of where your business wants to go and how you plan to get there. If your plan is more than ten pages long, consider creating a shorter version to accompany your employee handbook.

Each time you revise your business plan, get the word out to everyone on your team. Highlight the changes that you've made and explain why. If your business has an internal blog or newsletter, use it to describe the revised plan and its features. If you have an intranet, use it to publish the new plan, along with answers to a list of questions you think employees may have. (See the section "Keeping Your Plan Current," later in this chapter, for more info on updating your plan.)

Guiding and motivating remote employees

If some or all of your staff work remotely, using your business plan to promote teamwork is especially important. Chapter 14 is full of information on hiring and managing a remote team, including advice for determining if remote employees are right for your business. The answer may be yes if

>> Telecommuting is an important perk that will help you snare top talent.

>> You can effectively manage employees who work remotely.

>> You can clearly define the duties of and policies for remote employees.

>> You can easily measure the productivity of remote employees.

>> You've established and can align all team members, remote or on location, around a company culture that reflects business values, beliefs, and brand promise.

Remote employees may *not* be such a good idea for your organization if

>> Your company's creativity depends on employees brainstorming together.

>> The equipment required for working remotely is expensive to buy or maintain.

>> You'll have trouble motivating and managing employees who work outside the office.

>> The nature of your business involves frequent or spur-of-the-moment meetings.

EXAMPLE

A well-known Internet company made headlines a few years ago over the issue of remote work. The company had long encouraged employees to work at home. But a new CEO worried that its policy of allowing employees to telecommute jeopardized the kind of brainstorming that occurs when employees chat over coffee in the office. When she ordered telecommuting employees back to the office, many of them voiced their objections. So did advocates of social networking technologies outside the company, who see telecommuting as the wave of the future. Some critics warned that the company would have trouble hiring talented employees because of the new ban on telecommuting. Controversy ensued, but the CEO stood by her decision.

Was she right? Yes and no. A survey of employees nationwide, conducted a year after the controversial decision, found that people who worked up to 20 percent of the time from home were more engaged, enthusiastic, and committed to their jobs. They were also more productive, measured by the hours they put in. But the survey also revealed a point of diminishing returns. Employees who worked 50 percent or more time from home were more likely to feel disconnected from their company.

If managing remote employees makes good business sense, you should use your business plan to help guide them and keep them motivated in the following ways:

>> Give all remote employees a copy of the business plan, including the mission statement, vision statement, and goals and objectives.

>> Spell out policies regarding remote employees in the business plan.

>> Make sure remote employees are part of strategic planning sessions that affect their work.

>> Notify remote employees about changes to the business plan, even if those changes don't directly affect them.

>> Find every opportunity to remind remote employees that they're integral parts of the team.

Leading effectively

Effective teams demand strong leaders who can communicate the company's vision, inspire and influence others, and make things happen. The best leaders are people who move easily among the following three management styles, laying down the law when they need to but also eliciting help or asking for advice when appropriate:

>> **The boss:** Using this approach, the leader tells employees what to do, when to do it, and how to do it.

>> **The adviser:** With this style, the leader gives employees a fair amount of independence and responsibility, while stepping in to serve as the boss when help or advice is necessary.

>> **The colleague:** In this style, the leader sits down with employees for a free exchange of ideas in which all participants treat each other with equal respect and make mutual decisions.

Different kinds of companies and even different situations within each company call for the use of different leadership styles. If you run a design or advertising agency, for example, you need to serve as an adviser or colleague, giving people plenty of freedom to be as creative as possible, but you also need to be the boss who sets a clear vision and direction that everyone within the agency follows. If you start a local courier service, you need the ability to give instructions, direct people, and keep everyone on schedule, but you also need to remain open to ideas from your couriers regarding what they're hearing from customers and what could make the operation run more efficiently and effectively.

TIP

Use Form 17-3 as you weigh which management and leadership attributes most affect the success of your business plan. Always look for opportunities to practice those skills and traits. If tight deadlines are a fact of life in your business, develop ways to make colleagues aware of each deadline and make them comfortable meeting it. If creativity is the hallmark of your business, sit down with your colleagues to brainstorm the best ways to encourage it.

Sharing the vision

Your business plan presents the vision of what you want your company to become. By sharing it with everyone who has a stake in your company, you can create a sense of shared commitment and direction.

You don't have to ask everybody to read and reread your business plan on a monthly basis. You can use other methods to keep your vision, mission, and business goals front and center. The following are some examples:

- » Reproduce your mission and vision statements in company newsletters, the employee handbook, and on the flip side of business cards.

- » Refer to your business plan whenever appropriate — during marketing strategy meetings or new product development forums, for example.

- » Use the plan as a yardstick when evaluating programs and initiatives.

- » Use your business goals and objectives as a guide when setting employee objectives and conducting performance evaluations.

- » Actively enlist team feedback when you prepare to reassess and revise your business plan.

- » Turn to your plan if your company encounters a crisis; your mission and vision statements can serve as a useful guide when trouble arises.

Encouraging pride of ownership

People who own businesses usually work long hours, put up with tons of stress, and love every minute of it. They do all that because they've built something of their own — a company that reflects their talents and inspirations — and they're motivated by a strong pride of ownership.

Good leaders find ways to motivate employees so that they feel the same way, even when they're part of a sprawling multinational firm. Here are some ways that businesses inspire employees and give them pride of ownership:

- » Give them a piece of the company, using stock-purchase plans tied to individual or team performance.

- » Pay out year-end bonuses tied to company profitability.

- » Give employees full control and responsibility for particular programs, including the freedom to make key decisions.

- » Reinforce the sense that they own the successes of the projects by rewarding them for jobs well done.

REMEMBER

Although a performance bonus is always nice, employees value personal growth, recognition, challenging and meaningful work, and — above all else the most universally appreciated form of recognition — praise. Consider an employee of the month award, write-ups in the company newsletter, a round of applause at the next company-wide meeting, or a heartfelt gesture of thanks. When motivating employees, simple morale boosters can be more effective than money.

A major health-related website reorganized its writers and editors to create small editorial teams, each in charge of a specific content area or channel — men's health, diet and nutrition, children's health, fitness, and so on. The head honchos gave each team creative freedom to shape the channel and develop new features. The company then set up monthly meetings to review channel performance and recognize important achievements, such as award-winning stories. By virtually every measure, the quality of the website improved dramatically over the next six months.

The company then tried to go one step further. To create competition among the channels, managers started tracking the number of *page views* (the number of times people visited each channel) each month. That sounded like a good idea on paper. In reality, it spelled trouble.

The number of page views had little to do with the quality of a particular channel and much to do with the interests of the website's visitors, who tended to be women in their 30s and 40s. As a result, the men's health channel was always less popular than the women's health channel, regardless of the quality of stories or its special features. The result: Instead of motivating employees, the use of site traffic as a measure created a sense of frustration and unfairness among the teams. Fortunately, the company quickly abandoned the competition in favor of data reflecting the popularity of the entire website.

Although competition among teams can be a potent motivator, the approach can also backfire, creating resentment and hard feelings. When using team competitions as a motivating tool, make sure that everyone plays on a level field. As you establish how you'll judge performance — profits, unit sales, new site visitors, or other measurements — make sure you compare the work of the teams, not external factors that team members have little control over.

Developing employee skills

The success of your business plan depends on the quality of the people you attract and keep on your team, which means hiring qualified employees, of course, but it also means expanding the skills of people already on your staff.

Investing in your current team members is a win-win proposition. Employees get the opportunity to take on more responsibility, and your business gains an increasingly qualified (and loyal) staff.

To make the most of your investment in training, begin by defining which capabilities your company absolutely has to have in order to meet your goals and objectives. Study the company strategy and action plan sections of your business plan to identify skills your employees will need, including such general attributes as the ability to manage information, think independently, work in teams, and deal with change. But don't forget another key step: Ask employees how *they* want to expand their skills and capabilities.

TIP

With your critical skills list in hand, explore education and training opportunities that are best suited to your needs and budget. To help you get started, Form 17-4 offers a checklist of some of the most common training options available. Check off the options that seem most promising given your situation and budget.

Employee Training Resource Checklist
☐ Community college, university, and adult education courses
☐ Industry training programs
☐ In-house training programs
☐ Certification programs
☐ Internet-based education
☐ Independent learning programs
☐ Self-help business books and instructional guides
☐ Mentoring programs

© John Wiley & Sons, Inc.

FORM 17-4: Use this form as you investigate employee-training resources.

TIP

One of the most cost-effective ways to enhance the skills of your employees is mentoring. *Mentoring* occurs when experienced employees shepherd the careers of new hires or junior members of your team, and your business reaps the dual benefits of teamwork and company loyalty. If you decide to institute a mentoring program, realize that employees who serve as mentors make a personal investment of time and hard work. Plan to reward them accordingly. Among other options, free up their schedules in order to give them the extra time they need. Pick up a copy of *Coaching & Mentoring For Dummies* by Marty Brounstein (John Wiley & Sons, Inc.) for the lowdown on mentoring.

Other terrific training resources include self-help business books and podcasts, instructional guides, and educational websites. Subjects run the gamut from accounting and marketing to computer programming and customer service. Encourage continuous independent employee development by maintaining an in-house training library.

TIP

To increase involvement in employee training programs, consider offering job promotions, salary increases, bonuses, or other rewards to people who dedicate their personal off-the-job time to educational efforts that enhance their ability to contribute to your company's success.

Keeping Your Plan Current

This book is in its fifth edition for one very good reason. Nothing in the world of business or business planning stands still. Ten years ago, only a visionary few could have predicted that smartphones and mobile devices would radically alter the way people receive and send information, that businesses would be storing data not on disks but in the ether of the cloud, and that businesses could soar to multibillion-dollar valuations based not on physical assets but on globally reaching and Internet-connected networks. Ten years from today, as-yet unforeseen changes will have come along to further transform the competitive landscape.

Count on the upcoming sections to help you identify key indicators that signal when your company, your products, your competition, or your markets are shifting; knowing when it's time to tweak or totally revise your plan to respond effectively to change; and planning to keep your business plan current in the face of change.

The inevitability of business change

Don't for a minute think that, after you've finalized your business plan, you can tuck it in a drawer and get on with running your business. A business plan is a living, breathing document — at least it better be, if you want to stay nimble enough to keep one step ahead of the competition. The business-planning process is never over, so your business plan will always remain a work in progress.

The only constant in business is change, though the pace of change varies depending on your industry. If you manufacture high-speed telecom switches, your world is in constant motion. If you run the corner hardware store, change may come more slowly. But no business sector is immune to change at some level or another. (That corner hardware store better have a website up and running or it could be in trouble, for example.) And in virtually all businesses, these days, the pace of change has accelerated. (Check out Chapter 15 for more on detecting, reacting to, and managing change.)

EXAMPLE

For years, a medical practice was one of the most secure (and lucrative) businesses around. Everyone gets sick, after all, and doctors thought they had a well-defined, stable market for their services. Then along came managed care, and the business of doctoring changed dramatically. Today, healthcare reform is creating even more change in this industry, and in the health insurance industry as well.

For further proof of inescapable change, consider the family farm. Farmers have always been at the mercy of the weather, but for generations, farming remained a pretty steady and predictable business in all other ways. Enter big agribusiness and new, sophisticated agricultural technologies and the business of farming changed forever from top to bottom. Now, with growing interest in organic produce and local production, small farms are coming back. Who would have thought?

The good news is that change creates opportunities. In fact, more than likely you wouldn't be planning to start or expand your company if markets, customers, and competitors weren't evolving in one way or another. However, change also poses threats — from the arrival of new competitors to the enactment of stringent new regulations — which is a big part of why you need to make business planning an ongoing process.

Identifying critical metrics

Having a carefully constructed business plan is one of the most important keys to success. But to know if your plan is working as projected — and to identify where you need to alter or change course completely — you need to measure your results. Business gurus use the term *metric*, which basically means any unit of measurement. The most obvious business metric is profit. If your company is making money, you're doing fine, right? Maybe.

REMEMBER

Profit is only one metric. For a company that depends on the creativity and drive of its employees, morale may be just as useful a metric. For a service business such as a hair salon, customer satisfaction is a critical metric. For a company that sells highly precise instrumentation, quality control scores are the central measure of success. Don't assume that choosing the appropriate metric is easy. In fact, one of the biggest industries in the world, healthcare, has been struggling to do exactly that.

EXAMPLE

In the United States, healthcare metrics have tended to focus on what the experts call *process* — whether a doctor appropriately prescribed a blood pressure medicine to patient A or ordered an ultrasound for patient B. In some other countries, healthcare metrics focus on resources. A hospital gets top grades for having a certain percentage of nurses with advanced degrees or a certain number of MRI machines per 1,000 patients.

Trouble is, those metrics don't really say whether the treatment was a success. Patients don't care whether the nurse has advanced degrees or the hospital boasts a lot of MRI machines. They want to get well. So a new movement is underway to develop outcome measures based on what patients care about — how well and how quickly they recover, whether they experience complications, and whether the treatments are effective long-term.

The appropriate metrics vary widely from business to business. To come up with the best measures to gauge your success and guide you in the future, you need to think about all the aspects of your operation, including customers, employees, your public image, your production process, and more.

Take the time to consider every angle of your business operations as you determine how to gauge success. Use Form 17-5 as a guide.

Business Metrics Worksheet

Answer the following questions to begin to identify the most appropriate business metrics for your enterprise. *Metrics* are the measurements you choose that best gauge your progress in meeting goals and objectives.

Think about your customers:

1. What are the three most important things they want from you?
2. What are the three things they definitely don't want (damaged merchandise, rude treatment, long back orders, and so on)?
3. What do your customers say about you and your product in reviews?
4. What do you absolutely have to do to win and keep customers?
5. What additional products or services might they be interested in?
6. What reasons do your customers have for turning to your competitors?

Think about your internal processes:

7. How do you measure productivity?
8. How do you measure the quality of your product or service?
9. How do you measure efficiency?
10. If appropriate, are you taking advantage of web-based software to track your measurements?

Think about your employees:

11. How do your employees measure their own personal success?
12. What can interfere with employee productivity?
13. What can negatively impact employee morale?

Think about your bottom line:

14. What are the most important numbers you need to track?
15. What numbers serve as an early warning sign of problems in your business?

After you answer these 15 questions, review your answers. Pull out at least five metrics that you can use to measure your progress and your company's health. Then rank them in terms of importance. Don't worry if your list is a long one. Many companies begin to carefully track just two or three metrics and gradually add others.

© *John Wiley & Sons, Inc.*

FORM 17-5: Use this form to zero in on the measurements that are most important for tracking your business plan's success.

Monitoring your situation

Tracking all key metrics can help you keep your finger on the pulse of your business. Doing so can also help you monitor how well the objectives, goals, and strategies outlined in your plan are working. Even the best business plans need readjustments from time to time. How often? That depends on the nature of your business and the competitive environment. Scheduling an annual review of your business plan is a good general rule, but you should also consider reexamining certain parts of your plan on a more frequent basis. For example, if new competitors are popping up all around you, take a close look at the competitive analysis and customer profile sections of the business-environment component of your plan. If sales are falling short of expectations, update your marketing plan.

Even if your company is buzzing along precisely as planned, certain parts of your plan demand ongoing attention, on a semiannual or even a quarterly basis. Those sections of your plan include your

>> Goals and objectives (check out Chapter 3 for more details)

>> SWOT analysis (see Chapter 5)

>> Company strategy (see Chapter 5)

>> Financial projections (see Chapter 9)

>> Action plan (see Chapters 3 and 5)

TIP

If you already have a business-planning team in place, consider asking the team members to assume the ongoing task of reviewing — and possibly revising — key parts of your business plan during the course of the year. If you're on your own, create a schedule at the beginning of the year that sets out which parts of your plan you'll review and when you'll review them.

WARNING

In the rush of day-to-day business demands, you may be tempted to delay the review and revision of your business plan. Especially when your company is under pressure — from competitors, finances, and operational deadlines — you may want to postpone any kind of planning until your situation settles down. Don't. Giving your plan attention during critical times may well make the difference between pulling through and being pulled under.

Encouraging feedback

Your employees can provide valuable insights into how well your plan is performing. By listening to the people who actually carry out your plan — from top managers to entry-level hires — you can discover plenty about what's working and what isn't. Encouraging staff input taps a rich vein of ideas about how to revise and refine your business plan to make it even more effective. Some of the ideas you receive may be impossible to implement, and some may be downright wacky. But others are likely to be terrific and even invaluable.

In fact, employees can help you guide your company in the right direction. For instance, employees working on the front line may be the first to notice marketplace trends. They may be able to steer you toward prospective customers or customer groups worth pursuing. They may tip you off about competitors worth keeping an eye on or product problems that are worth analyzing. Employees working behind the scenes may have useful insights that lead to better processes or stronger strategic directions.

TIP

To solicit feedback from your employees, establish procedures that regularly encourage employees to offer their comments and suggestions. Some companies install an old-fashioned suggestion box. Others use their intranets to create virtual suggestion boxes, chat rooms, and online question-and-answer areas. If your business is small enough, you can employ the best approach of all, which is talking face to face with employees doing the work and dealing with customers to find out what's working, what isn't, and what the company can do differently.

Actively solicit suggestions and ideas by using memos, company-wide meetings, and employee questionnaires. In addition, invite employees to talk about the business plan during their performance reviews. Whatever methods you choose, consider asking for answers to the following questions:

» Is the company doing enough to communicate its vision, mission, and strategic plan to employees? If not, how would you suggest we do a better job?

» Are the business goals and objectives outlined in the plan clear and appropriate?

» Do your duties and responsibilities help support the company's goals and strategic direction?

» Can you suggest specific changes in the way you do your work that will help the company better meet its goals?

» Can you suggest ways to improve the company's overall operations?

» Do company procedures get in the way of doing your best job? If so, how do you suggest changing them?

» Are you aware of changes in the industry — including changes in customers and competitors — that the business plan should address?

» Can you suggest ways we can enhance the value we offer our customers?

>> Can you think of additional or better ways to produce and market our products and services?

>> If you were in charge of revising the business plan, what other changes would you make?

By soliciting suggestions and ideas from people at every level of your company, you not only collect constructive information, but you also enhance a sense of teamwork and shared mission, which go a long way toward making your business plan work and your business a long-term success.

Listening to customers

Many businesses have traditionally used customer surveys to gauge how well they're doing. Today, the Internet has made surveys easier than ever. For instance, many airlines send out an email survey after a trip is completed, asking passengers for feedback on everything from food quality to the friendliness of the service. Other businesses survey satisfaction following purchases or service visits, and yet others send out broader-reaching questionnaires using free online services such as SurveyMonkey. But old-fashioned ways of personally polling customers still hold sway.

Many restaurants and hotels deliver customer satisfaction surveys at the end of a customer's visit. Some businesses make it even more personal: To compete in the competitive world of car repairs, one ambitious mechanic we know makes a point of calling every customer within a week of his or her visit to see how everything went.

REMEMBER

Customer feedback can be one of the best measures of performance — and an effective way of checking to see if your plan is on track. In fact, your plan is a good place to start when crafting the appropriate questions to ask customers. In our experience, we've found that three parts of the plan are likely to yield useful questions:

>> **Your mission and vision statement:** Ask customers if you're living up to the overarching mission and vision you set for yourself. If not, ask customers for their insights on how you can do better.

>> **Your goals and objectives:** Focus on customer-specific goals and objectives. Use your customer survey to gauge if you're achieving the things you set out to accomplish. Again, if your customers say you're falling short, ask them how you can serve them better.

>> **Your marketing plan:** No one can give you more insight into the success of your marketing plan than your customers. Ask them how they first heard about you. Ask them whether the image conveyed in your marketing efforts matches their experience.

After you craft your customer survey, test it by asking a few people to complete the form. That way, you can make sure the questions make sense and yield the kind of information you're looking for. Distribute the survey to as many customers as possible. You may consider giving a small incentive to nudge people to take the time to fill it in, such as a discount on their next transaction with you or a chance to win a raffle. You can then compile the information from the survey and use it as a guide as you revisit your plan.

Planning for change

Some of the changes you confront will be fairly easy to navigate. But occasionally, changes come along that completely rewrite the rules of the game. Get ready to face a dilemma. Sometimes holding to your original plan through rough waters is the smart thing to do. Other times it's wiser to change course. You have to, as the song goes, know when to hold 'em and know when to fold 'em.

Sometimes clinging to the details of an established plan when business conditions are rapidly changing can sideline a business fast. Knowing when to stick to your mission, strategy, goals, and plans — and knowing when to make some quick or even sweeping changes — isn't easy. In many ways, it's a skill that determines the real leaders in business.

Metrics, staff feedback, and customer knowledge, all explored in this chapter, help unlock valuable insights that can guide decisions about business plan revisions. Sometimes the best strategy, in the face of disruptive change, is to start asking questions around the following issues:

>> Define the disruption you're experiencing and determine if it's likely to last long and whether it will have a long-term impact on your business.

>> Determine if the disruption presents opportunities if your business adapts and makes changes.

>> Assess your business capabilities to determine where you have strengths you can deploy as you adjust to address disruptive changes.

Beyond dealing with changes due to major disruptions in your business environment, stay proactive by forecasting and planning for anticipated change. Use Form 17-6 to get the process in motion. Not all the questions on our checklist will be appropriate to your business, but take the time to consider each one. In a medium-sized or large company, consider appointing a committee to review these questions and create a report.

FORM 17-6: Check off the questions on this list that are relevant for helping you manage change in your business environment.

REMEMBER

The more time you spend researching the forces that drive change in your business, the better you'll become at predicting those changes in advance. Just as important: The more time you spend improving your company's readiness for change, the more swiftly you'll be able to respond when it happens. As new technologies, globalization, and economic dislocations continue to transform the marketplace, the ability to respond to change will play an increasingly prominent role as one of the key capabilities for success. Turn to Chapter 15 for more information for navigating an uncertain future.

Nurturing Tomorrow's Leaders

If you intend to be in business for the long run, and we hope you do, think about who is going to support your leadership and perhaps one day step in to fill your shoes.

Don't worry: No one's planning your retirement party quite yet. But as your business grows, chances are good that one person at the top can't do everything. Even with a strong management team, the time will likely come when you have to expand the leadership of your company and loosen your reins. That's what growing a company — and creating a *succession plan* — is all about. How well you manage the leadership transition determines how successful your company ultimately becomes.

WARNING

Passing on the leadership mantle represents one of the most difficult transitions a leader can make. Relinquishing control is rarely easy; no one is asking you to rush the transition decision. However, too many entrepreneurs fail to establish a transition plan or to cultivate next-generation leaders. That's a big mistake for the simple reason that often the need for leadership change arises out of nowhere — prompted by anything from health to family issues to changing personal interests or conditions.

The issue of succession is doubly tricky for family-run firms because it brings up business and personal considerations. Some family members may not want to take over the family company; others may want to play a role but lack the training or experience. Planning is essential to ensure that the family member who assumes the helm is prepared and groomed for the job. For more on succession and family businesses, see Chapter 11.

TIP

Although the best person to eventually take over your company's leadership may, in fact, be a family member or a member of your existing team, don't begin with any assumptions. Look beyond the usual question: "How do I identify family members or rising stars in my organization who are most likely to become leaders?" Instead, face the leadership transition issue by taking these steps:

1. **Ask yourself, "Where is my business likely to need strong leadership in the future?"**

2. **To answer your question, review your business goals and objectives and your action plan, which indicate areas where strong leadership is essential.**

3. **Get out your most recent SWOT analysis or conduct a new one.**

   Your assessment of your company's strengths and weaknesses helps you target the leadership capabilities your company needs to develop in order to take advantage of opportunities while sidestepping potential threats. (Chapter 5 provides all the details).

4. **After you identify areas where leadership is critical, begin to consider people around you or recruit new hires that you can cultivate to take on future leadership roles.**

Forms

The following forms help you explain your company's strategy in your business plan. Go to www.dummies.com/go/businessplanskit to download them.

Form 17-1	**Goals and Objectives Assignment Chart**	An assignment chart designed to help you align management duties and responsibilities with major business goals and objectives.
Form 17-2	**Common Systems and Procedures Checklist**	A list of business systems and procedures common to many companies.
Form 17-3	**Checklist of Management and Leadership Traits**	A list of management skills and leadership traits you may want to develop to address future business needs.
Form 17-4	**Employee Training Resource Checklist**	The most common training resources for developing employee skills.
Form 17-5	**Business Metrics Worksheet**	Use this form to zero in on the measurements that are most important for tracking your business plan's success.
Form 17-6	**Checklist for Managing Change**	Use this form to assess your readiness for change and to identify ways to improve flexibility in the face of change.

5

The Part of Tens

Recognize warning signs that indicate your existing business plan needs an overhaul, including changes in your marketplace, sagging morale, unwelcome sales trends, climbing costs, and new competitive threats.

Stay proactive by watching for ten red flags that identify signs of trouble and alert you that it's time to revise your business plan before looming threats undermine your business success.

Give your almost-finished business plan one last review to ensure that it clearly describes your business model and your goals and objectives, to check your financial statements one last time to make sure the numbers are accurate and add up, and to verify that your business plan contains specific, actionable steps that allow you to achieve your goals.

Use a ten-point checklist to make sure your plan covers all the bases, lays out realistic goals backed by reasonable action plans, details sound financial forecasts, and speaks in a concise, jargon-free, and inspiring voice.

Chapter 18

Ten Signs That Your Plan May Need an Overhaul

Your business plan is your map, setting your course toward success. If conditions get choppy — or you lose your way completely — your business plan is the first place to turn. Flip to Chapter 4 to assess changing conditions, customers, and competition. Go to Chapter 13 for help steering around trouble and toward opportunity. Count on Chapter 15 for pointers on recognizing changes likely to affect your business so you don't get caught unprepared. At all times, watch for these ten red flags that your business plan needs a review.

Costs Rise, Revenues Fall

The clearest sign of trouble for almost any business is when costs are climbing and revenues are sinking. Yet, many business owners ignore the warning signs. Why? Because the shift doesn't take place overnight. Costs creep upward. Revenues drift downward. Too many business owners don't see what's happening because they aren't looking. Others hope things will turn around and go on hoping until it's too late. Keep a close eye on:

>> **Gross profit trends** to see whether your costs of goods sold are slowly climbing out of control

>> **Operating profits** to see whether your overhead and expenses are getting out of line or margins are changing

>> **Profitability** to see how much revenue makes its way to the bottom line

>> **Number of bids or inquiries** to monitor interest in your offerings

>> **Other measures,** such as the ratio of contracts won to bids submitted

Turn to Chapter 9 for a crash course on business financials. And at the first sign of a profit squeeze, revisit your business plan — starting with a hard look at your financial projections.

Sales Figures Head South

View sales figures like a customer poll. They'll alert you to fundamental problems, such as a disconnect between the features or services you offer and the benefits your customers seek, a glitch with quality control, a breakdown in customer service, or a marketing message that's not on target. If overall sales revenues fall — or sales for a product or service line miss your target — diagnose the problem. Then, revise the appropriate parts of your business plan — product design, operations, marketing strategy — to support your revised forecasts. Check back to Chapters 5, 6, and 7 for detailed advice.

You Don't Meet Financial Projections

Plenty of issues can knock financial projections out of whack. If your numbers aren't meeting your expectations:

1. Review the assumptions behind your original projections.

2. List every internal and external force that may be responsible for the variances.

3. Fix what you can and plan around what you can't, but don't ignore what the black-and-white financial statements tell you.

Don't waste time hoping that things will change. Update your financial projections based on the new reality and then revise your strategy and action plan accordingly. Chapter 9 covers financial statements. Turn to Chapter 15 for managing your company through times of turbulent change.

Employee Morale Sags

TIP

If you sense that employee morale is on the skids, talk to key people around you to find out what's wrong. Perhaps your goals and objectives are unreasonable, creating frustration rather than motivation. Or maybe there's a gap between the company's stated mission and your plan of action, causing confusion and indirection. When employee morale is at stake, address the problem immediately. Check out Chapter 3 for advice on crafting a mission statement that guides and motivates your team. Chapter 17 describes ways to use your business plan to keep everyone motivated and on track.

Key Projects Fall Behind Schedule

A business plan includes timelines for when action items need to happen. If you start missing key milestones, sit down with everyone involved to identify the source of the problem, including aspects of your business plan that may not be playing out as expected. Brainstorm solutions for getting back on schedule. If necessary, amend your business plan, revise your action plan, and notify all involved. Look in Chapter 3 for tips on creating reasonable goals and objectives. Chapter 17 offers advice for keeping your business plan on course.

New Competitors Appear

If a competitive assault rocks your company, take a deep breath and remember that competition isn't always a bad thing. It usually increases interest in your business sector, and it almost always forces you to focus on what you do best and how to do it as efficiently as possible.

Should a new shark enter your tank, immediately revise the situation analysis in your business plan. Start with a Strengths, Weaknesses, Opportunities and Threats analysis (see Chapter 5 for how to conduct a SWOT analysis) to uncover areas where your capabilities lag behind or surge ahead of the capabilities of your competitors.

Shore up the former and polish up the latter to overcome and even capitalize upon the changes in your business environment. Chapter 4 offers advice for staying a step ahead of competitors.

Technology Shakes Up Your World

New products and process innovations can turn your company upside down, for better or worse. A shift in technology can make existing products obsolete and create markets for new products or services almost overnight.

REMEMBER

With technological change comes the need to revamp business operations to address and incorporate technological breakthroughs, including the installation of new equipment and processes that can affect your company *and* its financial statements. Whenever a new technology appears on your business horizon, reassess your business plan — fast. Consider how the new technology may change the desires and demands of the markets you serve and how it may affect the way that you — and your competitors — do business. Lay out plans for how your business will incorporate and use the technology to your advantage. Chapter 15 explores everything you need to know about planning in a rapidly changing world.

Important Customers Defect

The defection of your best customers is an alarm signal that you can't afford to ignore. Here's how to respond:

>> Look for deficiencies in your product or service offering.

>> Ask departing customers why they left.

>> Query your salespeople and frontline staff for their insights.

>> Check out online reviews of your products or services.

Retool your business plan, paying close attention to how changes in your strengths and weaknesses may be affecting your ability to compete in your market. Chapter 15 helps you stay alert to changing customer perceptions. Chapter 13 goes into detail on revamping your strategy in times of trouble.

Business Strategy Does a 180

Slight course adjustments in your strategy are a normal part of doing business, but if your company does an unplanned 180-degree shift, something's wrong. Sit down with your management team — business plan in hand — to figure out why your original strategic direction isn't working. Take the time to do a complete diagnostic, and then plan a course change that addresses the problems you identify. Don't be afraid to make a major shift, if needed. Lots of businesses find their true path to success by learning from past mistakes and changing course.

Check out Chapters 5 and 6 for more on maintaining a flexible strategy. Turn to Chapter 13 to for information on pivoting your company to a new focus.

Growth Is Out of Your Control

A company *can* grow too fast — and that can mean trouble if you're not prepared. Customer service can suffer, or manufacturing may not be able to keep up with demand, for example. Some companies even find that their organizational structures no longer fit their new dimensions. If your business experiences growing pains, identify the parts of your business plan that need to change in order to accommodate the good news — and your increasing size. Chapter 4 helps you understand your business environment and chart growth patterns. Chapter 9 tells you everything you need to know about making financial forecasts.

Chapter 19

Ten Questions to Ask Before You Finish Your Business Plan

You're ready to dot the last *i* and cross that last *t* of your written business plan. But before you sign off, review the plan one last time. If you have the luxury to let your plan sit for a week or so before reading it with fresh eyes, that's even better. In our experience, some of the most important business plan refinements are made during the final review process. Use this checklist to zero in on the most important questions to ask.

Does the Plan Realistically Assess Your Business Idea?

We're all for enthusiasm, especially when it gives you the motivation and inspiration you need for the hard work of putting a business together. But a clear-eyed assessment of the strengths and weaknesses of the idea behind your enterprise is equally crucial to success.

Identifying weaknesses can help you develop a strategy that plays on your strengths and minimizes your weaknesses. Read over your plan, taking the point of view of a very skeptical investor. Make sure that it addresses every concern with convincing reasons why your business idea will succeed.

Do the Financials Add Up?

One of the biggest reasons new ventures fail is poor financial planning. No plan can prepare for everything, but your financial plan should be conservative enough — and honest enough — to give you some breathing room if the business or new product doesn't get off the ground as quickly as you want. Plan and review your financials. Make sure that the numbers are realistic. If you have any doubts, revise your financial forecast. For help, refer to Chapter 9.

Does the Plan Adequately Describe Your Customers and What They Want?

One thing that all successful businesses — for-profit and nonprofit, small and large alike — have in common is the ability to deliver what their customers want. To keep your customers satisfied, you have to know them as well as possible — who they are, where they are, what makes them tick, and what motivates them to buy (or in the case of a nonprofit, contribute). As you review your plan, consider it from the perspective of potential customers. Ensure that you've measured their wants and needs accurately and that your marketing approaches and messages will reach, engage, and inspire them to do business with you.

Does the Plan Establish a Clear Timeline?

An effective plan spells out what steps you need to take to achieve your goals and, just as importantly, when they need to happen. Without a firm timetable, projects and plans have a way of slipping. And in these competitive and fast-changing times, lost time can mean lost opportunities. Set a specific date for when you'll accomplish each action step described in your plan. Be sure that you specify the important milestones along the way.

WARNING

Your timetable should be ambitious, but not based on wishful thinking. Don't set yourself up for failure by creating a plan you can't possibly follow. Give yourself and your key players time to get the job done.

Does the Plan Spell Out Specific Goals and Objectives?

Abstract ideas and generalities have no place in a business plan. Your plan should be specific, especially in spelling out your goals and objectives. Each one should be supported by actions that will be taken, along with a precise way of determining when targets have been reached. Review your plan from the point of view of the key employees who will be asked to carry it out. Make sure that your plan is clear about what your business wants to accomplish. Check out Chapter 3 for more on goals and objectives.

Will the Plan Guide and Inspire Employees?

An effective plan lays out a strategic course that's clear and easy to follow. At the same time, it inspires employees by making them feel part of a team where everyone matters and every job is important. As you review your plan one last time, think about it from your employees' point of view. Does it clearly outline what your team aims to accomplish? Does it make a convincing case for success? Does it acknowledge (and encourage) the contributions of all employees? Does your mission statement offer inspiration as well as guidance?

Is the Writing Clear and Jargon-Free?

Your business plan should be understandable to as wide an audience as possible, from investors and employees to key partners and clients. To ensure your plan is clear and persuasive to anyone who reads it, rely as little as possible on industry jargon. Put yourself in the mind-set of a reader who knows little about your business but who just happens to have a spare million to invest in something that promises a big return. Is your plan easy to understand? Just as important, is it persuasive?

TIP

Sure, if you're writing a business plan for a new biotech venture, you may need to throw around terms like monoclonal antibody and randomized controlled studies. If your plan absolutely, positively requires technical words, include a glossary that defines these crucial terms in words that anyone, even your next-door neighbor, would understand. Such a glossary is helpful in making your plan understandable to everyone. It can also convince readers that you know what you're talking about when you throw around those high-falutin' words.

Is the Plan Concise?

It's easy to confuse the heft of a plan with substance. In our experience, the more concise and to the point a plan is, the more likely people are to read it and be motivated by it. Be on the lookout for empty phrases and unnecessary verbiage. If you find your own attention wandering as you read, look back over the section to see if there are ways to say the same thing in fewer words.

TIP

Sometimes it helps to have an editor read and review the final draft before it receives a final signoff. If you don't have an in-house communications team for the task, hire a freelance editor to read and red-pencil the plan. Sure, you'll spend a little extra money, but a good editor can catch confusing or embarrassing mistakes that would otherwise diminish the authority of your plan. From what we've seen, businesses that employ editors consider the money well spent.

Does Your Strategy Allow for the Unexpected?

By its very nature, a plan is an attempt to tell the future — or at least describe the future that you want to see. Your financial forecasts, your customer and competitor analyses, and your strategic plan are all based on assumptions about the year ahead. That's fine. But especially during these times of rapid change, make sure you've engineered some flexibility into your plan to account for uncertainties in the economy and the marketplace. As you review your plan one last time, be alert to places where your assumptions may be a little too glib. Beyond that, outline strategies and procedures you'll follow, should assumptions not pan out or should you face the unexpected. Turn to Chapter 15 for more details on planning for change.

What Would Your Competitors Think?

Imagine, as you review your plan, how one of your biggest competitors would respond to reading it. You can bet they'll be on the lookout for weaknesses in your strategy or glaring holes in your business forecast. Of course, they'll welcome any missteps you might take in assessing your customers or the marketplace you hope to dominate. Wherever they sense a weakness, they'll begin their own plan to exploit it. By putting yourself in your competitors' shoes when you review your plan, you may find weaknesses — or opportunities — you didn't recognize. Bolster your strategy or fine-tune your forecasts to anticipate competitors' countermoves.

Appendix

What You Can Find Online

The following sections are arranged by category and present a list of the files and software you can find online at www.dummies.com/go/businessplanskit.

All the business plan forms referred to in the book are included online. The forms come in two file formats:

>> Microsoft Word files: You can open these files if you use Microsoft Word 95 or later (for Mac or Windows).

>> Adobe Reader (PDF) files: These forms can't be modified, but if you have Adobe Reader, you can view and print them. Adobe Reader for Mac and Windows is included on the CD-ROM.

We organize the form files by chapter. Table A-1 lists them all by name and number.

TABLE A-1   **Forms at a Glance**

Form Number	Form Name
Form 1-1	Major Components in a Typical Business Plan
Form 1-2	Typical Business-Planning Situations
Form 1-3	Business-Planning Wish List
Form 1-4	Checklist of Common Business Plan Audiences
Form 1-5	Business Plan Target Audiences and Key Messages
Form 1-6	Business Plan Time Frame Questionnaire
Form 1-7	Business Plan Tracker

(continued)

TABLE A-1 *(continued)*

Form Number	Form Name
Form 2-1	Great Business Idea Evaluation Form
Form 2-2	Ideas Behind Successful Businesses Evaluation Form
Form 2-3	Business Challenges Questionnaire
Form 2-4	Turning a Gig into a Business
Form 2-5	Business Opportunity Evaluation Questionnaire
Form 2-6	Business Opportunity Framework
Form 2-7	New Product Innovation Questionnaire
Form 2-8	Personal Strengths and Weaknesses Survey
Form 2-9	Personal Strengths and Weaknesses Grid
Form 3-1	Basic Business Definition Framework
Form 3-2	Comparing the Most Common Business Structures
Form 3-3	Your Mission Statement Questionnaire
Form 3-4	Your Mission Statement Framework
From 3-5	Examples of Real-World Mission Statements
Form 3-6	Your Mission Statement
Form 3-7	Values Questionnaire
Form 3-8	Your Values Statement
Form 3-9	Examples of Real-World Vision Statements
Form 3-10	Your Vision Statement
Form 3-11	Goals and Objectives Flowchart
Form 3-12	Goals and Objectives Based on ACES
Form 3-13	Checklist of Common Business Goals
Form 3-14	Your Major Business Goals
Form 4-1	Industry Analysis Questionnaire
Form 4-2	Barriers to Entry Checklist
Form 4-3	Customer Profile Questionnaire
Form 4-4	Customer Intelligence Checklist
Form 4-5	Customer Snapshot

Form Number	Form Name
Form 4-6	Ideal Customer Questionnaire
Form 4-7	Distinguishing Traits of Ideal Customers
Form 4-8	Basic Market Segmentation Framework
Form 4-9	Channel Distribution Analysis Worksheet
Form 4-10	Market Segmentation Analysis Worksheet
Form 4-11	Business Customer Profile
Form 4-12	Our Biggest Competitors
Form 4-13	Competitive Intelligence Checklist
Form 4-14	Potential Stealth Competitors Questionnaire
Form 4-15	Competitor Tracking Form
Form 4-16	Our Biggest Competitors and Their Likely Moves
Form 4-17	Competitive Analysis Worksheet
Form 5-1	Business Strengths and Weaknesses Survey
Form 5-2	Business Strengths and Weaknesses Grid
Form 5-3	Business Opportunities and Threats
Form 5-4	Business SWOT Analysis Grid
Form 5-5	Quick Financial Projection Worksheet
Form 5-6	Freemium Business Model Considerations Checklist
Form 5-7	Pricing Considerations Checklist
Form 5-8	Business Model Questionnaire
Form 5-9	Elements of Your Business Model Worksheet
Form 5-10	Resources for Growth Checklist
Form 5-11	Planning for Growth Questionnaire
Form 5-12	Checklist of Common Owner Exit Strategies
Form 6-1	Product/Service Description Checklist
Form 6-2	Elevator Speech Planning Questionnaire
Form 6-3	Writing Your Elevator Speech
Form 6-4	Operations Planning Survey (Location)

(continued)

Form Number	Form Name
Form 6-5	Operations Planning Survey (Equipment)
Form 6-6	Operations Planning Survey (Labor)
Form 6-7	Operations Planning Survey (Process)
Form 6-8	Distribution and Delivery Survey
Form 6-9	Management Team Member Profile
Form 7-1	Positioning and Brand Statements Worksheet
Form 7-2	Six Brand-Management Steps
Form 7-3	Social Media Program Planning Checklist
Form 7-4	Product Strategy Checklist
Form 7-5	Distribution Strategy Checklist
Form 7-6	Pricing Strategy Checklist
Form 7-7	Promotion Strategy Checklist
Form 7-8	Customer Service Checklist
Form 9-1	Business Income Statement
Form 9-2	Business Balance Sheet
Form 9-3	Business Cash Flow Statement
Form 10-1	Is Self-Employment Right For You?
Form 10-2	Tasks and Time Survey
Form 10-3	Self-Employed Expense Checklist
Form 10-4	Evaluating Your Home Office Options
Form 10-5	Checklist of Business Networking Resources
Form 10-6	Checklist of Ways to Promote Yourself
Form 10-7	One-Person Business Checklist
Form 10-8	Strengths and Weaknesses Checklist
Form 11-1	Start-Up Costs Worksheet for Small Business
Form 11-2	Job Description Profile
Form 11-3	Job Recruiting Checklist
Form 11-4	Employee Retention Checklist
Form 11-5	Tips on Promoting Teamwork

Form Number	Form Name
Form 12-1	Checklist of Benefits of a Virtual Organization
Form 12-2	Challenges of Managing a Virtual Organization
Form 12-3	Remote Employee Hiring Checklist
Form 12-4	Job Description Worksheet
Form 13-1	Growth Strategies Worksheet
Form 13-2	Checklist of Common Warning Signs
Form 13-3	Selling Your Business Worksheet
Form 13-4	Business Transferability — Assessing Your Sale Readiness
Form 14-1	Nonprofit Planning Worksheet
Form 14-2	Examples of Real-World Nonprofit Mission Statements
Form 14-3	Ideal Individual Donor Questionnaire
Form 14-4	Checklist of Responsibilities for a Nonprofit Board
Form 14-5	Checklist of Typical Grant Proposal Sections
Form 14-6	Checklist of Nonprofit Marketing Strategies
Form 15-1	Identifying Key Drivers of Change
Form 15-2	New Technology Questionnaire
Form 15-3	Managing Changing Customer Expectations Questionnaire
Form 15-4	Adapting to Customer Demands and Desires Questionnaire
Form 16-1	Business Plan Components Checklist
Form 16-2	Business Plan Template
Form 16-3	Master Plan Tracking Sheet
Form 16-4	Business Plan Target Audience Guidelines
Form 16-5	Working Draft Checklist
Form 17-1	Goals and Objectives Assignment Chart
Form 17-2	Common Systems and Procedures Checklist
Form 17-3	Checklist of Management and Leadership Traits
Form 17-4	Employee Training Resource Checklist
Form 17-5	Business Metrics Worksheet
Form 17-6	Checklist for Managing Change

Index

Numerics

80/20 rule (Pareto Principle; law of maldistribution), 90

A

accountability
  B corporations, 54
  nonprofits, 299
accounts payable, 201
accounts receivable, 199
accrual basis accounting, 204
accrued expenses payable, 201
accumulated depreciation, 200
accumulated retained earnings, 203
ACES acronym, 71–72
Action plan (business plan), 11, 232, 250
adaptive website design, 167–168
alternative lending sites, 184
Amazon
  adapting to changing market, 50
  values statement, 65
angel investors, 188, 269
Appendices section (business plan), 11, 331
assembling business plan. *See also* business plan
  audience, 329–332
  finalizing plan, 333, 335
  forms, 335
  information resources, 321–324
  planning team, 325–329
assets
  current, 197–199
  fixed, 199–200
  liquid, 208
  liquidity, 197
  total, 201
audience
  addressing multiple audiences, 330–332
  business plan, 17
  making business plan information accessible to, 330–332
  niche marketing, 168–170

stakeholders, 329–330
Automattic website, 257

B

B corporations, 54
B2B (business-to-business) customers, 93
balance sheet
  building, 203–204
  current assets, 197–199
  current liabilities, 201–202
  estimated, 211–212
  fixed assets, 199–200
  intangibles, 200–201
  long-term liabilities, 202
  overview, 196
  owner's equity, 202–203
  total assets, 201
  total liabilities and equity, 203
bank funding
  commercial lines of credit, 183
  commercial loans, 182–183
  equipment leasing, 183
  overview, 181–182
  raising capital for established business, 268–269
  Small Business Administration loans, 183–184
beacons, 146
behavioral patterns (customers), 85
big data, 162–163
Bill and Melinda Gates Foundation, 286, 296
board of trustees (nonprofits), 293, 299
bookstores, as information resource, 321
bootstrapping (self-funding), 180
bottom line (net profit; net earnings; net income), 195–196
bounce rates, 162
BP (British Petroleum), 65
bracketing expectations, 311–312
brainstorming. *See also* idea development
  assembling brainstorming session, 37–38
  for effective fundraisers, 297
  LCS system, 36–37

C

capabilities
  altering distribution channels, 151
  data management, 145–146
  describing, 136–151
  distribution and delivery, 104, 108, 138–141
  grading, 105–106
  management, 141–143, 293
  matching to task, 106–107
  moving business, 149–150
  operations, 138
  organization, 104, 108, 143–145, 292–293
  overview, 104–105, 136
  pivoting strategies, 148–149
  research and development, 104, 108, 136–138, 293–294
  revising operations, 150
  testing, 146–148
capital. *See also* funding
  bank financing, 268–269
  crowdsourcing, 270
  investors, 269–270
cash. *See also* cash-flow statement
  cash reserves, 210, 299
  as current asset, 197
cash-flow statement
  assembling, 208–209
  changes in liquid assets, 208
  net change in cash position, 207, 208
  total funds in, 204–205
  total funds out, 205–207
CEO (Chief Executive Officer), 142, 292
CFO (Chief Financial Officer), 142
change. *See* drivers of change (driving forces)
Chief Executive Officer (CEO), 142, 292
Chief Financial Officer (CFO), 142
Chief Information Officer (CIO), 142
Chief Operating Officer (COO), 142
Chief Professional Officer (CPO), 292
Chief Technology Officer (CTO), 142
Chief Volunteer Officer (CVO), 292
CI (competitive intelligence), 97
CIO (Chief Information Officer), 142
cloak-and-dagger methods (competition), 96–97
cluster marketing (geodemographics; lifestyle marketing), 85

Coca-Cola, 65
collaboration tools (virtual business), 262
collateral, 182
collective business model, 51
commercial lines of credit, 183
commercial loans, 182–183
Common Systems and Procedures Checklist, 359
community-supported agriculture (CSA) programs, 181
company description, 245–246. *See also* describing business
competition
  assessing, 160–162
  cloak-and-dagger methods, 96–97
  direct competitors, 160
  forms, 102
  new competitors, 365–366
  researching, 43–44
  staying ahead of, 98–99
  stealth competitors, 97–98
competitive intelligence (CI), 97
conditions
  analyzing industry, 80–81
  defined, 79
  disruptive changes, 81–82
  entry barriers to industry, 82–84
  forms, 101
confidentiality (virtual business), 259
consultants/advisors, 22
COO (Chief Operating Officer), 142
cooperatives, 53
corporations. *See also* nonprofits
  B corporations, 54
  overview, 53–54
  S corporations, 54
costs
  controlling, 120
  as entry barrier to industry, 84
  overhead expenses, 206, 298
costs of goods acquired, 205–206
costs of goods sold, 194
CPO (Chief Professional Officer), 292
creativity
  boosting personal creativity, 28
  inspiring team creativity, 35–38
  virtual business, 257
credibility, as entry barrier to industry, 84

About the Authors

Steven D. Peterson, PhD, is coauthor, along with Paul Tiffany, of *Business Plans For Dummies,* which was nominated as one of the best business books of the year by *The Financial Times.* He is founder and CEO of Strategic Play, a management training company specializing in software tools designed to enhance business strategy, business planning, and general management skills. He created the Protean Strategist, a business simulation that reproduces a dynamic business environment where participant teams run companies and compete against each other in a fast-changing marketplace. He holds advanced degrees in mathematics and physics and received his doctorate from Cornell University. For more information, visit www.strategicplay.com.

Peter Jaret has written for *The New York Times, Newsweek, National Geographic, Reader's Digest, Vogue, Scientific American,* the *AARP Bulletin,* and dozens of other magazines. He is the author of seven books, including *In Self-Defense, From the Frontlines of Global Public Health,* and *Nurse: A World of Care.* He has developed written materials for the Electric Power Research Institute, Lucas Arts, The California Endowment, WebMD, Stanford University, University of California, Berkeley, Home Planet Technologies, and others. In 1992, he received the American Medical Association's first-place award for medical reporting. In 1997 and again in 2007, he won James Beard Awards for food and nutrition writing. He holds degrees from Northwestern University and the University of Virginia.

Barbara Findlay Schenck helps business owners start, grow, brand, market, and sell their companies. She is the author of *Small Business Marketing Kit For Dummies* and *Selling Your Business For Dummies* and the coauthor of *Branding For Dummies* and *Business Plans Kit For Dummies.* She also writes marketing and branding articles, speaks at conferences, and presents live, online, and taped marketing, branding, and business-planning workshops and programs. For more information on her background, books, and business advice, visit www.bizstrong.com.

Dedication

This book is dedicated to all entrepreneurs who have the courage and perseverance to take a good idea and turn it into a great business venture — thanks to the help of a solid business plan.

— Steven D. Peterson, Peter Jaret, and Barbara Findlay Schenck

Authors' Acknowledgments

Now that *Business Plans Kit for Dummies* is launching its fifth edition, we want to thank more people than we have room to list. A book like this is truly a collaboration, and the contributions of many talented editorial and technical people at John Wiley & Sons, Inc. are evident on every page.

This time around, we give special thanks for the support and encouragement we've received from our friend and acquisitions editor Stacy Kennedy, who put the team together; Michelle Sirois, our technical editor; Chad Sievers, our project manager; and to you and the hundreds of thousands of readers of the previous editions of this book, who make this newest edition possible.

Publisher's Acknowledgments

Acquisitions Editor: Stacy Kennedy, Tracy Boggier

Project Manager: Chad R. Sievers

Copy Editor: Chad R. Sievers

Technical Editor: Michelle Sirois

Art Coordinator: Alicia B. South

Production Editor: Vasanth Koilraj

Cover Photos: © www.BillionPhotos.com/shutterstock.com